Fire Officer Coaching

Vaughan Fire & Rescue Service
2141 Major MacKenzie Drive
Vaughan, Ontario L6A 1T1

First Edition

Published by
Fire Protection Publications • Oklahoma State University
Stillwater, Oklahoma

Project Manager: Rachel Hutchinson
Authors: James M. Gaston, Ph.D., CAE and Dr. Riley Harvill
Editor: Krystal Dickens, Ella R. Walter
Editorial Assistant: Tara Gladden
Production Manager: Don Davis
Design/Layout: Missy Hannan

All Rights reserved, No part of this publication may be reproduced without prior written permission from the publisher.

ISBN 0879392592
Library of Congress Control Number: 2005921819
First Edition
First Printing, July 2005

10   9   8   7   6   5   4   3   2   1   *Printed in the United States of America*

Oklahoma State University in compliance with Title VI of the Civil Rights Act of 1964 and Title IX of the Educational Amendments of 1972 (Higher Education Act) does not discriminate on the basis of race, color, national origin or sex in any of its policies, practices or procedures. This provision includes but is not limited to admissions, employment, financial aid and education services.

Contents

Vaughan Fire & Rescue Service
2141 Major MacKenzie Drive
Vaughan, Ontario L6A 1T1

About the Authors

James M. Gaston, Ph.D., CAE, has worked for municipal governments and trained city employees for over 30 years. He has served as Executive Director of the Texas Fire Chiefs Association since 1997 and holds the prestigious CAE, the highest credential in the association management profession. He was a 2001 recipient of the President's Award from the International Association of Fire Chiefs.

Jim was a city planner for ten years after earning a Bachelor of Science in Architecture in 1971. He earned a Masters of Public Administration in 1983 from Texas A&M and then managed real property assets for the Texas A&M University System for two years. From 1985 until 1992, Jim conducted training for city managers, public works officials, economic developers, and city planners while managing a funded center for the Texas Engineering Extension Service. Jim earned his Ph.D. from Texas A&M University in 1994 in adult learning and distance education. He served as Dean of Continuing Education at Palm Beach Atlantic College in 1996. He has taught at the undergraduate and graduate levels and has consulted on a number of public sector projects.

Dr. Riley Harvill lives in Dallas, Texas. As the founder of The Leadership Institute For Fire Executives (www.harbeck.com), he has consulted with over 200 fire departments around the country since 1991. He continues to deliver innovative training and learning programs for fire service personnel. He may be reached at 214/520-2921.

Acknowledgements

James M. Gaston, Ph.D., CAE

For over seven years I've talked with the people who hurry to help when citizens dial 9-1-1. I've listened to fire personnel ranging from big city fire chiefs to small town volunteer firefighters as they discussed the human relations problems that confront their organizations. I've listened to city managers, city council members, state regulators, Texas legislators, Members of Congress, the leaders of fire service associations, and fire service families. I've interviewed firefighters in their firehouses and I've observed them at fire scenes as they fought to save lives.

I would like to thank the men and women who have patiently taught me so much about the fire service. They introduced me to the culture and to the brotherhood. They opened the firehouse doors and the windows to their lives. They helped me learn their methods and technology, to understand their missions and their measures.

I've been studying the fire service for long enough now that I usually know the questions. It will be a while before I know many answers. It can't be comfortable for a firefighter or fire chief to be interviewed by a Ph.D. But they have answered me when I questioned, responded when I probed, and shared their humor with me. I enjoy their candor and I appreciate the volumes of information they have given me. Most of all I thank them for what they do.

I would also like to thank my wife, partner, and friend of nearly forty years, Dr. Sandra Gaston. She's the love of my life. She is my academic colleague and my ethical guide. She has helped me understand about organizations and how people work within them. Without her insight, intelligence, kindness, and steadfast support, I would never write anything worth reading.

Dr. Riley Harvill

To Rebecca, my soul-mate, and to Lizzy, Kate, and Jake who teach me what the purpose of coaching really is.

Preface

Riley Harvill, Ed.D.

I did not intend to be a coach. It just seems like that's what I have primarily done over most of my career. Whether it was in my role as clinical supervisor of graduate level psychotherapists-in-training or sitting across from a fire officer, most of what I have done can be characterized as coaching. And like many of you who are seeking to improve your coaching skills, I came ill equipped in my understanding of what facilitated lasting change in fire service organizations and what was necessary to help personnel improve their skills and performance.

Fortunately for my development, I often found myself working with exasperated officers who would practically sell their soul for harmony and better performance within the department. They were discouraged and wanted answers, magical solutions if at all possible. I had to dig. I had to improve my skills in order to help them. I got certified as an associate fire trainer as part of my development and began delving deeper into the dynamics of fire service culture. What I learned was that the accepted, command-style method of leadership and supervision is, in itself, contributing to the problems that fire officers often experience.

Fire service is, by tradition, *transactional command-style* in nature. By this I mean it is almost solely oriented toward accomplishing tasks through a series of verbal orders. Yet the problems most often encountered in firehouses are not due to the lack of knowledge in carrying out orders. Rather, they are based on a misunderstanding of why people behave as they do; their motivations. Performance problems are often the end result of relational issues that include:

1. How fire service personnel interact and feel toward one another.

2. The level of trust they have for their supervisors.

3. The degree of satisfaction and pride they have for their jobs.

4. The degree to which fire service personnel feel appreciated and encouraged.

The importance in considering relational factors is corroborated by the Gallup Organization. Over the past twenty-five years, the folks at Gallup have conducted, tape-recorded, and transcribed one and one-half hour interviews with over eighty thousand managers to find out what the best managers know from the rest. And what they discovered is that they know four things. (1) People don't change that much. (2) It is a waste of time to try to put in what was left out. (3) They should attempt to draw out what was left in, and (4) that that is hard enough (Buckingham & Coffman, 1999).

What Great Fire Officers Know

Great officers know that we are each motivated by something different and that these differing motivations cause us to behave differently, to possess different strengths, natural abilities, idiosyncratic comfort areas, and differences in, not only what, but how, we must improve. In other words, we cannot be something or somebody we are not. We are who we are and that's that. Sending the message that a person can be whatever they want is false. We all have both limitations and strengths.

Some fire officers spend inordinate amounts of time and money trying to make a gentle person more assertive, a too assertive person more gentle, a people oriented person more focused, a task oriented person more personable. But great fire officers don't spend time gnashing their teeth over these differences. Instead, they try to capitalize on differences by helping personnel accentuate their individual personality strengths so that they better fit their jobs and roles.

A well-respected and insightful chief reported that he put one of his lieutenants in charge of an education program aimed at increasing the public's knowledge of summertime hazards when kids are home from school. "I needed an upbeat kind of person and I asked for volunteers. My more bombastic female fire officer stepped up when no one else would. I should have assigned someone else instead. She treated our citizens like ignorant oafs and angered about two-thirds of the people with whom she had contact. I've known her for years. I know her nature. I made the mistake of thinking she would be different, that she would dramatically change."

This chief based his personnel decision on conventional wisdom that holds that people can change their true nature; that we all can be whatever we want. Nothing could be further from the truth. According to Buckingham and Coffman, the authors of the Gallup studies report entitled "First, Break All The Rules," conventional wisdom about management may be contributing to a variety of workplace problems.

"Their (manager's) ideas are plain and direct, but not necessarily simple to implement. Conventional wisdom is conventional for a reason; it is easier. It is easier to imagine that the best way to help an employee is by fixing his weaknesses. It is easier to "do unto others as you would be done unto…conventional wisdom is comfortingly, seductively easy."

"The revolutionary wisdom of great managers [officers] isn't. Their path is much more exacting. It demands discipline, focus, trust, and, perhaps most important, a willingness to individualize." (Buckingham & Coffman, p 12, 1999).

Most personnel problems in fire departments are the result of personality clashes, the types of problems that the transactional (command) style of leadership is least equipped to handle. Differing motivations mean that we seek to satisfy different needs. It is these hidden, largely unconscious needs that we have difficulty interpreting in other people.

For example, some fire service personnel get up in the morning and head for work in order to fulfill their need for social interaction. Others pull up their boots in order to exercise an element of power and control. Still others gain fulfillment as a knowledgeable *expert* in some area. All of these different needs create both subtle as well as easily recognizable differences in the way people interact, perceive authority, approach tasks, respond to stress, deal with change, handle mistakes, the pace in which they work, their enthusiasm, level of energy, tolerance for ambiguity, and the way they want to be supervised. Everyone is different!

Generically, we can say that these behavioral differences are created by differences in personality, but personality alone is not what puts behavior in motion. Motivation does. Another way to understand motivation is by understanding the purpose of behavior.

Belonging, Faulty Beliefs, and Fictional Goals

All behavior has a purpose (Adler, 1998) and that purpose is to accomplish a universal goal among people—belonging. Because we are social beings, the need to belong, to emotionally connect with others, exists in each of us. But how we strive for the sense of belonging varies and is based upon certain *faulty beliefs* (what we consciously or unconsciously expect to achieve by our behavior) and *fictional goals* (what we must accomplish in order to belong). They are *faulty* and *fictional* because they are not based on objective, empirical facts and accomplish merely a temporary condition of belonging, at best. Unexamined beliefs and goals often result in the kinds of workplace *symptoms* that require coaching. These symptoms include: underperformance, miscommunication, diminished morale, poor leadership, poor followership, lack of clarity in the department's vision, and unclear performance objectives. These are some of the more common subjects for coaching in fire service.

The table below illustrates some typical faulty beliefs, fictional goals, their resultant behaviors and effect on others.

Faulty Beliefs & Fictional Goals

Faulty Beliefs	Goals	Behaviors	Results
I am only satisfied when:			Other people:
I am first	Power	Demanding	Avoid them
I win		Commanding	Get angry
I am best		Accomplish at all cost	Fight back
			Become passive
			Get discouraged
I am enjoying myself	Fun	Talkative	Form good first impressions
I am noticed		Social	Think they are fun
I am praised		Easily bored	Get frusrated over their lack of attention to details
		Seek change	Want more commitment
		Avoid long-term commitment	Need them to be more serious
		Energetic	
I have intimacy	Intimacy	Perfectionist	Find them frustrating
I am loved		Self-righteous	Can't read them very well
I am understood		Unrealistic goals	Think they are good listeners
I am accepted		High moral standards	Wish they would take more risks
			Wish they would be more decisive and assertive
I please other people	Peace	Avoid confrontation	Get frustrated with their shyness
I do what I want		Reticent to disagree	Want them to extend themselves more and take risks
I have security		Bashful	
I am an expert		Passive	

In each of the examples above, motivation (Goal) is the source of the Behaviors. Different motivations and thus behaviors, are often the source of misunderstanding, frustration, and conflict among fire service personnel. Because we have only recently begun to examine behavioral differences from the standpoint of motivations, we continue to have difficulty understanding why people do what they do. This is no surprise since we don't even fully understand ourselves.

This book offers an approach for helping fire officers understand people and their motivations and, as a result, their strengths. It is an attempt to give officers a handle on how to accentuate the natural strengths of their personnel. Through the techniques and skills of coaching, fire officers will learn to enhance the gifts of their subordinates and provide the elements for a strong and vibrant workplace that rewards people for good work, allows people to do what they do best, listens to people, and treats them with respect.

The elements of just such a workplace were highlighted in the 1999 Gallup book called "First, Break All The Rules." In this book, the authors, Marcus Buckingham and Curt Coffman discuss the top twelve things that make for a "great" workplace. These include the following:

1. A good relationship with immediate supervisor (Relational)

2. The opportunity to utilize talent and/or do what one does best

3. A feeling that the job is important (Relational)

4. Clear expectations

5. Materials and tools to do the job

6. Giving/receiving praise/recognition at least twice per month (Relational)

7. A feeling that the supervisor cares about us as people (Relational)

8. Someone to encourage development and progress on a regular basis (Relational)

9. Opinions seem to count

10. Associates are committed to quality work

11. Having a best friend at work (Relational)

12. Having the regular opportunity to learn and to grow (Relational)

Of the above twelve elements, seven pinpoint relational factors as those that are essential for the creation of a desirable work atmosphere. Would these same elements have been desired forty years ago? Perhaps not; times have changed. Generational, cultural, gender, economic, and other societal factors have, no doubt, influenced what people see as desirable workplace elements. But the message to fire departments is clear; the transactional style, a style that was prevalent and successful in almost every kind of workplace through most of the twentieth century, may need a bit of tailoring-a nip here, a tuck there. While the transactional style is beneficial in accomplishing emergency tasks, it does not directly address many workplace issues that people say are important to them. Furthermore, when confronted with conflict, poor morale or underperformance, the transactional style's solution often is for officers to give more orders more often or louder.

This is called *first order* change. It has long been known that instead of solving problems and reaching the desired elements of a "great" workplace as noted above, first order solutions tend to exacerbate them. An alternative approach is necessary.

This book presents just such an alternative method. It is called coaching and combines traditional transactional leadership with methods and techniques that construct greater individual, team, and departmental performance. Coaching enhances relationships, improves morale, increases self-efficacy, and heightens encouragement. Coaching is based upon the following seven edicts:

1. All behavior has a purpose.

2. This purpose (motive) must be understood before good leadership and coaching can occur.

3. These motives and resultant behaviors are "privately logical." They may not make sense to the observer, but make perfect sense to the individual.

4. Changing behavior requires understanding why people do what they do.

5. Most people will follow orders and do what is minimally necessary, but will only excel when their needs are met.

6. People are drawn to great departments, but leave their superior officers. If they don't leave physically, they will leave mentally.

7. Personnel problems in fire service are due mostly to ineffective supervision and the fire culture itself.

What This Book Is About and Who It's For

Master the skills of this book and you will go a long way toward being an effective leader. Coaching and leadership are not dissimilar. In fact, I will suggest that those people whom you consider to be great leaders have learned to utilize the coaching skills presented in this book for the purpose of getting people to follow their vision.

Leadership is not some mystical ability that only a few people are born with. It is comprised of a learnable set of inner skills that form who you are, both your personality and your demeanor, and a set of outer skills that we associate with supervising and managing people. Great leaders aren't great leaders simply because they are famous, rich, or powerful. Rather they are what they are because they know how to relate to people, to encourage them, and to improve their performance.

Coaching

Even in traditional command-style work environments, leadership is more than giving orders and getting people to follow them. A supervisory style that focuses on people, their values, motivations, and growth can measurably enhance their performance-even during emergencies.

Great fire officers form constructive relationships with peers as well as subordinates—they each build off the other's strengths, they listen, and focus together in the right direction in terms of accomplishing the mission. Each is providing information to the other about what's going on so they can make better decisions. Together, they construct a leadership model that focuses on accomplishing tasks while developing people. The result is greater job satisfaction, improved morale, reduced turnover, improved succession planning, better service, and outstanding performance. Constructive leaders do more with colleagues and followers than set up simple exchanges or agreements. They behave in ways to achieve superior results by employing one or more of the "four I's":

1. Idealized influence — role models who can be counted on to do the right things

2. Inspirational motivation — enthusiasm and optimism that inspires and motivates those around them

3. Intellectual stimulation — stimulating innovation and creativity by questioning assumptions, reframing problems, and approaching old situations in new ways

4. Individualized consideration — stimulating growth through coaching and mentoring

Constructive leaders, as described in this book, are also mentors. They take a broader interest in their subordinates than simply the immediate resources to accomplish the present task. They are inspiring and flexible. They level with their subordinates and are focused on the future. They have a clear value and belief system that they convey to subordinates, are willing to challenge basic assumptions, and to think differently. They also take the time to know what problems and what strengths people have that can affect their achievement. It's much more than just getting the task done.

By contrast, command-style leaders, or so-called transactional leaders, focus on conveying orders. They clarify expectations and they ensure that needed steps are completed to accomplish a mission. It is the basis of leadership but by no means the entire package.

The constructive style builds on the transactional approach. Together, the two styles offer a broad range of leadership because they encompass a task focus as well as an emotional focus. Constructive leadership recognizes that behavior is explained by a variety of factors including motivation, emotions, and goals, not just rational reactions alone. Constructive leadership provides answers to essential human questions like: *Why am I doing this? Who does it benefit? Is my leader an ethical person? Does my leader have my best interest in mind? Do I believe in my leader? Does my leader know and respect me?*

Transactional leadership provides answers to the *how* and *when*, while constructive leadership provides guidance to the *why*. When combined in a unified manner, the two approaches create trust in leadership and help provide purpose to daily actions.

Fire officers learn leadership largely from operational experience. It's what they lived and developed as they proceeded up the ranks. Teaching constructive coaching at lower ranks may jump-start newer officers' growth as leaders. For lieutenants, having a constructive relationship with their battalion chiefs-and the rest of the unit-is crucial to understanding just what each individual firefighter can contribute to the broader departmental mission.

Constructive leaders display simple virtues like clarity of mind, basic goodness, wisdom, and fairness in dealing with others. When we meet people who possess such virtues, they automatically become leaders for us, whether they are in positions of leadership or not. These people often distinguish themselves in our eyes because of their extraordinary genuineness.

The Japanese use the term "*Hanshi*" for a high-ranking Jiujitsu instructor. The term has to do with perfecting one's inner nature. To be a great warrior, one must not only master the technique but perfect the way of being that is consistent with the servant leader-having a calm and centered inner spirit. Employees learn as much from the "master's" quality of being as from the "master's" knowledge and technical skills.

Constructive leaders are similar. Along with the developing inner spirit, constructive leaders consistently assess their:

1. Relationships with personnel,

2. Practice of recognizing and using each person's talents,

3. Practice of communicating <u>how</u> each person is important,

4. Practice of communicating expectations clearly,

5. Practice of regularly delivering genuine praise,

6. Practice of communicating caring to others,

7. Practice of encouraging professional and personal development,

8. Practice of encouraging and listening to others' opinions,

9. Practice of demonstrating and expecting quality work,

10. Practice of strategizing problem solutions with personnel,

11. Knowledge of human behavior, and

12. Ability to positively impact higher levels of performance.

Thank you for taking the time to read this book.

Riley Harvill, Ed.D.

James M. Gaston, Ph.D., CAE

When Riley Harvill asked me to collaborate on this book, I was excited to be able to contribute something of my academic and fire service experience to an effort so positive in its impact. The single most significant need in the fire service is for fire officers and firefighters to be able to work together more effectively. There is no skill that can improve the fire service more than listening. Dr. Harvill's constructive coaching uses creative listening skills to improve human interactions in the fire service.

I entered the fire service from an education and training background. After an early career in city planning, I studied public administration in graduate school. Even though I had served as a department head in a large city, I was shocked in graduate school to learn that much of the behavior I had encountered-and participated in-could be explained by bureaucratic theory and organizational development. What I had observed within the city organization was not only normal but to be expected.

The interpersonal conflicts and anxiety I observed in city halls over the years was also evident in the people I taught later as a trainer at a state agency. For seven years, I produced training and conferences for municipal employees in city management, public works, city planning, and economic development departments. Although the technical aspects of their jobs differed, the human relations problems were similar and persistent. The same organizational behavior problems plague the fire service.

I carried these lessons in human relations with me back into the classroom when I pursued a doctoral program in adult education. As I learned about adult learning theory and instructional methods, the question that was forming in my mind was about effective training to address healthy organizational behavior. Some learning is intentional and some is accidental. Some just comes to us in an epiphany, a moment of insight when we *get it*. How could municipal employee training be designed to improve organizational behavior?

During my doctoral research I discovered what most people already know, experience is the best teacher. It really doesn't take a Ph.D. to figure that out. But I wondered what it means to have an experience? Because I was in graduate school, I had time to consider that question. What does gaining *experience* really mean?

I am one of those people (constructivists) who believe that who we are and how we interpret events depends on our own life experiences. We are like chunks of clay that are shaped, molded, and colored by our experiences. The challenge to educators is to create experiences that stick to the chunk of clay in every student.

The question in my mind narrowed in focus to creating learning experiences in learning environments. We all have certain moments in our education that shape our lives for better or worse. What is it about an educational experience that leaves a lasting impression and becomes sustained learning?

In the fire service, I often hear that hands-on learning is best. But hands-on training has limitations. Training can only go so far until the risk and expense grow prohibitive. The costs of replicating reality in controlled environments are enormous and require more money than most local departments can afford. Unlike management training, people sometimes get hurt or even die during hands-on fire training.

Since most behavioral issues in the fire service and in city government are management problems rather than technical skills, it should be easier to create experience-based learning to teach those lessons. I have found that law schools and business schools use a teaching method that can be used effectively in other disciplines. They use teaching cases. Teaching cases are hands-on training for the mind. Maybe we should call them <u>minds-on training.</u>

A teaching case is a written scenario presenting a set of circumstances that pose a dilemma. In law school, the circumstances are the facts of the case and the dilemma hinges on some point of law. In business school, teaching cases establish an organizational scenario and students must recommend a successful course of action.

While I was teaching college, I assigned experience-based exercises in my courses. In one graduate class the students spent the whole course developing a training program for a hypothetical small business. I often required students to write new learning cases based on their own life experiences to present to the class. Experience, whether it is yours or someone else's, is the best teacher.

While teaching one particular course on instructional methods, I was confronted by a graduate student who thought she knew more about the subject than I did. It was an awkward hour for everyone in the class. I began the next class meeting with a case developed at Harvard wherein a student confronted a teacher in class. My graduate class had to resolve the hypothetical dilemma. In doing so, they resolved my very real dilemma and the graduate student had to accept the wisdom of her peers. We all learned from <u>that</u> experience.

When Dr. Harvill asked me to contribute to this book, I immediately knew what I could offer. I've read too many texts that go on and on without providing any minds-on experience. In addition to *Chapter Two, The Unique Challenges of the Fire Service Life*, I have prepared a series of brief scenarios and written dialogue between a coach and a fire officer to illustrate some of Dr. Harvill's points.

Think of these conversations as short learning cases where you need to understand the circumstances and then resolve the dilemma. Listen to the voices of the people involved and imagine what is going on out in the fire-house or over at city hall. How can a coach advise fire officers to behave in given situations? What can coaches do to help fire officers see solutions?

As you read a scenario, you are beginning to experience the dilemma on a superficial level. As you put yourself in the shoes of the participants, your involvement in the situation deepens. When you come up with a possible resolution to the conflict and put words into the coach's mouth, you are doing minds-on learning. At that point you have had a learning experience. I hope it sticks.

James M. Gaston, Ph.D., CAE

Bibliography and Recommended Readings

Adler, A. (1998). Hazelden Information Education; Reprint edition

Buckingham, Marcus and Coffman, Curt (1999). <u>First, Break All the Rules</u>, New York: Simon & Schuster

Prologue

Constructive Coaching's Bottom Line

Effective officer coaching must be both strategic and individualized. Good officer coaching not only develops effective future leaders, but also helps them retain key subordinates at a time when the fire service is seeing a higher rate of turnover. The end result is increased customer satisfaction, reduced costs from turnover, better personnel morale, and better fire service performance.

The rapid growth of fire officer coaching reflects its bottom-line benefits. To be effective, officer coaching must be both strategic and individualized. A balance must be struck between the needs of the organization and the needs of the individual. To engage and motivate individuals, officer coaching must be tailored to their needs and aspirations. To deliver service results, the coaching must be tailored to the strategy, vision, and values of the department.

Officer coaching that is strategic, that focuses on service/operational objectives as well as individual needs, is the key to achieving service results and better morale. This is in marked contrast to other approaches that concentrate on solving specific perceived problems with individuals such as changing their personality or making them more affable and approachable. Keep the spotlight on effective service results; other benefits are important but subordinate to the primary strategic goals of excellent service.

Perhaps the most important and direct benefit of good executive coaching is the development of highly effective future leaders. More effective leadership throughout the organization will drive many other important service results. For example, improved morale and better communication are two of the service benefits of improved leadership and therefore of the officer coaching that "drives" improvement in these skills.

Retention of highly effective firefighters is another outcome of effective officer coaching. Retaining key, competent people is an important retention, as well as succession, planning strategy. For example, a new hire can accomplish only 60% as much in the first three months as an experienced firefighter.

Our experience in developing officers/leaders reinforces the conclusion that Constructive officer coaching produces more effective leaders who facilitate firefighter job satisfaction, competence, morale, and citizen satisfaction necessary to drive better service and reduce costs. Moreover, by improving leadership skills throughout the department, officer coaching makes the organization a more attractive place to work for high potential people.

Officer coaching becomes strategic in the preparation that precedes the actual coaching process. Before the process begins, the coach must define the strategic context. This involves addressing a number of critical questions:

- What are the key operational and service challenges facing the department?

- What service goals are targeted by the department?

- What core values best define a common framework for how service results are achieved in your department?

- What leadership skills, knowledge, and abilities have been critical for success in the past? What is required in the future?

- How does the department determine whether the leadership candidate pool is available to lead effectively in the future? If the determination is made by civil service exams, are effective training strategies in place?

- Does the department have proven methods to attract, develop, and retain required talent? (Note: younger firefighters are changing jobs and leaving fire service more frequently!)

Once the strategic context has been mapped out, the actual officer coaching process can begin. From the point of view of the officers being coached, this is the personal component of the coaching process, where their own particular strengths and development needs are benchmarked against the leadership attributes needed to achieve the strategic goals of the department.

Chapter 1

Some Pre-Work Considerations

Some Pre-Work Considerations

If you are a new fire officer, you may be thinking that you know very little about coaching, especially if you have never seen coaching or been coached. Actually, everyone has experienced some aspect of coaching, in school, in sports, and in one on one or group training sessions. Any *"coaching"* you have received had one common goal - to make you better at something, either tangible or intangible. If coaching is new for you, you may be asking yourself several questions:

1. What is coaching?

2. What is the coaching process?

3. Who is a coach?

4. Who should coach?

5. Why coaching?

6. What are the various kinds of coaching?

7. What is the difference between training, coaching, and leadership?

8. Do cultural differences present specific coaching challenges?

9. Is there a kind of map that can guide my actions as a coach?

10. What are the most important coaching competencies?

11. What are examples of the kinds of challenges coaches face?

12. Are there strategies for working with difficult people?

13. How do I establish the way of things?

14. How do I know whether to focus on thoughts, feelings, actions, or spirit?

15. Why do coaching programs and relationships fail?

In this chapter we discuss a number of what we call *pre-work considerations*. These are elements that fire officers should consider and learn prior to supervising, leading, or coaching others. Answers to these questions are vital in establishing an effective coaching relationship.

1. What Is Coaching?

Coaching is both an opportunity and a risk. It is largely a teaching process beginning with parental nurturing of children and continuing through the lifecycle of organizational and personal interrelationships. A key principle proposed in this entire book is that coaching with fire service personnel is both an obligation and a responsibility of leadership. Through coaching (in some ways similar to mentoring), the wisdom and experience of the senior is passed to the junior, although this is changing somewhat. Nowadays, in this information era, it is not always the older person or even the more experienced person who is the coach. It may, at times, be someone who is younger, with less experience, but who possesses a level of expertise not possessed by senior personnel.

But coaching is not about fire-fighting skills. It includes passing on and discussing principles, traditions, shared values, quality, and lessons learned. Coaching provides a framework to bring about a cultural change in the way we view the professional development of competent future leaders. The road to the top in most organizations today is an uphill and bumpy ride. You simply can't float to the top. Coaching is a key way to help us get to our destination.

Coaching is perhaps the most powerful method by which we can shape the future. The term has become a buzzword, often carelessly shot into the air along with a dust cloud of other jargon from the unofficial, unwritten dictionary of those who consider themselves the cutting edge of modern fire leadership and management. But real coaching, properly understood, is much more than just another clipping from last week's Dilbert cartoon. Without an in-depth study of coaching, the capacity of an individual to coach is limited to the horizons of their own experience. Thus, coaching is literally a time machine that allows us to have a profound influence many years beyond today's busy and ordinary activities. It is safe to say that, just as sure as you are a partner in the fire service *brotherhood*, coaching can make a significant difference in the lives of your "brothers" around you.

A coach is a trusted advisor, teacher, counselor, and friend, often older and more senior than the person he or she helps. A coach is there when you need them. Coaching is an ongoing process. In departments, it can apply to all leaders and supervisors who are responsible for getting their work done through other people. It can apply to firefighters who want to promote. It can apply to officers who desire to become better leaders. The individual who is assisted by a coach is usually called a <u>client</u>- in essence, a student or pupil who learns from the coach. The process by which one person aids another in this type of relationship is known as coaching.

Regardless of how we choose to define it, coaching-if properly conducted-can have a most positive change in the life, attitudes, and behavior of the client. But what does this really mean? Does coaching differ in any way from teaching, parenting, or being a friend? This section attempts to answer these important questions in a practical way that will enable fire officers to implement the principles of coaching in everyday life. If we comprehend the principles essential to coaching, we will have in our grasp the tool kit that can make our "time machine" work. On balance, this section attempts to demystify the phenomenon of coaching by cutting through buzzwords and misconceptions to communicate a workable understanding of coaching and its practical implementation.

2. The Coaching Process

An effective coach must lead by example. When the coach serves as a real-world role model for the client (person being coached), the cliché that "actions speak louder than words" comes to life. Coaching requires significant amounts of time for coach and client to be in close proximity. Clients are always observing and learning from coaches. The opportunity to see how coaches actually deal with a variety of situations is an important part of the process because it takes things from the abstract to the realm of the practical and pragmatic application.

Coaches must behave at all times, both publicly and privately, as if the client were the coach's shadow. Part of the coaching process is the act of demonstrating for the client as he or she "shadows", as in mentoring, the coach, the proper methods, techniques, practices, and procedures that are part of the way the department functions. More than this, though, is the need for coaches to show clients how mature professionals deal with various challenges and opportunities. Coaches should be a model of composure, dignity, integrity, and professionalism, under all manner of conditions. Clients who shadow such role models will eventually come to understand, at a deep level, what he or she must be and do. Successful clients are those who are willing to listen, observe, learn, and grow from the examples of coaches.

An outstanding coach/mentor who personified the principles of ideal behavior was the great Jackie Robinson, baseball player and Hall of Famer. Prior to Robinson's presence in baseball, all American professional sports were completely closed to African-Americans. Skin color, not talent was the issue. But in 1947, Jackie Robinson broke the "color barrier" and became a major league baseball player for the Brooklyn Dodgers and a model of bravery for the rest of the world.

It was a hard, lonely struggle for this young man -- the one and only African-American in all of major league baseball. But Jackie Robinson was prepared. He understood and applied the four P's: preparation prevents poor performance.

Every day, he played all-star caliber baseball on the field and conducted himself like a true professional and gentleman both on and off the field. He carried himself with quiet dignity notwithstanding the most brutal indignities thrown at him. The only way he fought back was by playing baseball with an unsurpassed degree of dedication, drive, energy, and determination, game after game. In so doing, he gradually won the grudging respect of many former enemies, and demonstrated for countless other African-Americans that there was hope for them too. To this day, he remains a shining role model for everyone who must deal with racism and discrimination of whatever variety.

In time, Jackie personally coached/mentored other African-American baseball players who entered the major leagues through the doors he had opened, including teammates Roy Campanella and Don Newcombe. <u>He told them what they needed to know, but more importantly, he showed them.</u> His example proved to them, on a daily basis, what was needed to succeed. Because of his influence, it was easier for them and for everyone else who came later. He was the model for them to emulate personally and professionally. That is what coaches do.

Clearly, lessons of this type do not lend themselves to a quick one-time demonstration. This is not an easy, by-the-numbers, single-shot process. A person becomes a coach and a role model through persistent effort and interaction with the client over a considerable period of time. It may be that a coach can teach the basics of a task at hand fairly quickly, but the deeper lessons that distinguish coaching from simply teaching or training require prolonged involvement. You cannot model optimal actions over a broad spectrum of conditions all at once. It must happen naturally and in its own time. With enough time, and given a sufficiently wide range of circumstances, a relationship can mature from one of trainer-trainee to the more transformational one of coach-client. A memorable coach is like the point person on safari who cuts the brush with a machete in order to clear the path for those who follow. Memorable coaches exhibit caring for others. They are inspirational and high minded, with tremendous energy and a positive attitude toward making a difference in people's lives. This requires that a coach be capable of maintaining a give-and-take relationship with a client. In turn, memorable clients must be willing to learn, actively seek help, and apply what they have learned.

The fact is, we've had both memorable coaches and memorable clients and our experiences with them have been life changing. And, as different as they are as people, and as different as their approaches to life and work tend to be, they possess a common core set of skills, which includes empathizing, nurturing, teaching, organizing, responding, inspiring, networking and goal setting.

Empathizing

The ability and willingness to empathize are central to coaching. Only by truly understanding what the client is experiencing, and by identifying with what the client is feeling, can the coach know what is needed.

Coaching involves something more than teaching a skill. As has already been indicated, skills deficits are not the primary challenge. This extra ingredient is empathy, a measure of interpersonal involvement and caring. In fact, empathy is in many respects the Golden Rule in practice. We treat others as we would like them to treat us in similar circumstances.

An empathic coach will comprehend the types of challenges and struggles someone less experienced faces. A coach who remembers what it was like to be new and inexperienced will be far more effective in assisting others in that position.

When a coach puts himself or herself in the client's stiff, squeaky new shoes, he or she knows without being told which areas are likely to be causing discomfort and difficulties. Memorable coaches anticipate problems and needs and proactively take steps to smooth the path. Clients appreciate this, because it saves asking countless questions and it shows consideration for the client's need for self-respect. Empathy helps form a bond between coach and client, thereby fostering the kind of mutual commitment that characterizes coaching at its best.

Anne Sullivan, the teacher of Helen Keller, was one such empathic coach. Her steadfast determination to empathize with her very challenging student was her most notable characteristic. Sullivan overcame multiple daunting obstacles, a seven-year old, "spoiled," wildly undisciplined, extremely stubborn Helen Keller, who had been unable to see or hear almost all of her life! How would she ever be able to connect with such a pupil? How could she hope to teach her anything at all? Virtually all of the usual teaching methods were utterly useless.

Anne Sullivan is known the world over as the miracle worker because she did indeed overcome all these obstacles and succeeded in teaching Helen to an astonishing degree. Ultimately, Sullivan took Helen far beyond that first hurdle and taught her to read and write to such a phenomenal level that Helen graduated from prestigious Radcliffe College and became a famous author. Sullivan accomplished this monumental achievement largely because she tenaciously refused to be defeated, and gradually attained true empathy with Helen.

With tremendous persistence, she vicariously entered the dark, strange, silent world of her client and developed a combination of techniques that penetrated all those layers of separation between them. Once she achieved the initial breakthrough, Helen's indomitable spirit burst forth in an exultant tidal wave of freedom and carried both coach and client to undreamed of heights. Helen eventually summarized her experiences as Anne Sullivan's "client" in these words: "It was the birthday of my soul, the day my teacher came to me" (Personal letters, 1887-1901).

It is useful to keep this example in mind. The Golden Rule is a superb guiding principle for all coaches. Empathize with your client, and treat them as you would want to be treated. Comprehend, not merely their position, but also their actual circumstances. As Anne Sullivan showed us, this is the key to building bridges across even the widest chasms.

Nurturing

Nurturing encompasses a caring attitude, emphasis on development, and an understanding of the "law of the harvest." The coach nurtures the client as a gardener tends plants, providing seeds, nourishment, protection, and the room to grow, each in its turn, in the proper amount, and in its own due time. Most significant is that harvesting is a natural process that abides by certain principles, in a definite sequence. No gardener can grow award winning flowers without a sizable prior investment of time, talent, and labor. These seem to be obvious points, but they are often missed by people who are "too busy" to do more than go through the motions of coaching or who see coaching as merely a task and not the development of relationships.

If coaching is to be more than just going through the motions, the coach will have to tend to the real needs of the client. Seeds of knowledge must be planted and watered, cultivated with sufficient tools and the information necessary to use them properly, and given enough time for the seeds to germinate and take root. Only later can the flowers be weeded, and given more advanced nutrients and then still more time must be allowed before any blooms are expected. It is impossible for a gardener to receive on demand award winning blooms according to some artificially imposed "schedule" if the seedlings have been denied the time to mature and bear ripened fruit. This is the law of the harvest. Its components and its sequence are established by nature and are forever immutable.

To nurture a human being, similar natural laws must be obeyed. We cannot reasonably expect a "harvest" of expert-level performance from someone who has not had the appropriate training or the time to apply and internalize that training through actual trial and error. And in fire service, it is not the successful accomplishment of tasks that makes one great. Most firefighters are technically astute. Relationships and leadership ability are the areas most in need of nurturing. It is not enough to give a trainee a leadership position and train him/her through a manual. Manuals do not provide the necessary practical instruction on how to effectively lead people.

On a more intangible level, nurturing requires the coach to care about, and to care for, the client. This, too, cannot be faked or rushed or forced. If the coach is unwilling to learn what motivates the client, and to develop a degree of co-ownership of his/her aspirations, there will be a lack of nurturing.

There is a difference between nurturing someone and being a "mother hen." Good parents must let their children make some of their own decisions, including the inevitable mistakes, and learn to deal with the consequences. Through grappling with gradually increasing degrees of autonomy and living with the natural aftershocks of bad decisions, children eventually become responsible adults who gain independence from their parents. So, too, must good coaches allow their clients progressively increasing degrees of independence, together with the concomitant responsibility for their actions.

Any attempt to shelter people from all painful experiences will fail. No greenhouse environment, no matter how carefully constructed, can artificially protect its inhabitants, whether beans or human beings, indefinitely. Even if it could be done, the result would be people incapable of functioning as independent individuals in the real world. The key to effective nurturing is to maintain a balance between protecting the client and weaning them away from dependence. This is an imprecise process that requires coaches to continually monitor their client's progress and make the necessary adjustments. It does not lend itself to rigid timetables or cookbook recipes.

Only an actively engaged coach can know the client well enough to gauge the appropriate mix of sheltering and weaning.

Teaching

A central aspect of coaching is the process of teaching. Coaches teach their clients, first and foremost. Indeed, teaching in its fullest, most developed sense is the essence of coaching.

Many people, no matter how knowledgeable and experienced, are uncomfortable with teaching others. They often have had no training as teachers. They may have been trained by ineffective teachers themselves and assume that the methods that were used to teach them are appropriate for them now to use on others. They may have little interest in being a teacher, or they may not comprehend how the concepts that are so familiar and second nature to them are foreign, difficult, and time consuming for a novice to grasp.

There are many theories of education, each with their champions and critics. It is beyond the scope of this book to examine educational theory in depth. For our purposes, it will suffice to note that there is substantial evidence that by far the most effective teaching method, across the entire spectrum of subjects, is a common-sense approach known as direct instruction. For both short-term and long-term learning, in categories from mathematics to reading to logical reasoning, direct instruction has been shown to be a very powerful teaching method.

Direct instruction relies on time tested methods that seem obvious but are very often neglected by amateur and professional teachers alike. In essence, the best results come from teachers who: (1) organize the material into logical, step-by-step, building block units of manageable size; (2) correct students' errors immediately in a calm and nurturing manner; (3) frequently review all previously covered material and relate it to the current lesson; (4) include generous amounts of practical exercises on which students can flex their developing intellectual muscles; and (5) often test students' comprehension, formally and informally, and give them detailed feedback on their progress. With these basic principles constantly in mind, anyone can be an effective teacher.

It is crucial for coaches to spend some time developing a realistic plan for teaching their clients. This requires empathy, in that the expert coach must put himself or herself in the place of the novice client and determine what information needs to be conveyed, in what sequence, and over what period of time. The coach must realize that this material is totally new to the novice, and that most people need to see or hear unfamiliar material several times before they truly learn it. A one time explanation is not enough, particularly when there is a great deal of material involved.

People differ in the ways they learn most readily. Some people learn by reading; some learn by watching others perform the task in question; some learn by listening; and some learn by doing, armed with a basic overview of the material. Thus, every effective training program includes ample practical exercises whereby clients have the opportunity to test and expand their knowledge of previously presented oral and written material. These exercises must be done with the coach's participation to correct errors swiftly, offer helpful tips, and answer questions as they arise.

Because people vary in how they learn, it is a good idea to use all of the above methods, in combination, with any given client. At least until and unless it becomes clear that a person finds some methods far more effective than others, a coach should provide a mixture of all of these approaches (reading, shadowing, listening, and doing) to give the client the best possible chance to learn.

Teaching must also progress in a logical, building block manner. Coaches should begin by thoroughly establishing a solid foundation of the simplest, most general concepts and skills. These must include understandable definitions of all terms and acronyms, which often are used so profusely by experienced people that they fail to realize that others are unfamiliar with the vocabulary of this strange new language. It is a good idea to <u>provide a written handout that defines all the key terms and acronyms in layman's verbiage</u>.

Only when satisfied that the client has a firm grasp of the basics can the coach build upon this foundation and add the next layer of complexity. It is very easy for unskilled teachers to get off track and jump erratically from concept to concept, but that spells disaster for the learning process. This happens because the coach knows so much more about the topic than the client, and his or her brain automatically fills in all the gaps in the subject matter. By empathizing with the client and organizing a plan of action, the coach should be able to determine which concepts depend on a foundation of basic knowledge, and to teach both basic and advanced topics without skipping around and leaving gapping holes in the lessons.

Socrates, the great teacher and philosopher of ancient Greece, made a very powerful teaching tool famous. Socrates asked questions of his students, including Plato, and through their answers and his skillful use of follow up questions, he led them to think through the material for themselves. Day after day, the streets of Athens were the stage for this remarkable, interactive learning process. Plato became an immortal philosopher in his own right under the expert tutelage of his coach and mentor Socrates, and later, Plato coached another great thinker, Aristotle, who then coached Alexander the Great. Such is the nature of coaching, as one generation learns from the preceding coaches and then teaches the succeeding generation. Through his influence on his illustrious followers, Socrates profoundly affected the course of Western civilization.

This Socratic method of questions and answers is a very effective way to teach. It is often used in law schools today, because it causes students to learn a new way of thinking, not merely new information. It compels both teacher and student to be involved and actively engaged in the educational process. There is no room for passivity when there is a continual interchange of ideas, questions, and responses. The stereotype of the traditional lecture dominated classroom populated with near comatose students lulled to sleep by a droning bore of a teacher is the antithesis of a lively, stimulating Socratic dialogue.

Coaches should incorporate this technique of periodically asking their clients questions and, based on their answers, assessing the need for either additional questions or further instruction. This is an excellent way to test a student's progress, quickly, frequently, and informally, and provide crucial early warning of problem areas that require more attention from the coach. If the student hasn't learned, the material hasn't been taught.

If a student can thoroughly explain the material to the teacher, in the student's own words, the evidence is strong that the material has in fact been taught and learned.

It is also absolutely essential that coaches periodically review previously presented material with their clients. All successful teaching programs include frequent reviews of previous lessons, with logical ties to the areas currently being studied. Repetition is an important component of learning, and coaches simply have to take this into account. Again, it is all too easy to forget to conduct reviews, or to assume that they are unnecessary. If the lesson is important enough to present the first time, it is important enough to review. If it is not reviewed, there is a high probability that it will not be learned. Remember, people internalize new information best when the material is presented in multiple ways (reading, observing, hearing, and doing) and at multiple times (reviewing). In instructional terms, what is required are real events, initiatives, and experiences capable of changing the coaching trajectory, i.e., making coaching more central to the ever increasing role of the leader as a teacher. Keep it simple, keep it practical, and ensure that leaders are doing the actual teaching. The teaching purpose of coaching/mentoring should be cultural, rather than structural; personal development is the first priority—the kind that produces enhanced knowledge of attitudes, resulting in new and improved behaviors. Credibility and competence are the two essential things that clients are looking for in this aspect of coaching.

Organizing

A coach must be organized to be of much help to the client and must also help the client become organized. The systematic, methodical approach is essential, both in preparing an effective coaching program and in building the "protégé" into a more effective individual.

An organized coach will know at the outset what he or she wants to achieve and will focus every aspect of the program toward that goal. As the saying goes, "If you don't know where you're going, how will you know when you get there?" By developing a desired end state before beginning the coaching process, a coach gains the ability to gear every effort in that direction. Organization and planning are a vital part of a good teaching/coaching program. The time and effort spent organizing thoughts and materials into a logical, building-block, sequential plan of lessons all aimed at a definite, precisely defined target of what needs to be learned, will pay big dividends in the form of improved learning and the quicker, better performance that follows.

Coaching is too important a journey to commence without a prior investment of time and effort to develop an organized road map or plan of action. Coaching involves real people and real commitments between them, on a continuing basis. It is worth the time spent to organize a coherent, individually tailored plan.

Organizing may not be the most emotionally rewarding facet of coaching, or the most fun. People tend to prefer to spend their limited time actually interacting with clients or engaged in other activities that feel more like action and less like paperwork. But if you neglect to organize your efforts, you are unlikely to achieve the best results. In essence, the time you devote to organizing saves a lot of time and energy. It minimizes or eliminates the resources squandered on irrelevant or secondary activities, while focusing maximum attention on the real goal and the key stepping stones along the way.

A topic by topic breakdown of the important ingredients of the process provides a ready-made outline to keep you on track and aimed at the target. An outline compels you to examine the essential facets of an effective coaching approach. It leads you to devote some time to planning a method of addressing each aspect of the coaching process, armed with an understanding of what should be achieved. Similar to a good checklist, an outline provides some assurance that major components will not be inadvertently left out or given inadequate attention. This is all part and parcel of what it means to organize.

Finally, because one significant lesson all coaches should teach their clients is organizational skill, it is necessary first for the coach to learn and use this tool. As mentioned previously, a coach must model the desired behavior.

Responding

Coaching is a communicative process. It is not a method for shooting information at a person who writes down every word. The ideal coach is not a guru perched motionless atop a remote Himalayan mountain peak, dispensing wisdom periodically. Coaching involves genuine two-way communication between coach and client on a protracted, continuing basis.

Coaches must truly listen to questions from their clients and respond to them fully. This requires active listening from clients. Coaches should follow up with more questions after the initial question to ensure their clients understand the answer and are satisfied with it. It is important to remember that the primary customer in any coach-client relationship is the client. Who knows best when there are relationship problems, inadequately answered questions, or a pace that makes effective learning impossible. The coach must respond to the client's needs if the coaching process is to succeed.

Less obviously, but also very important, the coach must respond on multiple communication levels throughout the coaching process. The client may be reluctant to voice certain concerns or to ask too many questions.

An effective coach must be alert for nonverbal indications and cues. It takes some diligence, sensitivity, and perceptiveness for a coach to develop the capacity to respond in this manner. A client who discovers the coach is sufficiently in tune to respond even to unspoken questions and problems will be more likely to appreciate that coach and to bond with him.

A coach should be available much of the time. Particularly in the early phases of a coaching relationship, a coach must be prepared to devote sizeable amounts of time and has to be physically present and actively involved with the client if the process is to work. Many aspects of the coaching process require frequent interaction and the continual exchange of information.

Do not confuse responding with being reactive or sitting back waiting to answer questions. A responsive coach does not merely react, but is proactive. Coaches must anticipate needs, problems, and concerns, and try to take care of them in advance. This is one area where another key principle, organization, is particularly helpful. With proper organization, a coach can foresee many of the usual pitfalls along the way and do as much as possible to build precautions against them into the coaching plan.

Jaime Escalante demonstrated the principle of responsiveness in a most remarkable way, as memorialized in the film *Stand and Deliver*. He stunned his colleagues when he left his high paying position in the computer industry to become a mathematics teacher in a low-income Hispanic section of Los Angeles. What he found when he entered his classroom was a disheartened collection of underachieving, streetwise teenagers whose minds and hearts were on anything but mathematics. But Escalante was determined to use all of his considerable skills to make a difference for these young people, regardless of the cost to him personally in terms of time, effort, lost income, and frustration.

Escalante decided to teach his students calculus, not just high school mathematics, although many people would have considered that an achievement in itself. To make this happen, he knew he had to respond to his class not as a class, and not as a cluster of stereotypes but as unique individuals. He worked hard to explain calculus from the most basic principles, illustrating his points with real life examples from his students' own experiences. He appealed to their ethnic pride by stressing the illustrious history of Hispanic achievement in higher mathematics. He tailored his teaching methods to the needs of each student and if that meant supplemental review sessions in his own home over dinner, then that is exactly what he provided. Even after he suffered a serious heart attack, he refused to relax; his students needed him, and he was not about to let them down.

The results of Jaime Escalante's work were so phenomenal that they became the subject of a popular motion picture, hardly the place one would usually expect to find a high school calculus class! His inner-city students performed like superstars on the difficult Advanced Placement calculus examination and earned a huge head start on their college mathematics careers. Escalante repeated this feat year after year, coaching/teaching ever-increasing numbers of students from his previously obscure school to reach unheard-of achievements in calculus. Moreover, his responsiveness to and total involvement with each student helped them in many aspects of their lives, not just in academics. Under his care, they proved to the world and to themselves that they could excel in any forum, against any odds. That is the impact of a coach/teacher who responds to each client/student on a meaningful, individualized level.

Inspiring

A coach should be more than a good role model, teacher, and helpful acquaintance. Important though all of those are, true coaching encompasses something extra, an element of inspiration. The coach who can inspire will have a profound, deeply rooted effect for perhaps an entire lifetime. When inspired, a person is powerfully motivated to transform himself or herself into something better than before. Inspiration is the key to the most fundamental, core level transformations.

Inspiration is one way in which leaders differ from managers. A leader has a broader vision and a far-reaching drive that goes beyond the more limited focus on daily operations that is the typical province of managers. The best coaches will also be good leaders because similar qualities are required of both.

To some extent, inspiration is a matter of chemistry and does not lend itself to conscious analysis or application; but there are things a coach can do to enhance this important element of the coaching process.

It is useful to read about leadership, especially in-depth discussions of some inspirational leaders. Reading a few case studies of effective leaders will lend at least an intellectual understanding of some of the key factors that can form the foundation for more pragmatic, action driving steps.

Probably the most significant factor contributing to one person's ability to inspire another is integrity. The coach must have, and be perceived to have, integrity. No one is apt to be inspired by a hypocrite. We are moved by people we admire, and we admire people who exemplify qualities we want to have. Honesty, consistency, and commitment to correct principles are traits we can all strive to incorporate into our approach to life. Over time, with sufficient testing in stressful situations, these traits will add up to integrity, and help us to inspire those who look to us for guidance.

The other central element of inspirational character is a selfless, altruistic nature. People who are willing to sacrifice their own self-interest for the good of others tend to inspire others. Altruism is a noble quality refreshingly different from the usual human tendency to ask "what's in it for me." We trust and admire people who have proven themselves to be unselfish, and that naturally leads to our being inspired by their example.

Example, as usual, is crucial. Although a client might be inspired by the coach's words, that will soon wear off if the coach's actions fail to support what is said. If the coach is the type of person others might wish to emulate, and if the client has ample opportunities to observe the coach handling difficult situations, the inspiration will follow.

A contemporary coach who embodies the principle of inspiration is Marva Collins. This famous educator has taught generations of impoverished, disadvantaged, inner city children from the roughest neighborhoods of Chicago. Collins has never been content just to achieve an orderly classroom, although many would consider that a major victory under the circumstances. Despite the discouraging predictions of hordes of self-styled educational experts, she has taught thousands of poverty level African-American children to read, write, compute, and achieve several grade levels above their age group. More than this, she has instilled in them a genuine love of Shakespeare, Dante, the Greek philosophers, and many other things typically assumed to be far beyond the grasp of her young pupils. Under her guidance, African-American children as young as 3 or 4 years old learn to read, memorize, and recite lengthy passages, and analyze sophisticated themes from the great thinkers of civilization. She has proven her maxim, "Any child can be a real achiever," thousands of times over.

Marva Collins is, of course, a master teacher. Her no nonsense, low budget, back to basics approach has worked wonders, especially when combined with her unconquerable faith in the worth of every child and her absolute refusal to accept failure from herself or her students. She has twice, 20 years apart, been featured in glowing reports on the television news magazine program "60 Minutes." She has twice been formally invited by presidents of the United States to be Secretary of Education, invitations she declined because she did not want to leave her inner-city classroom. She is in constant demand as a speaker and is the author of several successful books. She has achieved her astonishing results, where so many others have failed, in large part because she knows how to inspire her very youthful clients. Her students see her everyday working endlessly with total dedication and genuine love with each individual child, no matter how difficult and resistant to change the child may be. They see her doing the same things she exhorts them to do, including reading and re-reading every book she assigns them. They see her, an African-American woman from a small town in Alabama, refusing to throw any "pity parties" for herself no matter how much prejudice and discrimination is thrown in her path.

They see her devoting her time, talents, indeed everything she has, including her life savings, to Westside Preparatory and the other schools she has founded. They see her demanding the same lofty standards from herself that she expects from them, excellence and achievement, hard work and persistence. And they see that she never gives up on them, just as she tells them every day never to give up on themselves. Day after day,

Marva spends time with every student, one on one. She cradles a child's face lovingly in her hands, looks into the young eyes that, in her words, "hold wonder like a cup," and says, "You are a very, very bright child. You are going to succeed. You are going to produce. I will never let you fail. I promise you that!" As one of her former students recalled on "60 Minutes," 20 years after he had been in Marva's classroom, "When somebody does that every day for 2 years, it transforms you!" That is the impact an inspirational teacher/mentor can have. Teachers/Mentors such as Marva Collins achieve titanic accomplishments because they inspire. And they inspire because they live the principles they teach. Every coach must aspire to do the same.

Networking

A good coach introduces the client to other people who can also provide support, information, and resources. Networking is vital to effective functioning in the real world, and the coach should give the client a head start on establishing those key contacts.

It takes years to cultivate and build a network of friends and associates of sufficient breadth and depth to be useful in a wide range of situations. One of the greatest resources an "old head" has is a network of people who can help cut through the usual tangle of red tape and quickly obtain the desired result. These contacts are enormously valuable shortcuts who effectively reduce untold hours wasted in researching issues from scratch or running into bureaucratic roadblocks. In some cases, it is literally impossible to accomplish a given task without the extra boost a good network can supply. When something must get done, reliance on such a network is a tremendous force multiplier.

Of course, a coach cannot simply deliver a network to a client as if it were a notebook. Relationships are nontransferable, at least not directly transferable. But it is possible to act as a go-between and a facilitator. The coach should personally take the client to meet as many contacts as feasible, one at a time, in their respective work areas. These meetings should be rather informal, under pleasant, ice-breaking conditions, with an eye toward helping the client establish a relationship with each contact.

The very act of physically accompanying the client on a series of personal visits to meet and chat with contacts is a valuable lesson, because it will demonstrate the importance of getting out from behind the desk, escaping from the office, and interacting with people face-to-face. Particularly in this electronic age of e-mail, voice mail, cell phones, and faxes, it is very easy to lose the personal touch that is so central to effective networking. No matter how high-tech our society becomes, human beings relate much more naturally to each other than to any other means of communication no matter how convenient or timely. Coaches/Mentors must show how to use, cultivate, and keep a network flourishing, now more than ever.

The coach should supplement a personal visit to each contact with a list of people, addresses, office locations, telephone numbers, and e-mail addresses, complete with a brief description of who they are and what they do. The network is too important to entrust it entirely to the client's memory; a written record will be a valuable insurance policy for the clients to rely on. Plus, the list may serve to jog the mentor's memory of each contact and lead to further helpful insights.

In addition to sharing a personal preexisting network with the client, the coach should teach the client how to build upon this nucleus and add contacts of his or her own. The art of being a professional friend, exchanging legitimate favors, and serving as a prized contact for other people, is a vital lesson for the coach to convey. This is the type of real world practical skill that is an ideal subject for coaching.

Goal-Setting

Many young and inexperienced people fail to understand the importance of setting proper goals and objectives or they lack the expertise to make their goals realistic and attainable. Coaches set goals, teach the need for goal-setting, and help their clients master the process of establishing and effectively pursuing goals.

First, an integral part of the organizational aspect of coaching is to set goals. Very early in the relationship with the client, the coach should carefully establish some tangible goals to achieve with the client. As always, the goals should be worthwhile, specific, attainable, measurable, and have a timetable. This is critically important, because the goals will be the target for everything that is done from that point on, the end towards which all efforts are directed. Once the goals are established, the coach should periodically monitor progress toward attaining each goal (and milestones along the way) and make any necessary adjustments to the goals.

All of the coaches discussed in this section are outstanding examples of people who set highly challenging, worthy goals and then did everything necessary to achieve them. Jackie Robinson, Anne Sullivan, Jaime Escalante, Socrates, and Marva Collins knew exactly what they wanted to achieve, and they devoted themselves to their goals with magnificent persistence and dedication. Their single-minded pursuit of deeply felt goals, goals that motivated them from the very core of their hearts, enabled them to achieve dizzying heights, against incredible odds.

In addition to setting and stressing the importance of goals for the coaching process, a coach must also teach proper goal-setting techniques. Many young people confuse goals with wishes, and fail to grasp the elements that are essential to transforming mere wishful thinking into an attainable and worthwhile plan for the future. Also, in today's culture of instant gratification and minuscule attention spans, some people have never learned the discipline that is so central to the determined pursuit of a clearly defined goal. It is not uncommon for people to be unfamiliar with the very concept of deferred gratification, let alone be able to implement it. A coach's work is not done until the client moves beyond that level into the realm of a mature goal setter and goal achiever.

An excellent way of doing this is to meet privately with the client and let the person talk about background, goals (both near and long term), and hopes and dreams. The coach can share present and past goals with the client too, and in so doing illustrate by example some of the factors the coach/mentor has used in his or her own goal setting. This will highlight some of the elements the client may have omitted, and vividly demonstrate how they contribute to making goals realistic in concept and reality in execution. It should become apparent to the client that there are significant differences between workable goals on the one hand and pleasant but less reality-based dreams, hopes, or wishes on the other.

The coach should teach the principles of effective goal-setting and guide the client to gradually develop and refine goals, objectives, milestones, measures of progress, and to a plan of action.

Through the study and evaluation of these coaching principles as practiced by several notable examples, you can gain a working understanding of what it takes to be a coach. Ultimately, however, it is only through actually trying these principles that you will truly learn what they mean. The learning curve will probably be neither smooth nor easy. But "coach" is not a title we can give to ourselves or have bestowed upon us through a simple administrative act. It is an honor that must be earned everyday as we diligently strive to apply each of the principles.

If we succeed, it will be because we have learned how to use coaching as a "tool kit for our time machine." Through effective implementation of the tools that are the coaching principles, we will influence the future and change the course of events in ways both great and small. As coaches, our greatest reward may be one day to witness our clients in turn become coaches.

A major challenge of contemporary departments is to nurture the talent and interest of all personnel so that the needs of both the employees as well as the public can be met. To achieve this worthy goal, leaders must take seriously their obligation to coach their people, if they expect them to meet the needs of society in a world as complex as we live in today. Coaches must have the vision to develop the leadership potential in fire service personnel for the global and highly inter-dependent world of the future.

3. Who Is a Coach?

A coach is a person who facilitates learning that results in performance enhancement or personal growth. A coach is a trusted role model, adviser, wise person, friend, steward, or guide—a person who works with people, teams, and organizations to tap into dormant potential and enhance performance. A coach is someone who is trained and devoted to guiding others into overcoming repetitive, unproductive patterns, gaining personal awareness, overcoming interpersonal "blind" spots, and increasing self-efficacy.

The most profound way to learn both tangible skills and intangibles, like values, is directly from other people who already possess those qualities and who are available to offer guidance and counsel. The fire officer rank is a natural springboard for coaching because subordinate personnel are looking for leadership and guidance from you. As a fire officer, you have a built-in opportunity for positively influencing your subordinates and for being a change agent. But just being an officer does not equate with being an effective coach. It requires some basic yet vital skills for developing your subordinates and getting the most out of them.

4. Who Should Coach?

Coaching skills and the coaching process are important for anyone in a supervisory position. You don't have to have the label *"coach"* in order to use coaching skills. The main qualification is that the coach must possess some skill, knowledge, or ability beyond that of the client.

The primary non-academic qualification for coaches is the desire to see people break out of unproductive patterns, manage change, learn new skills, embrace new roles in response to change, and stretch into unfamiliar territory. As a coach, you are someone who does not ask your subordinates to do something you would not do. Rather, you are someone who consistently sets your own *stretch* goals and strives toward your own personal growth.

5. Why Coach?

An organization's culture is the collective (conscious and unconscious) attitudes, beliefs, values and behaviors that define "how we do things around here." However, leaders set the tone, pace, and expectations for a culture as they role model what is expected, desired, and/or tolerated in the department. Truly effective leaders:

1. Set clear direction (vision, mission, strategy, goals) for the Department, and do so as collaboratively as possible.

2. Role model the core values of the department, and

3. Coach people to alignment and optimal performance on the above.

What has been largely missing so far is the ability of leaders and managers to coach and create a coaching culture. As leaders become skilled at the leadership practice of coaching (the antithesis of 'command & control' management) and authentically become a coach for their teams, they experience powerful benefits. They also set the tone and expectations for coaching to become a legitimate leadership and team practice within and across the department.

As this transformation occurs, a "performance-focused, feedback-rich" department develops, establishing a competitive advantage over other departments that adhere to a more traditional command and control style.

Creating a coaching culture is THE NEXT STEP in the evolution of the high-performance department. Through this transformation, officers and leaders become skilled coaches for their teams. Then, the teams also learn the practice of coaching, gaining a new, integral way of interacting with one another.

When an entire organization is "on the same page" and shares a common coaching language and approach to working together and solving problems, we see the following results:

- Leaders become more effective in their roles.

- More open and trusting relationships are formed.

- Interpersonal and organizational conflict is more quickly resolved.

- Teamwork and true collaboration become easier-and expected.

- Learning is captured and shared across the team more willingly, thus reducing errors and cycle time.

- Creativity and innovation are unleashed and more energy is focused on solving customers' needs.

- Resistance to change is greatly reduced - more people actively support change initiatives because they are involved.

- Departmental values are revitalized and become meaningful.

- People receive the developmental time and attention they need in order to grow.

- The department becomes a better place to work and personnel consequently become more engaged in their work and in serving the mission of the department.

- People have more fun and turnover is reduced.

What is the value of these dynamics changing? Your department's bottom-line performance is directly improved and sustained through competitive advantage.

It does not take a futurist to see that the world is becoming more complex. The amount of information that gets thrown at us each day is growing; the number of daily decisions required of us is multiplying, and the rapidity of change we must assimilate is now beyond a rapid pace. Fire service personnel are expected to do more with less and, when lives are at stake, there is no room for error.

Few people can consistently handle the pace and amount of change that is required to perform at an optimal level and remain competitive. New leaders are increasingly finding themselves in pressure-packed situations where they are expected to rapidly turn around under-achieving departments or create better performance even though impediments to that performance often lie outside their control.

Another important reason for using coaching comes from the fact that the fire service industry has witnessed many management failures. Over the past twenty years, fire departments promoted many technically astute employees who had little experience in managing people. The result was less than ideal. What worked in the technical aspects of departments-stubborn drive, ignoring competing interests, dogged pursuit, and compulsivity-were not the kinds of leadership characteristics that generated creativity and enthusiasm. In fact, hard-driving, competitive, individuals have been criticized for not being people oriented and encouraging. In such conditions as these, coaching skills are proving to be an invaluable resource for leaders who want to accomplish departmental tasks by empowering everyone to provide input and maintain accountability. Coaching can provide a customized, one on one crash course in management and leadership. In addition, there are several other reasons for coaching that warrant discussion. A fire department will benefit from coaching by increasing Cost Effectiveness, Flexibility, Transfer of Learning, Mentoring, Skills Practice, and Feedback.

Cost Effectiveness

Fire departments spend millions of dollars on training each year. Some of it is cost effective in that it is well designed and targeted to meet specific needs. But much of it is "shotgun" in nature, an approach that is used in the hope that some of the pellets will hit the target. In reality, some people need some of the training some of the time. But departmental philosophy often holds that everyone needs all of the training that is offered. This is expensive. The departmental costs of coaching are much less than classroom and group training because coaching is an approach that is targeted to a specific need with a limited number of people. The goal is to help someone or a smaller number of people change to meet a specific challenge.

Flexibility

The name of the game in departments today is flexibility and the ability to adjust quickly. Economic and community conditions, including customer (the public) demands, change rapidly. When the economy is prosperous, departments strive for rapid growth. When market conditions are sluggish, departments attempt to add value through improved customer relations. Efforts are aimed at meeting demands through existing products and services. Both conditions require a flexible, on-time learning approach that maximizes time and shortens the learning curve. Coaching is ideal for this.

The intent of *"Traditional"* classroom training is to put everyone on the same page and create uniformity of thought and action. This is an effective way to handle many training objectives where compliance, not originality, is the sought after goal.

Transfer of Learning

Another detrimental factor for departments is the low rate of transfer of learning from classroom training. Some estimates are that less than 20% of stated objectives are remembered within seven days of training. Within sixty days, there is less than 5% retention of stated objectives. Time and retention are inversely related, which does not speak well to the relationship between cost effectiveness and the retention of learning.

Obviously, to retain information, training must be presented more often, yet for those who use the skills only on a sporadic basis, even this approach does not guarantee a high rate of learning retention. Conversely, coaching provides a much higher rate of transfer because the skills and knowledge are targeted and immediately used on the job. In fact, skills and knowledge that are not immediately required are usually not the grist of coaching conversations. Even when the coaching conversations are focused on affective or cognitive change, and less related to targeted behaviors, there is an ultimate benefit in changing behavior.

Mentoring

Mentors take a special interest in their protégés. In fact the definition of protégé is one whose welfare, training, or career is promoted by an influential person. Used interchangeably with the term *coaching*, the idea of mentoring is as old as Greek Mythology. In Homer's *Odyssey*, the King of Ithaca, Odysseus, left his young son, Telemachus, in the care of Mentor, a wise and proven teacher who had agreed to raise the boy until Odysseus could return. Mentor modeled the manhood skills that Telemachus needed, and the young prince grew as a whole person, a leader, and a man of integrity. Both coaches and mentors have the competence to pass on knowledge and skills through example, inner authority, and dialogue.

Skills Practice

Although team or group coaching will be discussed later in this text, it bears brief discussion here. This is a type of coaching in which a team or group of individuals comes together. Certain benefits can be derived from team and group coaching that are not available in one-to-one coaching, namely the opportunity to practice skills safely. For example, *group* (a group of fire officers) coaching allows officers and firefighters to practice new skills and behaviors in a supportive environment before trying them on the job. The range of new behaviors to explore is nearly infinite. Participants can enhance their presentation skills, learn to mediate conflict, practice new supervisory skills, role-play meeting leadership, practice cross-generational and diversity communication skills, and learn delegation methods. Practicing these interactions and skills greatly enhances a participant's chances for job success. In addition, team coaching teaches officers better communication skills, increases their understanding of personal style differences, delivers effective 360° feedback practices, and gives them experience in team building.

Feedback

The opportunity for feedback is another group or team coaching function that bears mentioning. Groups provide an opportunity for members to receive feedback. Group feedback often is more powerful than individual feedback because feedback from only one person, even if it is a supervisor, is more readily dismissed (Jacobs, Harvill, & Masson, 1994) "Group feedback partly differs from feedback during an individual session by generally being more powerful. When only one person is giving feedback, the receiver can dismiss that person's viewpoint. When six or seven people are saying the same thing, it is hard to deny what's being said. Often [fire service personnel] have an unrealistic perception of themselves, and feedback from [others] can cause them to expand and alter their self-perceptions (pp 4-5)." And certainly supervisors can more readily dismiss the feedback of only one or two of their employees. But feedback is harder to ignore when six or seven people are saying similar things and saying them in the spirit of good will. And in those teams in which members experience mutual trust, feedback is an invaluable precursor to altering behavior and practicing new behaviors. We will discuss the importance as well as the rules for confidentiality later in this book.

6. Kinds of Coaching

Most people think the term *coaching* refers to one-on-one interaction between a coach and a client. In fact, there are five different kinds of coaching: *individual, pair, team, group, and organizational.* All possess somewhat overlapping learning objectives, but each is unique as well.

Individual Coaching

The choice of individual coaching indicates that a given set of learning objectives applies to only one person. But there is perhaps more variance in the ultimate goals of individual coaching. In addition to outer work that is skills and work process focused, individual coaching lends itself to inner work that is related to self-efficacy, self-esteem, perceptual accuracy, and interpersonal attractiveness.

For example, in an effort to avoid what has been termed "new leader dilemma" (being terminated within eighteen months for failing to grasp the new role), newly appointed leaders often employ individual coaching in order to gain both inner and outer resources. Many must adjust to their new positions by improving their self-efficacy in an effort to learn not only new skills that fit the position, but also new concepts like political intelligence, the ability to diagnose the organizational atmosphere, and an awareness of the commitment level of employees to follow a vision. Individual coaching lends itself to the apprenticeship model where a teacher is personally committed to the personal growth of the protégé for the purpose of advancing the work begun by the mentor. The relationship can be quite intimate and trust is an essential component for this relationship to achieve maximum results. It is through a professionally intimate and trusting relationship that the coach/mentor is viewed as attractive and credible. Ideally, the protégé should be aware of the coach/mentor's admiration and interest in his/her professional growth. It is this state of mutual admiration and trust that provides the foundation for feedback and learning.

Pair Coaching

According to several biographical sources Steven Jobs and Steven Wazniak could have benefited from pair coaching had it been in vogue during their start up of Apple Computers. Jobs was the salesman, the man who desired a public presence and wanted to compete head on with IBM. If he was fire, Wazniak was ice. Steven Wazniak was the person more interested in quality. He was more low-key, caring less for the public eye and instead sought to build a dependable product. The potential was incredible, but the two men hit an impasse as a result of their personal style differences and the result was the abandonment of their relationship. Eventually, neither was part of the Apple empire until much later when Jobs was again brought back to head up the company.

Pair coaching is a unique method for a number of situations. For example, pair coaching can:

- Help a battalion chief and a lieutenant form a partnership that maximizes the strength of their relationship or help the two people gain direction in their departmental mission. A supervisory style that focuses on people, their values, their motivations, their growth can measurably enhance their performance—even during emergencies. Constructive coaching builds on the transactional approach. Together, the two styles offer a broad range of leadership because they encompass a task focus as well as an emotional focus. Constructive coaching recognizes that behavior is explained by motivation and emotional factors, not simply rational reasons that are implied with the traditional transactional leadership approach. For lieutenants, having a constructive relationship with their battalion chiefs, and the rest of the unit, is crucial to understanding just what each individual firefighter/EMT can contribute to the broader departmental mission.

- Be a powerful way to help a leader and one of his or her supervisors to strategically plan for departmental or team improvement.

- Provide a process for dealing with conflict.

Team Coaching

For the purposes of this text, the term *team* refers to a department or smaller segment of a department in which the members have regular contact with each other and share common goals and mission. Members of work teams are familiar with each other and exhibit some of the same roles, conflicts, strengths, and challenges, as do families. Of course, some teams are more enmeshed and possess more family-like characteristics than others, and perhaps none more so than fire service personnel who literally share living, eating, sleeping, and bathroom facilities with each other while on duty.

Intact teams always present challenges to the team coach. The more enmeshed the team, the more likely it is for resistance to rear its ugly head in the face of change. Conflict rises in direct proportion and is more common, as are secrets, sub-grouping (cliques), and triangulation (a response to anxiety involving a third person to relieve some of the pressure experienced between an individual and another person or group).

Thus, an effective team coach must possess skills and knowledge in the psychology of group development, family dynamics, and conflict management. Possible coaching goals include identifying the impediments to performance, challenging individuals to take responsibility for both individual and team visions and mission, and instilling a heightened atmosphere of service to others.

Group/Shift Coaching

While similar to team coaching in that there are more than two people involved, groups don't necessarily have regular daily contact with one another and may only share in the completion of the overall vision of the organization or professional association. These groups may be composed of managers or supervisors of the various departments, various emergency management units, or an organization composed of fire chiefs from around the state. The goal of such groups is usually educational or visionary in nature and membership varies more frequently than does the membership of intact teams. For these groups, coaches are involved in the design and delivery of learning development programs as well as in strategic planning for the enhancement of the entire organization or professional association.

Career Coaching/Succession Planning

Succession planning is becoming a more vital function in today's fire departments. Retaining and promoting quality fire officers not only saves money, but also ensures continued excellence in service. More specifically, the roles of fire officers who are involved in career coaching within fire departments include:

- Creating succession plans for the organization: Identifying and adjusting "job-fit" between the organization and the employees.

- Facilitating personal insight: Assessment of personal style and guiding fictions. Increasing awareness of personal "blind" spots, and gaining knowledge of the motives underlying behavior.

- Educating: Teaching interpersonal communication skills, providing information, and relaying information regarding learning opportunities.

- Action planning: Setting, implementing, and revisiting goals.

- Counseling: Problem-solving, identifying self-defeating behaviors and "knee-jerk" reactions, resolving conflicts, conducting interventions in cases of inappropriate behavior and other remedial corrections of individual and team functioning.

7. Differences Between Training and Coaching

There are both similarities and differences between training and coaching. While both are used to help people learn something, training-with some exceptions-is limited to the systematic presentation of information. Examples include the presentation of facts, ideas, laws, concepts, and case studies. Although experiential activities are often a part of many training experiences, they would be examples of the use of coaching as part of the training curriculum. A coach is more hands-on and active than most trainers. Trainers rely more on the participants assimilating information presented to them. Coaches focus on participants learning sets of skills.

Arson investigation classes provide a good example. Typically, the classes begin with classroom lectures and reading material. The trainer might explain the criminal statutes governing arson, describe the motivations of arsonists, and talk about juvenile fire setters. The class would hear about methods arsonists use to set fires and the types of evidence resulting from certain chemicals and liquids. The trainer would likely show slides and video of arson fire scenes. At the end, participants would be tested to see if they could answer questions over the material presented.

A larger amount of information can be presented to large numbers of participants in a minimal amount of time using classroom lectures. The presenter may be brilliant, the best source of material in the discipline with current examples and excellent graphics. Or the presenter may be dull, reading the outline from bad slides in a monotone. We all know what happens in classrooms. Some participants are interested and others are not. While some take notes, others sleep in the back row. Some are good at taking tests and others have testing anxiety. It's the traditional model.

The other part of learning about arson investigation must happen in the field. A coach will lead the participants to one or more arson scenes and demonstrate the needed investigation skills. The coach will show participants how to spot the fire's origin, how to observe the charring pattern on walls and doors, floors and ceilings, and what to look for in terms of the fire's evolution from room to room. The coach will demonstrate how to take a sample of flooring or debris and seal it in a container marked as evidence.

Then the coach will encourage each participant to practice those investigative skills. The coach will watch them, point out better ways to collect information, work with each person hands-on. As an evaluation of the learning exercise, the coach may arrange for participants to demonstrate their skills on a new fire scene or a special prop made for the evaluation. Participant gets evaluated and their performances are critiqued so all of them can learn from the mistakes and successes of the others.

Coaching takes more time than training. It requires individual attention and the opportunity for participants to observe skills being demonstrated. Then the coach must motivate participants to practice the proper performance of skills before evaluation. Coaching is interactive. In a coaching relationship, there's no way to sleep in the back row.

8. Do Cultural Differences Present Specific Coaching Challenges?

Unquestionably, Yes. Some of our own best personal and professional coaching experiences have been through our relationships with clients of a different culture than ours. Understanding cultural differences is a must, especially for managers and supervisor who, sooner or later, will direct the activities of culturally diverse employees. Most departments that do have diversity programs have ones that focus on understanding, and appreciating differences such as culture, ethnicity, race, gender, class, religion, lifestyle, age, or nationality.

Because coaching involves an active approach, it is important to be aware of the various cultural backgrounds of clients. If you feel you are not well versed in multicultural issues and coaching considerations, it is necessary that you seek out course work, workshops, readings, and life experiences that will broaden your understanding. The American Society For Training and Development (ASTD) and the Society For Human Resources Management (SHRM) are both excellent sources for cultural knowledge and training opportunities.

The set of guidelines in Appendix I comes from the Association for Specialists in Group Work, a subgroup of the American Counseling Association. These guidelines outline what a leader needs to know in regard to counseling diverse populations. These guidelines are thorough and easily apply to the work fire officers do in their leadership and coaching. In the appendix, you will notice that I have replaced "group worker" with [coach] in keeping with the subject matter of this book.

This document offers a set of suggestions and is a starting point for coaches as we become increasingly aware, knowledgeable, and skillful in coaching diverse people. It is not intended to be a "how to" document. It is written as a call to action and/or as a guideline and represents a commitment to moving forward with an agenda for addressing and understanding the needs of the people we serve. It is suggested that this document serve as a living document that changes as our knowledge and skills in coaching diverse people increases.

9. Is There a Map to Guide My Coaching?

Yes, there are several, and it is important that you borrow from various sources to derive your own approach. The primary approach of this book comes from one that I have found to be extremely effective over the past twenty years: Adlerian Psychology. Alfred Adler, a contemporary of Sigmund Freud, created one of the most comprehensive approaches in use today. Adlerian, as it is commonly called, is a theory of personality development, as well as a theory of psychology.

I use this approach every day in my coaching work because it is comprehensive and lends itself to the use of additional, supportive approaches. Other approaches that I incorporate depending upon the kind of coaching and the particular challenge facing the client include the group dynamics of Kurt Lewin (1935), the cognitive psychology of Aaron Beck (1976), Albert Ellis (1962), and the individual psychology of Alfred Adler (1934).

The coach's style is perhaps equally important as the guiding approach. Trust, enthusiasm, honesty, coaching experience, and what Mary Beth O'Neill (2000) calls "signature presence" are vital regardless of the particular approach. The style outlined in this book is highly active and often directive. This is not an approach or a field that lends itself to a non-directive, mostly listening kind of style. It takes too long. Fire departments require performance and efficiency from their leaders and employees, and rightly so. Reacting slowly to change damages performance and puts lives at risk.

Whether coaches adhere to one or several approaches is a purposive decision and should be based on the coach's personality and personal beliefs about the origins of poor performance and how personal and organizational change comes about.

If you have not adopted a stance on what stimulates change, it may be important to first consider the following stimulus questions:

1. What are the factors (personal, organizational) contributing to poor performance?

2. What are the habits (inner and outer habits) of high performing people?

3. What is your belief about what generates high performance? Personality? Habits? Knowledge? Self esteem? Self-Efficacy?

4. What are your personal beliefs about human nature? Are people basically good, untrustworthy, self-starters, never satisfied, moving forward, prone to destruction?

5. Are people driven (from past events) or goal striving (moving toward the future)?

6. Why do people do what they do?

7. Are there basic needs we all share?

It is the premise of this book that coaches should adopt their own personal theory of human development and intervention. Theories answer all of the above questions and act as a guide for designing coaching interventions. This will be discussed in great detail later in this book.

10. What Are the Most Important Coaching Competencies?

In her book, *Executive Coaching With Backbone and Heart*, Mary Beth O'Neill (2000) makes an important connection for coaches. She indicates that business results and human processes must always remain linked. In support of this stance, it is the premise of this book that by definition, coaching is intended to:

1. Help clients perform to their personal best.

2. Help departments create and hold a competitive advantage through high performing employees.

3. Create an atmosphere of ongoing learning through mutual accountability and feedback at all levels of the department.

4. Instill the spirit of service to one another and to the community at large.

To accomplish these objectives, coaches should possess a number of competencies as listed in the Appendix. Although by no means exhaustive, these competencies provide a targeted guideline for coaches in their professional development (O'Neill, 2000; Hargrove, 1995; and Hudson, 1999).

11. What Are Examples of The Kinds of Challenges Coaches Face?

There are literally thousands of possible challenges coaches could face, in fact, as many challenges as there are people. So, in no way is this book capable of covering all of them, nor would you want to read about them all. But it may be helpful to mention some prominent ones. Challenges can be those that require *remediation*, meaning that a behavior, action, or attitude has been designated as problematic and needs to be corrected, or *proactive*, meaning that the coaching is used to forestall a problem or build strength toward a targeted goal. Remedial coaching addresses inappropriate behavior, ineffective leadership, or recurring errors. Proactive coaching is often involved in preparing for leadership, learning a new position, preparing for a new product launch or leading an ad hoc team. Here are some additional examples:

- A person is promoted to a supervisory position yet has strictly a technical background, so must learn to manage people quickly.

- An older, experienced fire officer suddenly confronted with young firefighters just out of the academy, less than half the officer's age, must learn to supervise different generations of firefighters.

- Reorganization places a people oriented, outgoing officer under the watchful scrutiny of a notoriously introverted and uptight chief. The officer must develop a relationship of mutual respect that will allow continued success.

- A driven, task-oriented officer gets feedback that her supervisory style is too harsh, cold, and aloof. Firefighters are discouraged and quitting. How will she learn to lighten up and yet still get things done?

- A lateral move for a supervisor means getting acquainted with the idiosyncrasies and personalities of the staff. How can this be done and avoid delays in both personal and teams effectiveness?

- A lieutenant's plate is full yet the battalion chief continues to give her more assignments. She must learn to delegate some of the tasks and oversee them to successful completion.

- The makeup of a department has changed due to retirements and new recruits. The supervisor must learn to manage conflict within generational differences.

- A veteran fire-fighter/EMT of twelve years has recently been promoted to lieutenant and now is in charge of former peers. His first performance evaluation was sub-par. His battalion chief said that his leadership skills are weak. A coach is brought in to help him create professional boundaries and exhibit stronger leadership.

- A lieutenant of a newly built sub-station is the consummate energetic leader. Typically, his energy is infectious around the station, but lately he has hit a snag as the municipality and department grows. He is frustrated that his staff doesn't share his enthusiasm, and energetic spirit. "It's probably my own unrealistic expectations," he said, "but they wait around to be told what to do. We need a coach to come in and work with us."

- A chief of a large metropolitan department indicates that he has a battalion chief who is "a beast" when it comes to getting tasks accomplished. "That is his best quality," the chief says. "His weakness is that he is the same when it comes to interacting with people. I'm losing some awfully good employees and the turnover is costing a lot of money."

12. Are There Strategies for Working With Difficult People?

Yes. Why people sometimes behave in stupid, self-defeating, and divisive ways is mind-boggling to say the least. It is vital to keep in mind that most rotten behavior is, if not created, certainly maintained by an ongoing, cyclical system of interactions. This point is vitally important! People do what they do because it works (according to their own perception) within the context of other people.

Think of the relationship between the air temperature in a room and the thermostat. Each influences the other. When the temperature rises, the thermostat kicks on the air conditioning unit, which lowers the temperature, which lowers the thermostat and shuts off the unit, and on and on. The term cybernetics was developed and named (from the Greek word for helmsman) by Norbert Weiner, a mathematician at MIT. During World War II, Weiner was asked to work on the problem of how to get guns to hit moving targets. From that work he expanded his ideas about cybernetic systems—systems that are self-correcting—to the way people operate.

At the core of cybernetics is the concept of the feedback loop, the process by which a system (firefighters on shift) gets information necessary to self-correct in its effort to maintain a steady state or move toward a goal. This feedback may be information regarding a shift's performance relative to its external environment or regarding the relationship among the system's (shift's) members.

Feedback loops can be negative or positive. This distinction refers to the effect they have on deviations from a steady (homeostatic) state within the system, not to whether they are good or bad or beneficial or not. Negative feedback reduces deviation or change; positive feedback amplifies it. In the fire service, negative feedback can serve the function of diminishing negative, dysfunctional behavior, such as conflicts, poor performance, complaints, or poor service, and bringing the shift back to homeostatic normal.

Because cybernetics developed out of the study of machines, where positive feedback loops led to destructive *runaways* in which the machinery would break down, the emphasis was on negative feedback and the maintenance of homeostasis in the face of change. The system's environment would change—the temperature outside a house would change—and this change would trigger the negative feedback mechanism to bring the system back to homeostasis—the air conditioning or heat would go on.

As applied to fire service, cybernetics focuses attention on several phenomena:

1. Rules which govern the range of behaviors that the shift can tolerate (i.e., the shift's homeostatic range).

2. Negative feedback processes that shift (or department) members use to enforce those rules (e.g., reprimands, put-down humor, silence, complaints, gossip, passive-aggressive behavior).

3. Sequences of shift interaction around a problem that characterize the system's reaction to it (i.e., the feedback loops around a deviation); and

4. What happens when the shift's (or department's) traditional negative feedback is ineffective, triggering positive feedback loops.

This cycle of mutual influence may continue for years and is almost always unconscious in that neither party acknowledges their role in the ongoing conflict. Before very long, an interesting phenomenon occurs; conflict becomes the new norm and negative feedback includes those behaviors and interactions that maintain the conflict instead of solving it.

Negative feedback takes on a life of its own, largely because it is unconscious and subject to habit. In addition, deviations from the norm create anxiety in one or more of the shift members. The tendency is to return things to "normal" in an effort to reduce the anxiety, even if the interactions and relationships are destructive to the outsider.

Since you will read more in-depth discussion later, suffice it to say that the most important strategy involves you, not the difficult other person. What might you be doing over and over that gets you the very result you don't like?

- Do you sometimes respond with negativity and pessimism? Do you notice that people respond by withdrawing?

- Do you make jokes when someone complains? Do people stop taking you seriously?

- Do you please people when you would prefer to disagree? Do people take you for granted? Do people fail to perform at their optimal level?

- Do you tend to isolate yourself from others or hold back from offering your opinion? Do others tend to bark orders at you?

Consider the following question: what does the behavior of the other person—behavior that seems completely illogical—communicate about their needs? We discuss this further later on.

13. How Do You Establish the Way to Performance Improvement?

The role of the coach is to establish and create a setting of mutual respect, of dialogue, of inquiry, and of goal setting on the way to performance improvement. In coaching, the bottom line is performance enhancement and, to the extent possible, targeted changes are measured. Goaling (goal setting) conversations between coach and client consider answers to the following general questions:

- What do subordinates say they want from coaching, keeping in mind that their goals may have to be woven among the organization's goals.

- How might they be contributing to what is not wanted?

- How will what they want make a difference to them?

- How will fire service personnel know that their problem is solved?

- How will they know they are on track?

- How are they experiencing some of what they want now?

By the same token, fire officers (as an example) have a role in creating and coauthoring a process that leads to performance improvement. The goal of coaching meetings is to facilitate alternative possibilities and experiences for:

1. Helping fire officers see the influence of their immediate sphere of influence—the system.

2. Helping fire officers learn how to positively impact the system, given the reality that challenges are systemically influenced

3. Helping officers overcome what they are doing that gets them the responses they do <u>not</u> want.

14. How Do I Know Which to Focus Upon: Thoughts, Feelings, Actions, or Spirit?

The answer is that all must be the focus at one time or another. One is never separate from another. Some leaders possess knowledge of the necessary actions (behaviors) but cannot seem to use them at critical moments. Some leaders are highly spiritual or religious but completely lack the essential leadership or management competencies. Some consistently misread people's intentions and have perceptual difficulties while others struggle with anxiety or anger or low self-esteem.

Management research has shown that the quality most people desire in leaders is credibility, grounded in respect, and the number one value they look for in a leader is integrity.

> "Will this shift to more compassion and collaboration last, or is it temporary? Will life return to the hyper-competitive 24/7/365 world of September 10, 2001? Will profits replace people as number one on the corporate hit parade? Not according to what we've learned. The competencies of self-awareness, self-management, social awareness, and interpersonal skills are ascendant. Today there's much more demand for leaders who are exemplary coaches and individuals who show respect for people from many different cultural backgrounds." (Kouzes, J. & Posner, B., 1993).

If there are discrepancies between what coaches do and what they say, it affects the power of their word, which in turn affects coaches' ability to effectively impact people. For words to carry power, coaches need integrity, the kind of integrity that comes from the congruence between thoughts, actions, feelings, and spirit. People need to experience coaches as being trustworthy and true to both what they espouse and the way they live. When coaches' words have power, people know where they stand and start having confidence in their ability to lead them. Regardless of what the vision or values of a coach/leader may be, unless the coach/leader is seen to embody them in his or her own words and actions, the soul of the fire department will not be moved.

15. Why Coaching Programs and Relationships Fail

By and large, departments don't advertise their failures, especially when there is considerable prestige connected with them. So you won't read much about coaching programs that fail to deliver the goods. Even the academic literature contains only a handful of studies that examine programs or coaching relationships that don't deliver. Yet understanding the cause of other people's failure is often the key to one's own success.

Both coaching programs and relationships fail due to a variety of causes and problems, which can be categorized into 1) Contextual; 2) Interpersonal; or 3) Procedural. Let's look at them in this order.

1) Contextual Problems with Coaching Programs and Relationships

Contextual problems for schemes relate primarily to issues of clarity of purpose, or to the supportiveness of the organizational environment. For relationships, the key issues are again clarity of purpose, along with expectations by each party of the style of coaching to be adopted.

The importance of clarity of purpose is illustrated by a case of a large urban fire department that recently incorporated a coaching program and required coaching relationships between fire officers and their respective staff officers. Participants knew that it was somehow related to the department's initiative of replacing the performance evaluation process, but nobody explained how coaching was to contribute to this goal. Most of the relationships faded away within a few months, as both sides waited for the other to tell them what they should do. Clarity of purpose about the program - why it is being done, what is expected of participants, what the respective roles and responsibilities of coach and client are, and what the desired outcomes are - is directly correlated with clarity of purpose in the individual relationships.

Coaching also requires a reasonable level of support from within the department. There have been examples where coaches and clients have effectively been penalized for taking working time out for their meetings, because there is no specific allowance for coaching relationships. Lack of expressed interest by command staff is also likely to undermine coaching programs.

Clarity of purpose within the relationship is critical for energizing the relationship. Most relationships require a clear sense of purpose and a defined transition, which the client wishes to achieve. The clearer that transition is, the more focused the discussions and the easier it is to relate day-to-day issues to the larger goal. Even in relationships, where the primary objective is for the client simply to have an occasional sounding board, unless that is agreed up front, one or both parties will feel dissatisfied.

It should be obvious that coaching for a driver requires a different approach from that for a fire officer. Equally, different cultures demand different approaches to coaching. Yet departments often assume that perceptions of coaching are pretty standard. In reality, there are at least two major schools of coaching and failure to clarify what is intended can cause confusion, argument and major misalignments of expectation between participants and between the organization and the participants. The two schools can be characterized as:

1) *Traditional* School of Coaching: United States-originated, involving a considerable level of sponsorship or hands-on help, tapping into the authority or influence of the senior partner, with a focus mostly on career progress and primarily a one-way learning experience.

2) *Developmental* School of Coaching: Much more of a two-way learning partnership, with the expectation that the client will do things for him or herself, with the focus more on developing the less experienced person's capability, and owing its origins more to European experience.

Multi-national corporations, which have attempted to introduce coaching around the world without taking these differences in coaching style properly into account, are surprised when they meet resistance. It is a fundamental error to assume that everyone will have the same understanding of what coaching is and what coaches should and shouldn't do. We have seen examples of program failure both from European-based companies attempting to introduce programs in their United States subsidiaries and vice-versa. Even in regions, the understanding of what constitutes coaching can be radically different; in France, it can be seen as almost entirely sponsorship based; in large parts of Asia-Pacific, a compromise between the two styles may often be required (or even, in one case, two mentors, one in each style!).

2) Interpersonal Problems with Coaching Programs and Relationships

Interpersonal problems for coaching programs arise from the reactions of people, who are not included in the pairings - for example, the client's direct supervisor or peers. Within the coaching relationship itself, the primary issue tends to hinge around incompatibility of personalities and personal values between coach and client.

Failure to engage superior officers and promote the program's benefits to them is a common omission. Involving both officers and chiefs in the design and overall management of the coaching program helps, as does briefing them about the advantages to them of having someone with whom the client can discuss *in confidence* how the client manages his or her key working relationships (and especially how he or she relates to their superior officer).

In very informal programs, or programs with low clarity of purpose, resentment from people not included is common. So too, is the gossip, especially with regard to cross-gender pairs. Openness about the program and why it targets particular groups of people helps to overcome such problems.

3) Procedural Problems with Coaching Programs and Relationships

Procedural problems arise from the way the coaching program or the relationship is managed. We often see programs that are heavily over-managed. In one case-presented by the department concerned as a "best practice" method-coaches and clients were given discussion sheets to create uniformity in what they talked about. The spontaneity and individual focus of effective coaching were smothered by this over-attention. In another case, the opposite occurred. An enthusiastic training officer simply told people they were to be coach and client and left them to it. When relationships ran into difficulty or participants needed advice, there was no provision to support them and the training department was too busy running the next objective.

At a relationship level, coaching sometimes fails to establish an appropriate balance between being directive and laissez-faire. Indeed, a core skill for a coach is to recognize when to lead and when to enable the client to lead discussions. One of the most common complaints by clients is that the coach talks at them, rather than engages them in reflective dialogue. Less common, but equally dysfunctional, is the coach who never gives advice and is unable to adapt style to the client's needs at the time.

How can you avoid the major pitfalls?

Preparation: Time spent thinking through what the program is meant to achieve and how each aspect of it should be managed, supported and measured will be amply repaid later. Engaging the stakeholder group in the planning identifies barriers to success and occasionally radically changes the nature of the program.

Selection: Not everyone makes a good coach. Some departments have assumed that the qualities of an officer or chief are such that they should automatically be able to perform the coach's role. In practice, many officers or chiefs are unable to escape from the habit of telling and advising. Many also lack the depth of self-awareness that characterizes an effective coach. In general, the more convinced someone is that they are a "natural" coach, the more lethal they are likely to be.

Good practice avoids any suggestion of "shotgun marriages." It does not give people completely free choice of a coach, because people tend either not to seek enough challenge in the relationship, or to choose someone upon whose coat tails they can hang. Typically, a "program coordinator" offers a selection of possible coaches, from which the client chooses. In this way, the client feels some ownership of the relationship and how it is to be managed.

Of course, the logical assumption is that the client's coach should be the direct supervisor, that their direct relationship naturally facilitates the coach/client relationship. Perhaps, but in many cases the relationship between direct subordinate and superior officer may hinder coaching success. The client may find it difficult to open up to the coach or to trust that what is shared will remain confidential. The history of the relationship, particularly in a command-and-control style, may not be conducive to a collaborative coaching approach. The department should foresee this challenge and base the match between coach and client on several factors including:

- Client's preference
- Coach's preference
- Personality assessment

Training: The most successful in-company coaching programs train both coaches and clients and at least provide a detailed face-to-face briefing for officer coaches. In our experience, the figures are stark. Without any training at all, less than one in three pairings will deliver significant results for either party. Training coaches alone raises the success rate to around 65%. Training both and educating officer coaches about the program pushes the "success" rate above 90%, with both parties reporting substantial gains.

Process Ownership: One reason for training both parties is so that coaches have the expectation to and gradually acquire the confidence and skills to manage the relationship; and so that coach/mentors know how to help them do so. Developmental coaching in particular, demands that the coach helps the coach to help them, by understanding the process and contributing to it.

Post-Training Support: Initial training is rarely enough to give coaches more than a basic level of competence and confidence. Experience of hundreds of programs in more than three dozen countries shows that they both want and need access to continued expert advice on how to do the role and develop their skills; and that they greatly value the opportunity to share experience with other coach/mentors.

<u>Measurement:</u> Effective, appropriate measurement, especially at key points in the first 12 months, not only helps keep the program on track, but also stimulates coach and client to good practice -- for example, reviewing the relationship and what each is gaining from it.

16. So What's the Bottom Line on Coaching Programs and Relationships?

Estimates of what proportion of coaching programs fail to deliver significant benefits vary widely, depending on how success or failure is assessed. A good working estimate, however, would be that at least 40% of coaching programs and relationships do NOT meet one or more of the following criteria:

- Achievement of a clear business [service] purpose (e.g. improving morale and communication)

- Achievement of most clients' personal development objectives

- Learning by most of the coaches

- Willingness of both parties to engage in coaching (as coach or client) again and many coaching programs and relationships meet NONE of these.

A positive sign, however, is that more and more fire departments are becoming knowledgeable about coaching and recognize the value of anchoring it firmly in priority service and operational needs. In addition, many of those departments that have experienced initial failure, are now taking a more considered, mature look at the process and resourcing it properly.

Bibliography and Recommended Readings

Barna, George. <u>Turning Vision into Action</u>. U.S.A.: Regal Books, 1996.

Collins, Marva. <u>Ordinary Children, Extraordinary Teachers</u>. Charlotte, VA: Hampton Roads Publishing Company, 1992.

Collins, Marva and Tamarkin, Civia. <u>Marva Collins' Way</u>. New York: J. P. Tarcher, 1990.

Conant, Jennet and Marbach, William, D. "It's the Apple of His Eye." *NewsWeek*, 30 January, 1984: 54-57. Gelman, Eric and Michael Rogers. "Showdown in Silicon Valley". *NewsWeek*, 30 September, 1985: 46-50.

Covey, Stephen R. <u>The 7 Habits of Highly Successful People</u>. New York: Simon & Schuster, 1992.

Editorial. "You Can't Float to the Top." Government Executive (June, 1998).

Edwards, Nicholas Ramon Menendez, and Tom Musca. Stand and Deliver. U.S.A.: Scholastic, 1989.

Engelmann, Siegfried and Douglas Carnine. Theory of Instruction: Principles and Applications. ADI Press, 1991.

Engelmann, Siegfried; Haddox, Phyllis and Bruner, Elaine. Teach Your Child to Read in Easy Lessons. New York: Simon & Schuster, 1983.

Geiger-Dumond, Adrianne and Boyle, Susan (March 1995). "Mentoring: A Practitioner's Guide." Training and Development.

Gibson, William. Miracle Worker. New York: Bantam Books, 1984.

Goodell, Jeff. "Eve Jobs." *Rolling Stone*, 16 June 1994: 73-79.

Halliday, Davi. "Steve Paul Jobs." *Current Biography 5* February 1983: 204-207. Morrison, Ann, M. "Apple Bites Back". *Fortune* 20 February 1984: 86-100.

Hunt, David. Mentoring: The Right Tool for the Right Job, A Not-So-Quick Fix. Hunt Associates, 1994.

Keller, Helen. The Story of My Life. New York: Doubleday, Page and Company, 1905.

Kleinman, Carol. The Career Coach. Chicago: Dearborn-Financial Publishing, 1994.

Kram, Kathy. Mentoring at Work: Developmental Relations in Organizational Life. University Press of America, 1998

Lash, Joseph P. Helen and Teacher: The Story of Helen Keller and Anne Sullivan Macy. American Foundation for the Blind, 1997.

MacLennon, Nigel. Coaching and Mentoring. U.K.: Gower Publishing, 1995.

McClenahen, John. "One-on-One Career Coaches." Government Executive.

Scott, Linda, M. "For the Rest of Us: a Reader-Oriented Interpretation of Apple's 1984 Commercial". Journal of Popular Culture 1984.

Sculley, John. "Interpretation of Apple's 1984 Commercial." *Journal of Popular Culture* Summer 1987: 71-78. "Odyssey." *Personal Computing*, December 1987: 201-209.

Uttal, Bro. "The Adventures of Steve Jobs." *Fortune*, 14 October 1985: 119-124.

Chapter 2

The Unique Challenges of the Fire Service Life

The Unique Challenges of the Fire Service Life

When an emergency happens, frightened citizens know to pick up the telephone and dial 911. They know that rescue personnel are dispatched from the local fire station. They know ambulances and fire trucks race through the streets with flashing lights and sirens. They know firefighters will save them and paramedics will take care of them.

Fire departments are staffed with people dedicated to saving lives and property, even at the cost of their own lives. A common saying in the fire service is that they *put their lives on the line*. But another fire service mantra is that they *want everyone to go home to their families at the end of the shift*. This is the dilemma made so clear by the World Trade Center attack. The fire service constantly seeks a balance between speed and personal protection, between duty and safety, between bravery and self-sacrifice.

Public Service Calling

Citizens expect firefighters to be strong enough to charge into situations everyone else would run from, to face infernos, collapsed structures, tangled wreckage, and deadly hazardous materials. Yet they must be gentle enough to breathe life back into a drowned toddler. Firefighters must be emotionally stable enough to face fatal incidents routinely, yet retain respect and empathy for the victims.

With all of the public adoration of firefighters, there comes a price, their lives as role models "raise the bar" for them as public employees. Fire departments live in the glare of public scrutiny like all public services, where a moment's indiscretion can become front-page news. A firefighter's slightest misstep can bring dishonor to the whole department and damage public perception for years to come. The media can turn the hero into a "goat" in less than a news cycle.

After dealing with the aftermath of human tragedy, they must be professional enough to return for the next shift, to answer the next tone. Society expects such dedication from firefighters. It is an extraordinary calling.

Another public service mission is growing more prevalent as well. A whole generation of Americans has grown up with firefighters visiting their schools each fall during fire prevention week. Many elderly people have had firefighters come into their homes to check smoke alarms or even install new ones. Others have participated in a wide variety of public education programs for children or adults. The fire service has taken on the mission of public educators as well as first responders. Fire prevention and life safety programs have saved untold numbers of lives.

These images play well in the media. On television news, human interest stories include excited children waving to the fire engine in the 4th of July parade or firefighters in clown make-up entertaining second graders during a school visit. A voice-over describes how the local fire department participated in a community event that day. These pieces make great public relations for the fire department and run well at the end of the local news program.

But nothing grabs viewers at the top of the news program like flames licking the night sky with flashing lights on fire trucks in the foreground. It is human drama with great visuals to lead the ten o'clock news. The media shows families driven out into the night air with only the clothes on their backs. Video shows firefighters hurrying around with hoses, lights reflecting off their bunker gear. Paramedics wait by an ambulance to treat injured residents or firefighters. Whether the incident involved a kitchen fire in one unit or destroyed a dozen units in a building, the message is the same. Firefighters came to the rescue.

But there is another side of the fire service, shielded from the public. Except for those who are close to firefighters, it is as unseen as the dark side of the moon. The public had glimpses of this other aspect of the fire service during the media frenzy following September 11, 2001. Even though thousands of citizens were rescued from the World Trade Center, the media focused almost exclusively on the recovery effort. In a few cases, the fire services were portrayed accurately in fiction and documentary programming. During these productions, the dark side of the fire service was illuminated. Haunting scenes will remain with all of us of dust-covered firefighters frantically digging with their hands through the rubble then standing silently in respect when victims were found. The overwhelming grief as firefighter funerals continued day after day resonated throughout the fire service brotherhood.

The Brotherhood

Although the term *brotherhood* is rife with gender bias and macho connotations, no other word sufficiently describes the culture of the fire service. Women have joined the brotherhood in limited numbers and many have gained the well-deserved respect of their colleagues, but it is still a predominately male profession. More than that, it is a culture of strong young men working, living, and sometimes dying together.

The tradition that attracts men to the fire service and keeps them on the job for decades is a relationship that often surpasses literal brotherhood. Firefighters would willingly sacrifice their own lives to prevent the death of another firefighter. Part of that bond develops during their indoctrination. In academy training they begin to fight fire together. They learn to depend on each other for their personal survival in deadly environments.

Firefighters exist in a state of continuous readiness. They must train constantly on tactics and the use of equipment. Firefighters come to understand a common body of knowledge that represents the practice of firefighting in their departments. They have to know the risks and threats within their service areas and in areas where they provide mutual aid. They must maintain a high level of physical fitness if they are to avoid becoming victims themselves. Preparation for action is an important way the brotherhood is reinforced.

Volunteer firefighters lack the experience of living in the firehouse since they respond from their homes or jobs. What they lack in terms of closeness, they supplant with an extra helping of self-sacrifice. Their bond is strengthened by responding when the pager goes off and by donating their time for training together. Actually, many career firefighters volunteer for other departments on their days off to gain experience or simply to be of service.

Firefighters learn that self-sacrifice is one of the obligations of the profession, a blood oath to the brotherhood. It shows in their emblems, their ceremonies, and their quasi-military discipline. But most of the bond develops over time as firefighters work together as a team, live together at the firehouse, and experience tragedy together.

The Family

Beyond the brotherhood is a larger fire service culture that includes the families of firefighters, retirees and their families, people who serve in support roles, and their families. This broader culture is described as the *fire service family*. It extends far beyond the first responders to the millions of people who work with them and care about them. As in all families, there is joy and there is pain. There are good days and bad. Like all families, there are new babies, aged relatives, wild kids, crazy uncles, love and dysfunction, but the fire service family mostly lives on the "dark side of the moon."

When members of the brotherhood are hurting, the fire service family feels the pain. Firefighters experience high rates of divorce and a disturbing frequency of heart disease. Whether or not they admit it, first responders experience trauma on the job. They share experiences that are deeply disturbing, such as the recovery of burned bodies, decomposed drowning victims, and people crushed or dismembered in accidents. Sometimes the dead and injured are innocent children. Firefighters have to suppress their natural reactions to such horrors and continue doing the job. While the incident is ongoing, their natural responses have to be repressed and dealt with later, if at all.

This is something members of the brotherhood know from their training and experience. The fire service family seeks to understand what firefighters are living through in order to help them cope. Some firefighters think they are immune, that they have grown a hard shell to protect them from what they experience. Others think traumatic memories are locked away in a mental room. They just *never go there*. Some think they are used to it after so many incidents only to find that the next call gets to them.

A discipline has developed within the fire service family to work with this problem called critical incident stress management. Over the past decade, there has been a greater understanding of critical incident stress and the importance of education and training in reducing negative impacts on first responders. Much of the displaced aggression prevalent in the fire service may be attributable to critical incident stress.

When critical incident stress from work is combined with typical off-duty stressors like marital problems, financial obligations, or child rearing, the impact can be dramatic. The results can range from suicide or family violence, to depression or inability to work in emergency situations. Physical, cognitive, behavioral, or emotional symptoms appear, usually in combination. A firefighter experiencing a crisis sends anxiety throughout the firehouse and out into the broader fire service family. Once a firefighter reaches the crisis stage, damage may be permanent.

Firefighters need to be trained to expect critical incident stress, especially when the media attention on an incident prolongs the event for them. If fire officers are prepared, they can prevent some of the long-term effects of daily exposure to tragedy. Firefighters should know that critical incident stress has a cumulative effect. This aspect of their work will probably impair their long-term physical and mental health. Call it an occupational hazard.

Paramedics and firefighters who assist with medical calls are even more susceptible to critical incident stress because they actually touch the victims. It is more difficult to objectify victims when physical contact has been made. First responders and their families must understand that sights, smells, sounds, textures, weather, locations, and any number of other triggers may set off a reaction to critical incident stress. Coaches need to be aware of potentially unresolved stress in fire officers and must prepare to deal with it effectively.

Most experts agree that physical exercise, a work routine, and talking about the incident soon afterward, help manage critical incident stress. The brotherhood serves many of those purposes. If firefighters will talk about their feelings, sometimes a difficult thing for young men to do, they will see that their coworkers who shared the experience may be having trouble with it too. These "tailboard" talks or firehouse debriefings can do much to prevent the incident from becoming a festering problem. If they carry on with their routine work together, maintaining the apparatus and equipment, preparing reports, training, and include plenty of physical exercise, the impact of the critical incident may lessen still further. The brotherhood can offer relief from the symptoms in a safe, closed environment.

Professional therapists can also be brought in from outside the department to facilitate healing. The fire service family can also help with a nurturing and continuing informal support. Pre-incident education for firefighters and the fire service family should be a top priority.

Ins and Outs and Isms of the Fire Service

Understanding that the fire service is different from *civilian* life, it is useful to consider what to do about it. The basic tool is conversation. Honest, open dialogue coaxes preconceptions and beliefs to the surface. There are signals coaches can watch for that indicate which path conversations might take. A phrase or even a word may set off your alarm.

There are some **Ins** and **Outs** and **Isms** that help describe underlying predispositions in fire officers. Coaches should watch for indicators that these misconceptions are at the root of a problem.

Ins That Can Do You In

Intolerance: Fire officers are like other Americans when it comes to prejudice. Some people in the fire service are very tolerant of the cultures, customs, sexual preferences, and religions of other folks. Some are not. The increasing diversity in the fire service allows no room for intolerance. The communities served by firefighters vary widely, often requiring special knowledge of languages, customs, and religious practices. Fire officers who treat any citizen as second class, do themselves and the fire service a great harm. Those who treat employees with intolerance are inviting legal action.

Intolerance should be obvious to a coach fairly soon into the conversation. Fire officers usually signal their distaste for other cultures with phrases like *those people* or by using pejorative labels. Others are subtler, resorting to coded words, connotations, or even gestures to describe some trait of a class of people. The point is that intolerance is unacceptable in the modern fire service and coaches must work to eliminate it in their meetings with fire officers.

<u>Inflexibility:</u> There was a time, not too long ago, when firefighters fell off tailboards of speeding fire trucks, fought fires without SCBA, and were transported to the hospital in a white hearse with a red light on top. Many fire officers today are survivors of such practices, yet they stubbornly resist changes in the fire service.

In an industry where technological advancement poses daunting challenges, it also offers fantastic new tools. Yet there are still fire officers unable to access a web site because they are afraid of the computer keyboard. There are fire officers who are unfamiliar with foam fire fighting systems because they have always *put the wet stuff on the red stuff* and see no reason to change. One challenge to coaches is to ensure that inflexible officers are replaced with officers who embrace change and can evolve with modern practice.

Change is frustrating sometimes because it happens way too fast. The computers you purchased last year, after a considerable fight over the funding, are too slow for today's simulation software. The radios you were so proud to get two years ago are suddenly incompatible with everyone around you. The SOP your firefighters' association signed off on after a labor-management struggle was just made obsolete by new regulations. So, what is the cure for fire officers with a bad case of inflexibility? Don't allow them to hide in their caves. They need to be around other people, young, competent fire officers and firefighters, young ambitious officers, and young aggressive sales reps. Young people are the future of the fire service and they can have a dramatic, positive effect on the present.

<u>Indiscretion:</u> No matter how many times a fire chief bites the bullet at budget time or successfully implements an unpopular city policy, the first time the fire department causes a public embarrassment, the chief's job is on the line. A fire officer of the year can quickly become the department's biggest liability when some indiscretion makes the news.

As the old saying goes, you shouldn't do anything you wouldn't want to see on the front page of the local paper. For public employees, especially in leadership positions, a scandal can cause irreparable career damage. The harm can come on many levels, from less desirable duty assignments, missed raises or promotions, discipline or probation, to outright termination from service.

Most indiscretions are just plain stupid. They involve office politics, bad habits, or sexual liaisons. The severity of the outcome depends less on the offensive act than on the amount of embarrassment it causes to the city manager or council. A minor mistake may be blown so out of proportion that jobs are lost, while a major screw-up may result in a slap on the wrist. The severity also depends on who commits the offense and where they stand in departmental politics at the moment the offense becomes public.

Indiscretion can damage a fire officer's career when the officer's bad habits become excessive. Over the years, some habits grow out of control. The social drinking becomes excessive or gambling losses attract loan sharks. These problems end careers. They threaten health and families. These indiscretions lead to divorce and debt. When bad habits become excessive, fire officers can lose more than their jobs.

Nothing matches sexual misadventures when it comes to publicly ruining careers. The combination of sex and the workplace is nearly always lethal to someone's career. Sexual harassment law has expanded to the point where a lot of behaviors that used to be tolerated now create a hostile workplace. Actual sexual behavior, even between consenting adults, is now strictly prohibited in most fire departments.

Regardless of what bad habits a fire officer might have, the rule should be moderation. There is no such thing as a *minor* indiscretion. When bad behavior reaches some undefined threshold, action will be taken to punish the offender. Almost anything done to excess will cause problems.

Ineffectiveness: The last of the *Ins* is worse than intolerance, inflexibility, or indiscretion. Ineffectiveness does long-term damage to the fire service and the career of the fire officer. It is failure to perform, failure to do the job of planning, monitoring, and evaluating. Ineffective fire officers are either unable or unwilling to do those things that are required to make the department function at its best.

In a profession where responding is the primary function, it is too easy to become reactionary rather than visionary. Planning in the fire service is too often tactical instead of strategic. Fire officers are easily isolated from the other city departments because of their dispersed locations and strange working hours. Integrating the fire department into the city's vision for the future is essential. If the city is planning decades into the future by zoning land use, aligning streets, and designing utility systems, shouldn't the fire department be estimating the future demand on its services too? Shouldn't the fire chief be demanding the dedication of future station sites as developers carve up the countryside?

Managing the daily operations of the department consumes most fire officer time. But managing ongoing operations tends to be a bureaucratic process of satisfying the least common denominator. There are those things that *must* be done, like responding to emergencies, staffing positions, supplying the firefighters and paramedics, and essential repairs. Then there are those things that *should* get done, and usually are accomplished. Then there are those tasks that would be *nice* to complete, if you had the time. There may even be a stack of things that might get done if hell actually freezes over that day.

The process of daily management tends to lower the bar. It is a logical progression. Because tasks expand to fill the time available, daily management rarely gets beyond the *must* be done and *should* be done lists. Unfortunately, organizational planning is in the *nice* to do list. When daily monitoring and management reach the point where nothing gets accomplished except the must be done list, on a continuing basis, the fire officer is ineffective. This isn't management; it is short-term survival.

The third measure of effectiveness is (1) planning, (2) monitoring, (3) evaluating. There are several systems built into the fire service that require ongoing evaluation. Reports must be prepared that cite budget numbers, overtime use, run statistics, fire loss estimates, EMS billing collections, training hours, maintenance costs, and so forth. One of the most thorough evaluations comes when ISO rates the community for the insurance industry. An ineffective fire chief either fails to collect the necessary data, or fails to analyze the data to judge departmental performance.

Outs That Can Force You Out

Along with intolerance, inflexibility, indiscretion, and ineffectiveness, there are other factors that exist that will force a fire officer out of the job. A couple of these **Outs** are discussed in fire service magazines but a couple of them aren't. Regardless, these are the types of problems that your friends may not mention to you because they are too polite or because they don't want to endure the consequences of stating the obvious.

Out of Shape: One of the most tragic statistics in the fire service is the frequency of heart disease. When fire officers reach their forties or fifties, their physical conditioning often declines significantly. Excess weight, chronic anxiety, lack of exercise, and a genetic predisposition to portliness have resulted in thousands of fire officers who can't see their shoes and couldn't reach the laces to tie them anyway.

In addition to the health issues, the image of the fire service is damaged by out of shape fire officers. The public is less confident in their fire and rescue services when fire departments are represented by out of shape fire chiefs.

Out of Touch: The modern fire service is subject to continuous change just like the rest of American society. New practices and equipment are introduced every month. New fire risks and rescue challenges are always being presented. Emergency medicine changes daily. And, of course, government regulations and court cases can change the law overnight. Keeping current is a challenge for the most dedicated fire officers.

This is one area where computers can make fire officers' lives easier. Communication is so much easier online than through any other media. There are sources online for almost any information fire officers need. There are agencies, organizations, and companies ready to supply the latest information in an easy to access, always available format. Email is the most efficient way to communicate with most professionals today because it is asynchronous. You don't have to be connected at the same time, like you do on the telephone. Ask a question via email and it gets answered at the first opportunity. Many fire officers have discovered that the solution to being out of date is simple -- *learn to use the Internet effectively.*

The second way to keep up with the state of the fire service is to participate in training and conferences. There are more conferences available than any one person can attend, so choice is the key. Officers that stay in touch select conferences where the best resource people will be available and the best networking opportunities will occur. They attend specific training that focuses on the immediate needs of their departments but they don't neglect training that concentrates on improving their own professionalism.

<u>Out of Line:</u> Sometimes fire officers find themselves on the wrong side of a situation because they have taken actions that exceed their legitimate authority. Invariably, these situations seem to involve personnel. As much as fire officers like to be in charge, they are actually constrained by the ever-evolving body of labor law. Decisions to employ, promote, discipline, or terminate employees are like minefields. You have to get across them but you never know where to step next.

Since fire departments are seen as good organizations to work for, there are usually more applicants than positions open. The domination of fire service by white males makes the personnel issues even more difficult because minorities and women sometimes get recruited and receive preferential consideration during the hiring process. Aptitude tests, physical testing, and promotional exams open lots of opportunities for officers to step out of line during employment and promotion decisions.

When discipline needs to be applied, fire officers too often misjudge where the line is and they step across. Labor organizations make bad matters worse when a fire officer is already out of line. Even when a firefighter has done something clearly against departmental policies, the union may fight the punishment because they see a flaw in the way the disciplinary procedure was handled. Labor has a natural advantage in such proceedings because discipline is usually discretionary, punishment may vary in terms of length and severity. It is difficult for a fire officer to be *objective* when dealing with personnel issues so it is easy to be out of line.

<u>Out on a Limb:</u> The fourth way to be **Out** is by speaking your mind at the wrong time, wrong place, or to the wrong people. Politics is a strange and ruthless pursuit. Some people are really good at political maneuvering; others are innocents among the wolves. It is difficult for fire officers with integrity to bite their tongues all the time and occasionally, the truth spills

out just when it shouldn't. As a fire officer, being outspoken will get you out on a limb even if what you say is absolutely true. The problem about being out on a limb is that someone is always prepared with a saw.

The art of local politics isn't taught in any school. It is rarely studied as a subject of training. So, how do fire officers learn the political ropes? Some get political experience by being in union leadership. In that way they can learn how city council races operate and who the power elite group is in their community. Others have private businesses on their off-days or work in organizations with political ties. Many fire officers learn politics by watching city managers and fire chiefs come and go. They learn from the mistakes made by those who go before them.

The primary lesson in local politics is to know when to keep your mouth shut and your ears open. Quiet people in quiet rooms make real decisions in local government. Very few people have access to those rooms or those discussions. The more fire officers listen, the less likely they are to speak out of turn, and the more they will be trusted around people with political power. The shortest route to the end of the limb is to repeat what was said in confidence.

The next shortest way out on the limb is to defend an unpopular political position in a public forum. Like all city officials, fire officers are asked to speak at civic clubs and the Chamber of Commerce. They get quoted at emergency scenes and during Fire Prevention Week. There are plenty of opportunities to catch the media's ear, and it is tempting sometimes. But beating your drum when there's no band around can draw more attention than you need. It is better politically to state your point quietly, in private, with someone who can access the decision makers for you. Fire officers should take the lead in a public debate only when they are directed to do so by the city manager and, even then, should remain understated and professional.

Isms Will Get You Every Time

The brotherhood and the fire service family have a public image as America's heroes and the salt of the earth. But there are four **Isms** (ageism, sexism, racism, and classism) that bring out the worst in human relations and the fire service is not immune from their effects.

These *Isms* are pervasive in American society. Even though the law speaks volumes on each and we profess as a culture, to fight them, these *Isms* persist. Whether we acknowledge our *Isms* or not, they haunt our everyday lives, destroy relationships, and damage careers. Those who coach in the fire service must watch for the signs of these *Isms* and guard against their influences.

Ageism: People around the world treat age differently. Some cultures value their children above everyone else. The children are their gifts to the future, a legacy to their continuing society. Other societies value the elderly. To them, older people represent wisdom and experience. The elderly in those societies have earned the deference of everyone else. There are probably some societies where, at least in theory, each individual is equally valued.

Society in the United States is based on *equal protection under the law*. But we know the guarantee of equality is not easily enforced. In fact, much of our daily activity is guided by age categories. School is the first we encounter. Until they are about 18 years old, children are categorized based primarily on age rather than their intelligence. Children do not enjoy the same rights as adults in terms of personal choice or freedom of speech.

Government programs often use age as the primary determinant of eligibility. Social Security and Medicare, for instance, are primarily for the elderly. Retirement saving is tax sheltered. There are tax credits for people of child-rearing age. School lunch programs are for children. There are age limits that exclude the young, like for driver's licenses and purchasing liquor.

In our culture, business values young adults most of all. In our capitalist society, young adults are the best consumers. Older adults are next in line because they make replacement purchases, they are the biggest consumers of health care, and they own homes. The elderly come next because some of them are wealthy and all of them require medical care. Last come the children. They watch cartoons and influence food purchases.

What does *Ageism* have to do with the fire service? First of all, firefighters and paramedics must serve people of every age and they must understand the needs of each age group. Secondly, the fire service is a young person's profession. Many departments have minimum and maximum ages for employment. Firefighting and emergency medical care require strength, agility, and stamina. These physical characteristics decline with age even with the best of workout regimes.

Sexism: Several thousand women now work in the fire service alongside men. The number is still a small percentage of the total but it is a significant minority in terms of cultural changes. Women have earned a place in the fire service in spite of the barriers raised to prevent it. The necessary changes are not easy to make. Firehouses have had to be modified or designed to accommodate both genders. Male firefighters have had to understand that women bring different skills to the job along with their different physical characteristics.

The brotherhood has not been quick to accept women in the fire service. Sometimes the presence of women has resulted in actual sexual conflicts and sometimes the problems are only imaginary. The fire service family has had to adjust to the concept of women working, eating, and sleeping in close proximity to men. Our society still views the fire service as a nontraditional career choice for women.

But the law is clear. Changes have been made in the hiring process to eliminate tests that unfairly discriminate against women. The law protects women because there is very real discrimination against them. Physical ability is now judged by the actual demands of the job, not the macho image of earlier years. The culture of the firehouse is changing to eliminate those behaviors that create workplaces hostile to women. The result is a more professional workplace and a more professional approach to service delivery.

Racism: People are pretty much the same the world over but life would be much easier if everyone had similar skin color and physical features. Groups would still find some reason to hate each other and start wars to dominate other groups but at least one excuse would be gone. As it is, there are people in just about every community who look different than the majority of other people and they are marginalized because of their appearance.

Racial differences are easy to categorize because they are easy to see. Race is one of the worst reasons to discriminate against someone because it is one of the least meaningful distinctions between people. Racial prejudice is one of the most difficult preconceptions to deal with because it is based on ignorance and fear.

The tandem issue of racial prejudice is ignorance of other cultures. When combined with diverse physical features, cultural differences reinforce the stereotypes that feed hatred. People who are different from the predominant race and who are also from a different culture not only look different but act differently. When the powerful want to exploit people for profit, to find cheap labor, or steal resources from the land, racism is a perfect justification. Although economic systems are too often served by racial prejudice, the roots of racism are misunderstanding and fear.

Classism: Ask yourself this question? Do poor people get the same level of service in your city as wealthy people receive? Do your firefighters try as hard to save a two-bedroom wood-sided house as they do to save a brick mansion? Are your paramedics as polite to a homeless person in rags as they are to a business executive in an Armani suit?

If the answers to those questions point to a difference in service delivery, then classism is a problem in your department, just as it is in the fire service in general. It is an unfortunate fact that well-dressed, educated people are treated with more respect than badly dressed, illiterate people. The property of wealthy people is cared for better than the property of poor people. Privileged people and disadvantaged people are not *supposed* to receive different levels of service from public agencies, but they often do.

Very few firefighters aspire to become poor. Usually, people in the fire service are upwardly mobile. It is natural to respect those you hope to emulate and to disrespect those you want to leave behind in the social system. Some folks think that poverty is self-imposed, that they *do it to themselves* and that privileged people *earn* their status. But more often than not, poverty and wealth are accidents of birth. There is a reason most United States Senators were millionaires before they were elected. They were born into privilege, into the upper class. Regardless of the self-made man mythology, it is far more difficult for a poor child to succeed than it is for a rich child.

Examining Coaches' Preconceptions

As coaches in the fire service, there is a need to enter the conversation with as few biases as possible. Whether you are a consultant coaching fire officers or an officer coaching your staff, you come to the table with your own set of preconceptions about people and society. We are all products of our upbringing and our adult experiences. Others mold and shape our attitudes by their words and actions. While education and understanding can change those preconceptions, we still have visceral reactions that have no connection to logic.

Transforming the way we construct meaning is a tough task. It requires an uncomfortable kind of self-examination that challenges long-held beliefs. Questions to ask ourselves:

- Are we intolerant of some people?

- Do we cling to outmoded ways of working and resist innovation?

- Do we think our bad habits are under control?

- Are we overly opinionated or politically motivated?

- Do we sometimes accept instead of analyze information?

- Do we think women are inferior to men?

- Do we disrespect people of other races, ages, or social classes?

If coaches exhibit none of these traits, they are in the wrong business. They should be saints instead. In order to effectively assist other people, coaches must face their own preconceptions and use that understanding to transform themselves into better human beings.

Chapter 3

Understanding the
Fire System

Understanding the Fire System

The Triangle Relationship

A bunch of firefighters are a family in all ways except biology. This fire "family" tremendously affects how people think, feel, and act, but each individual varies in his/her susceptibility to "group think" and groups vary in the amount of pressure they exert for conformity.

In any family-like group, the three-person relationship system or triangle is the most important one to understand. It is considered the building block or "molecule" of larger emotional systems because a triangle is the smallest stable relationship system. A two-person system is unstable because it tolerates little tension before involving a third person. A triangle can contain much more tension without involving another person because the tension can shift around three relationships. If the tension is too high for one triangle to contain, it spreads to a series of "interlocking" triangles.

Spreading the tension can stabilize a system, but nothing gets resolved. People's actions in a triangle reflect their efforts to ensure their emotional attachments to important others, their reactions to too much intensity in the attachments, and their taking sides in the conflicts of others.

Paradoxically, a triangle is more stable than a dyad, but a triangle creates an "odd man out," which is a very difficult position for individuals to tolerate. Anxiety generated by anticipating or being the odd one out is a potent force in triangles. The patterns in a triangle change with increasing tension. In calm periods, two people are comfortably close "insiders" and the third person is an uncomfortable "outsider." The insiders actively exclude the outsider and the outsider works to get closer to one of them.

Someone is always uncomfortable in a triangle and pushing for change. The insiders solidify their bond by choosing each other in preference to the less desirable outsider. Someone choosing another person over oneself arouses particularly intense feelings of rejection. If mild to moderate tension develops between the insiders, the most uncomfortable one will move closer to the outsider. One of the original insiders now becomes the new outsider and the original outsider is now an insider. The new outsider will make predictable moves to restore closeness with one of the insiders.

Departmental Conflict

Triangles contribute significantly to the development of departmental conflict. Getting pushed from an inside to an outside position triggers the feeling of being excluded and creates frustration, anger, and even depression.

What does this have to do with coaching? Practically everything. Coaches must come to coaching with an accurate picture of what is taking place. For example: to what do you typically attribute firefighter problems, misbehavior, or under performance? Your answer to this question is very important. If you believe, down deep, that people screw up or under-perform because of one form of stupidity or another, then your coaching will take on a controlling, often critical nature. Furthermore, you will find yourself getting frustrated that your clients aren't improving. It's no different in leadership. Those leaders who lack trust in the good intentions of their firefighters and who over control and criticize them, constantly battle performance problems, repeated mistakes, and poor morale.

On the other hand, if you believe in the basic goodness of people and view morale and performance as subject to a variety of interactions and relationships, then your coaching will take on a more developmental, helpful, growth inducing form and you will be on the track to true leadership and coaching greatness.

Coaching strategies based upon a linear model offer, at best, temporary, band-aid solutions to change. The following are some examples of the way we tend to interpret performance challenges within a linear model. If left unexamined, these assumptions will most likely lead to coaching failure.

- Employee underperformance is an indication of laziness.

- Poor performance means the individual needs training.

- Employee complaints are simply an indication that some people cannot be satisfied.

- Effective explanations for poor performance or misbehavior are those that have been boiled down to a single cause.

- When someone performs poorly, reprimands are the corrective action of choice.

- If the reprimand doesn't work, a stronger, more forceful reprimand will.

- The lower down the ladder a person is, the less capable he or she is of assimilating information.

In each of these examples, little consideration is given to the product of a system of complex and evolving interactions or the impact that the broader system of employee interactions and relationships has on the emotional/intellectual well-being, and thus the level of performance, of people within an organization. On the contrary, linear assumptions like those above assume that the source of problems, whether underperformance or conflict, stem from a deficit in a single person or a single source. Thus, the solution is a simple one, to force change in that one person or source. Taking this approach ignores the process of how and why problematic employees emerge as well as the impact they have on other team member's performances.

Sir Isaac Newton's well known third law of motion and gravity which states that "with every action, there is an equal and opposite reaction, only begins to tell the story of how relationships and interactions themselves can create problematic workplace symptoms. More accurately, it is the triangle (the smallest version of the web) that provides a better model for understanding problem relationships in the workplace.

To further understand triangles, it's helpful to remember that relationships are not static. Any two people in a relationship go through cycles of closeness and distance; it's when they're distant that triangles are most likely to develop. These cycles reflect not only good times and bad in relationships, but also people's needs for autonomy and connectedness. The most common workplace process that operates in the formation of a triangle begins with any form of stress or discomfort whereby one individual connects with someone else as a way of gaining an ally and temporarily reducing stress.

Coaches who are called to intervene often battle a confusing array of explanations regarding what the issue really is. Sifting through these explanations for actionable insights can be like finding a needle in a haystack.

One of systems approaches greatest contributions to coaching and organizational change is to stress the importance of understanding people's behavior and performance within a social context. As an outside consultant/coach or one of the organization's leaders, your challenge is the net result of a web-like structure of social interactions (multiple triangles) with fixed, habitual patterns of interacting and behaving.

Prior to the recognition of a systemic perspective, poor performance was viewed in isolation, completely apart from the person's network of relationships. So, the only available explanation was that the person was defective. Once you begin to view people within the sphere of influence of their social context, their behavior will seem less strange, and will come to be understood as an inevitable, even necessary aspect of the way they or an entire team interacts. The following example should help to further illustrate and contrast the linear versus systemic interpretations.

Recently I was called to consult and coach with a large suburban fire department. The problem, as stated by the chief was the sheer amount of complaints coming out of the local firefighters union and directed against the command staff officers.

"They are a bunch of malcontents and slackers," said the chief as he closed his office door.

One by one, as I talked with the chief, the command staff officers knocked on his door and requested permission to put in their two cents. The entire command staff group agreed with the chief that the lower level officers and firefighters were lazy and unmotivated.

Discussion revealed that the firefighter union representatives had repeatedly gone to the media to complain about changes in promotion procedures, the lack of communication with regard to the construction of a new fire house (and thus additional officer positions), the rationale behind the recent termination of some firefighters, and the chief's refusal to sign off on a workman's compensation injury report. Needless to say, the relationship between the command staff and the firefighters was distant at best. For this department, things were going well if a month passed and there was no new scathing media articles or investigative reports on the local evening news. Discussion with the city manager shed some light on his interpretation as well. In sum, he supported the chief and the command staff.

Finally, interviews with the firefighters resulted in the usual content-laden stories about how they had been mistreated by the command staff. They had no opinion or insight into how ongoing interactions within their ranks or how their interactions and the avoidance of interaction with the command staff could be exacerbating the conflict.

Let's summarize the cause/effect explanations that are exacerbating the problem and preventing the fire department from seeking an effective solution.

- Placing the sole responsibility for blame on the firefighters prevents the command staff from examining the impact of their actions as a contributing factor.

- It also prevents the command staff from considering possible stress created by city or departmental policy changes that serve as a trigger to triangulate using the media as the third party.

- Viewing the firefighters as dumb is fatalistic and a part of a feedback loop that serves to perpetuate each side's view of the problem rather than create a long-term solution. Such one-sided views offer a one-way solution only, that being to continue to ignore and put down the firefighters. This, in turn, perpetuates the firefighters' frustration. They, in turn, blame the command staff through the third party media. Both sides contribute to a feedback loop whereby the explanations for problems as well as the solutions are both habitual and ineffective and produce the same consistent results.

- The city manager's explanation is similar and offers only a one-sided view that fails to consider that work performance symptoms are a result of an ineffective system of interactions that result in the inability of people to get their emotional, intellectual, and spiritual needs met at work.

How an individual, team, or department carries out its tasks is not nearly as important as how well. Teams/departments are not static entities. They are the recipients of a continual process of change, as are their social contexts—particularly clients and customers. Coaches must look at human beings within this context of change and ask themselves "what does the current crisis reveal about the requirements stemming from change that they are unaware of as yet."

Frankly, crisis is an ally to the coach. It says that "something has changed and the client is using the same coping methods, the same ways of relating as before, but the same methods no longer work." A primary function of the coach then is to study that gap between what the old ways were and what the new demands require. Consider the following scenario as a way of illustrating the web like influence of systems.

Bill Charles was a renowned chief of one of the fastest growing suburbs in the U.S. Once a sleepy little town, the suburb became prime property and the population tripled inside ten years and was expected to increase over 1000% over the next twenty-five years. The town was once so small that, at one point, Chief Charles doubled as mayor. Through his "walk-tall-and-carry-a-big-stick" style, he was loved, hated, envied, and feared depending on whether he was saving you from a fire or berating you for an infraction of one of the department's (actually his) rules.

The call for coaching came from the new city manager, that Bill was being referred because of his demeanor. Although he was always brash, bordering on arrogant, he was supported because of his community service, long-family presence in the community and his tireless work ethic. Recently, however, he had made some highly inappropriate sexist comments and some angry remarks during meetings.

> *"I want you to help this guy to stop with the embarrassing comments,"* fumed the city manager *"I can't believe he pulled that verbal stunt in front of the new council. I felt like firing him on the spot."*
>
> *"Has this ever happened before?"* asked the coach on the other end of the line.
>
> *"Not to this extent. I mean he's always been brash, but I think his success has gone to his head."*

This is a relatively common example of the way problems are interpreted—it's one person's fault. Fix him or her! And it is also an example of how identification of the real problem gets twisted. In speaking with this city manager, it was clear that he labeled the problem as one of Chief Charles' arrogance. Thus both the blame and the responsibility were placed at Bill Charles' feet. Probably a big mistake! Labeling Chief Charles as the problem actually perpetuates the problem and creates a roadblock to improvement. Without the proper intervention, this city manager will continue to blame the Chief and merely use more of the same solutions to the problem that will make the problem worse.

The initial, more cautious systemic approach dictates that the coach should hold out for more information and view the challenge from a broader perspective. How? By investigating the client's sphere of influence. The example illustrates a term called negative feedback (the tendency for systems to remain the same).

Another example of a linear solution involved the coaching approach with a battalion chief named Seth Long. Chief Long was referred for coaching because of his poor management of people. Consultation with Seth's chief corroborated that Seth was a pleaser who had difficulty making decisions and holding his subordinates' noses to the grindstone. The coach agreed to work with Chief Long but focused only on his lack of managerial fortitude. No focus was placed on the larger system, particularly the fire chief.

In the short run, Chief Long began to improve in his ability to be a stronger leader. But the coach missed an important ingredient. The fire chief was a caustic and negative micromanager who overly delegated and overloaded Chief Long with little encouragement. In time, the battalion chief, in an effort to please his boss, took on all responsibilities, pleased as a way of coping with anxiety, and again appeared ineffective.

The fire chief threw up his hands and said, "I knew it. Seth is not capable of managing people."

He stepped up his micromanagement of Seth Long because he viewed the battalion chief as incapable. The perception that Chief Long was incapable of managing people could be labeled as "negative feedback" that maintained the familiar, old system. When responsibility was not assessed elsewhere, others, who might be responsible, felt little anxiety for improving their performance. Of course, this was ultimately a destructive diagnosis because the real influences of the poor performance were not addressed, the situation remained unchanged, and a sacrificial lamb was offered up for remediation while others sat back comfortably free of self-examination.

As is typical of the homeostatic nature of systems, the real potential problem remained hidden. As of this writing, the situation is worse than ever and the chief decided to abandon coaching as a potential solution. Had the coach been more cognizant of the power of the system, he would have broadened his approach to include the chief as both a source of the problem as well as a portion of the solution.

Now, let's go back to Chief Bill Charles and the city manager. What followed next with the city manager, and then with the client, Chief Charles, was vital for coaching success. If the coach could formulate an effective hypothesis of the problem, the client and coach would stand a much better chance of not only improving his behavior, but also positively impacting a larger sphere of connection. But the systems approach suggested that the real problem was only partially connected to the stated problem. Thus, the first step in coaching was to formulate an accurate hypothesis of the problem.

As is implied above, things are usually much deeper than they first appear. In this case, while Chief Charles was certainly arrogant, there were confounding influences that contributed to his behavior. He did not behave in isolation. According to systems theory, the chief's "arrogance" is initially viewed as a symptom of something else; an outgrowth of dysfunctional interactions within the system. What this "something else" is is not initially known. While it is a symptom of a larger, systemic problem, that is about as specific as possible at this point. Not to worry though, probing questions and your own observations will later provide clarity. What is important is to avoid knee-jerk conclusions while remaining open to discovering what the contributing factors are. One thing is for sure; effective coaches do not form opinions too early without conducting a broader, more thorough analysis of these potential influences. In the example above, the coaches should begin immediately upon talking with the referring city manager. Although avoiding knee-jerk diagnoses is imperative, the sooner the coach can formulate a hypothesis, the sooner the issue can be remediated. The following are some questions to ask and the reasons for asking them:

Question	Rationale
• Has this happened before? When?	Specific history of the problem
• When and under what circumstances?	Detailed history and broader perspective
• What are possible triggering events in his life?	
• What was your initial response to the embarrassing comments?	System's response
• What was the company's response?	System's response
• Did you reprimand him? How? Have you reprimanded him like this before?	System patterns

Question	Rationale
• What was his reaction to the reprimand?	Possible patterns that further influence behavior
• What was your reaction to his reaction?	Possible patterns that further influence behavior
• How would you view this if you were in his shoes?	
• Did his behavior and/or performance improve? How?	Patterns and motivation
• What explanation does he give for his behavior?	His perception of the issue
• Have you outlined a performance/behavior improvement plan for him?	
• How specific were you with behaviors and timelines?	
• What was his reaction?	Supervisor/system support
• What are consequences of his failure to improve?	Direct supervisor's response
• How will you know when things improve?	

You'll note that many of the questions are systemically focused as opposed to linear. A systemic focus assumes a broader sphere of influence; that a person's behavior affects another person who, in turn, reacts and affects another and so on. In this sort of web-like system of influence, the "real" problem is never the behavior of one individual although invariably, the challenge will be presented in a linear fashion, i.e., you make me angry, he hurt my feelings, she did this to me. Do not fall prey to this cultural mantra. Systems theory teaches us that when we behave, we have an effect on others who, in turn, react further affecting the system, and so on. From a systems perspective, the real problem tends to be the way things get reacted to, not what is said, but the way things are said. Thus, most communication is non-verbal. It is the way something is done, the voice tone, the facial expression, body posture, leaving someone off an invitation list, skipping over someone's comments during a meeting, a cold hello in the morning. These are the non-verbal behaviors that are left up to interpretation by the receiver and, depending on what kind of filter the receiver uses to form his/her interpretation, determines the non-verbal reaction and the process continues on. Some estimates indicate that 80% of our communication is non-verbal. But we are poor interpreters of non-verbal behavior.

Let's continue formulating our hypothesis. Remember, our job is to formulate actionable insights so that our coaching efforts have maximum impact on both the individual being referred as well as the larger team or organization.

Let's continue with the example of Bill C. and look at the rest of the telephone conversation with the city manager and see how the analysis develops as the conversation continues using some of the questions above.

> *"O.K., so Chief Charles has always been brash," the coach said. "The mere fact that you recognize this indicates that it has been of some concern."*
>
> *"Well, yes," the city manager said. "People complained that he was not patient, did not promote good team spirit and was not very encouraging."*
>
> *"Who was the recipient of these complaints?"*
>
> *The city manager said, "Hell, I was; he answers directly to me."*
>
> *"And how was it for you to hear these complaints about Chief Charles?" the coach asked.*
>
> *"Between you and me," the city manager replied, "I was livid. Here we had high visibility, the kind that every department strives for with the council and he pulls a stunt like that. Now I can't trust him around council members. I feel like I have to be present whenever he's around them. Frankly, I'm trying to hide him now. These are sophisticated people; something this town has never seen before. Please understand, I have the greatest respect for Bill. We wouldn't be where we are today without him. But he just cannot do and say those things with outsiders.*
>
> *"How did you handle it?"*
>
> *"Oh, I exploded after that. I can't even go into what all I said. I think I finally told him to go as far away from me as possible."*
>
> *"I see," the coach said, "and there were complaints from his subordinates. What were those?"*
>
> *"That's a whole other matter," the city manager said. "Frankly, some of the people who complained about him are slackers looking to avoid accountability."*
>
> *"So how did you handle those complaints?"*
>
> *"I had a guy come in to do some communication skills improvement."*
>
> *"Did it help?" the coach asked.*

"For about a week. I thought I would get a break from all the bickering. My gosh how it takes up my time."

"Sounds incredibly frustrating," the coach replied. "What was your reaction to these complaints?"

"I probably didn't handle things in the best manner. I should have consulted with him more, perhaps suggested some leadership training or coaching for him a couple of years ago."

"What did you say to him?"

"I think I told him not to worry about it too much," the city manager said. "I was hoping the complaints would just go away."

"So what do you think triggered his inappropriate sexual comments in the presence of those people?" the coach asked.

"Actually, I think he's mad. My office at city hall is several miles from the fire station. Hell, I can't be on site to supervise the department. That's not my role anyway. And I've been pushing for the creation of some new positions in Human Resources to handle people problems and performance issues in the city. Can you believe Chief Charles applied for the job? Unfortunately, because of his arrogant nature and the longstanding grumblings about him, we didn't feel that we could take him out of his position. This position requires too many people skills. He doesn't have them."

"Did the chief ever receive performance evaluations or have coaching discussions that targeted performance improvements?" the coach asked.

"I'm afraid not," the city manager replied. "It's on the agenda, but we haven't addressed our performance evaluation process yet."

Okay, let's summarize what we know at this point.

- There have been longstanding complaints about Chief Charles.

- There has been little or no supervision of the fire department.

- Employees who had complaints about Chief Charles had nowhere to go except the city manager.

- The city manager was overwhelmed and responded in a hands-off manner, reacting with anger or disinterest, but failing to seek solutions.

- Chief Charles has not received coaching or been supported in making leadership changes. The non-verbal communication has been that he is incapable of improving.

The landscape of the concern has broadened considerably as a result of the coach's pattern-probing questions. Note that the coach has not probed into any goals or objectives yet. This is because the goals are likely to change as the concern morphs from being Chief Charles' problem with arrogance (which was the initial stated problem) to what now appears to be a larger concern with a lack of supervision, training, and coaching. Within just a few minutes, the issue has grown from fixing the chief's attitude to improving the fire department's and city's process for training, career planning, and performance evaluations. Now the coach has several new possibilities for impacting the organization. They may be listed in this manner:

- Broadly speaking, Chief Charles needs to improve his leadership skills including his ability to encourage his employees.

- The organization may need help in hiring the right type of person to fill the new administrative position.

- The city manager may need help in embracing firmer boundaries. Further questioning may reveal that this city manager is not strong in his own leadership skills or possesses a weak leadership presence. If this is the case, the present challenges may appear again in the future.

- Down the road, the fire department could benefit from improved relationships. Perhaps a focus should be on effective followership in partnership with effective leadership.

- Create a coaching culture in which employees receive support, encouragement, and strategies for improving their performance.

As the landscape of influence broadens, the coach has an ethical responsibility to intervene where the problem(s) really lie. It is always a good idea to look to the highest level of influence for the source of the concern. While, sole responsibility for poor performance should not be placed at the feet of the boss, it is more likely that this problem will re-emerge if the highest level of influence receives no insight or intervention. Just like a physician who treats the underlying systemic cause as opposed to merely the symptom, so must the coach look beyond the stated problem. This is because much of the time the referring person, even if that person is the client, is responding out of frustration and holds a narrow view of the origin of the problem. It is our nature that when stress is high, there is an attempt to fix blame externally and to find a simple external solution as quickly as possible. Blame is unfortunately and unnecessarily placed on a single individual or source.

Now let's take a look at our conversation with Chief Charles. In the same manner, probing questions assess who, what, when, where, how, how much, and how often. The goal is to formulate as broad a view as possible of the contributing factors.

> "What have you been told about why you are here today?" the coach asked Chief Charles.
>
> "I made the mistake of hacking off the city manager," the chief said.
>
> "Yes, he indicated that you used offensive language during a council meeting."
>
> "It didn't upset the council members," the chief said. "The city manager just has an issue with me."
>
> "How so?"
>
> "I think it's a basic personality conflict," the chief explained. "He's laid back and I'm not. He's a people person and I'm not. I upset people on occasion because I expect results. He doesn't like mess."
>
> "Specifically, what was your reaction to the city manager's reprimand?" the coach asked.
>
> "I laughed at first," Chief Charles said. "I know each and every one of those council members; I've had lunches and dinners with them. They've used the same language and shared risqué stories too."
>
> "What was the city manager's reaction to your laughter?"
>
> "He hit the ceiling. The guy is wound too tight."
>
> "How do your employees view you, Chief?" the coach asked.
>
> "Well, I know I could do better there," the chief replied. "Like I said, I'm not really a people person. I'm tough, like General Patton. I want to see results and I want to see them right away."

Summary

Let's pause here and consider what we have thus far. Clearly Chief Charles should not be using foul language or sexist jokes even if it has been acceptable in the past. That's the first issue. There is no need to address it as yet since the coach is not yet in the intervention stage and does not have a psychological contract for work. It is merely enough to recognize it at this point. Secondly, Chief Charles mentions the existence of a "personality" issue between himself and the city manager. Personality conflicts don't occur merely because people differ in their styles. Rather, they occur as people interact with each other and attempt to interpret the meaning of the other person's actions and demeanor. When actions are interpreted negatively, there is a response of frustration or anger. Therefore, the personality conflict must be addressed in some fashion. Thirdly, Chief Charles as much as admits that he could improve in his management of his employees. He has some glaring "blind spots" regarding the way his behavior impacts other people. If this issue is targeted for improvement, additional questioning will identify what improvements are needed under what circumstances.

O.K., what can we hypothesize at this point? And what actionable insights can we postulate for performance enhancement?

- Chief Charles would greatly benefit from one-on-one coaching to improve his people and managerial skills.

- Chief Charles should receive one-on-one coaching to eliminate his inappropriate language.

- At some point, Chief Charles' team may benefit from team coaching. This is not definite as yet because oftentimes teams improve along with the leader.

- The city manager probably needs some coaching himself. Goals should be to improve his own coaching and managerial skills.

- The performance evaluation system should be overhauled to take on a coaching/mentoring approach. Employee performance goals should be established and reviewed frequently. Targeted improvements should be shared between employees and supervisor.

- It appears that there is not an empowering kind of atmosphere that facilitates input and shared decision-making.

Good followership is lacking, but we will hold off on this one to see how it might improve as leadership improves.

Chapter 4

Understanding the Challenge

Understanding the Challenge

"Success in the knowledge economy comes to those who know themselves, their strengths, their values, and how they best perform." -Peter Drucker

Let's say you have worked hard to train a good command staff. Assistant Chief Jones has worked with you for three years. His communication style is direct. He has many good ideas and is good at starting projects, but weak on finishing what he starts. Assistant Chief White, on the other hand, is good at details. He finishes what he starts, but seems to lack initiative. Assistant Chief Morales is a great team-builder and keeps the team motivated. His only weakness is time management. He has to be reminded to finish his projects on time. Assistant Chief Gonzales is bright and intelligent, but is not sociable. He prefers to stay in his office and send e-mail messages to those he works with.

In my younger days, I had a narrow approach to managing others. I believed people who did not respond to my management style were defective. I evaluated everyone with the same broken yardstick. I was wrong.

I now subscribe to the theory that there are several different, but predictable, work styles or behavior patterns common in people. In fire service, as in any workplace, firefighters and officers unaware of these behavior patterns will unintentionally damage their personal effectiveness. When an officer understands these unique differences, then they are in a more powerful position. They are better able to manage, understand, and lead people toward higher levels of productivity, lower frustration, higher morale, and better retention rates.

Many departments are turning to behavior assessments and personality trait testing for both firefighters and officers. Back in the late '90s, only 5 percent of my client departments used some type of assessment. Today, that figure is climbing to 45 percent. Assessments can help:

1. Individuals identify their strengths, know which jobs they are best suited for, and design a development plan to overcome shortcomings.

2. Human Resources managers and fire officers predict a new firefighter's success before they are hired.

3. Command staffs understand the temperament and work style of individual firefighters.

4. Officers can give performance feedback to people in a style they understand and accept for improving performance and accelerating professional development.

5. People enhance communication, understanding, and improve personal relationships.

6. Training officers select, hire, develop, and motivate super fire service people.

One client department uses assessments to improve their hiring and recruiting process. Previously, they made hiring decisions based on the candidate's resume and then hired the person based on their "gut" reaction. Once hired, many of these new people created friction, had bad work ethics, and their attitudes had a negative impact on their co-workers.

By using assessments, they created a visual benchmark (a graphic) of their "top" performers. They used another profile to identify the values, emotional competencies, and behaviors needed for success based on the requirements needed by each department.

They had a roadmap for success. They identified the behavior patterns, communication styles, motivations, and attitudes of their top personnel. In other words, they cloned their top performers. These assessments measure individual attitudes, values, personal interests, and behavior with 85 percent accuracy. Now the department is able to screen out applicants who may have good interview skills and have a great resume, yet are not suited for the job. The process saves them thousands of dollars in costs and reduces a lot of frustrations.

Most assessments available on the market today can be administered on the Internet and generate an amazing amount of detail on diverse behaviors, skills, and competencies, including:

- General characteristics

- Value to the organization

- Checklist for communicating

- Don'ts in communication

- Ideal work environment

- Perceptions
- Keys to motivating
- Keys to managing
- Areas for improvement
- Ranking of 12 leadership competencies
- Action plan for improvement

Successful officer development programs first begin with self-analysis. When you understand behavior styles, then you have a roadmap for improved potential and enhanced communication. The Extended DISC® for example identifies eight unique behavior patterns/styles people fall into:

1. Implementor — insures actual fulfillment by concrete measures

2. Conductor — guides, directs, manages, shows the way

3. Persuader — induces, argues others into an opinion

4. Promoter — initiates and advances new growth, undertakings

5. Relater — connects, establishes relationships between people and events

6. Supporter — advocates, maintains, tolerates, defends

7. Coordinator — brings together, joins for a common goal or action

8. Analyzer — studies the factors of a problem/situation in detail to arrive at a solution

As consultants, we work with groups of fire service personnel who experience difficulty working together and meeting objectives. We've worked with many departments who all possess notoriety for infighting. After completing behavior assessments on everyone, the problems are clear. In one particular department, the chief and two assistant chiefs possessed the same personality style; all three of them were confrontational. Their natural tendency was to go overboard to argue their points, they fought for sport rather than for principle. After they understood their natural tendencies, they were able to adapt, interact, and lead more effectively.

Developing people is less expensive than firing them. By understanding behavior differences, a department can align a fire officer's motivations with the department's mission. Assessments also help individuals reduce conflict and get along better. Furthermore, coworkers appreciate each person's unique strengths and abilities. With this knowledge departments and officers can maximize the abilities of their workforce in ways to help make all firefighters star performers.

Being unconscious of our motives, needs, and wants means that we are moving through time and space in a kind of fog, unaware of our limitations and how these create difficulties for us and other people as we interact. The problem is not our personality style, but rather the fact that many of us do not choose more effective behaviors from among the other personality styles. The conscious choice of behavior is one mark of an effective leader.

In settling on where the coaching is going (purpose/goal), you must first understand where you are, or in your subordinate's case, why she is where she is. Why is she having this challenge at this point? What personal "blind spots" are impeding her from seeing the solution? What inner resource is she failing to tap into? Is she open to learning, to self-exploration?

Granted, finding out why someone behaves as they do may feel a bit like finding a needle in a haystack. Fire service personnel are trained in fire rescue, not to understand the human mind. A lot of officers have reported that they find human behavior confusing! Even for psychologists and human resources specialists, understanding the origin of poor performance can seem daunting. Therefore, it is important to boil some things down to a more understandable and useable form.

Motivation Determines Behavior

Motivation is another word for goal. To understand why people do what they do, we must understand what goal they are striving for. In general, there are four goals: power, fun, intimacy, and peace.

Each motivation results in different patterns of behavior.

An officer seeks power and challenge. He or she may be termed a <u>Driver</u>. Predictably, this officer works with an intensely focused purpose and is blunt in his/her interactions with others. Peers, subordinates, and even chief officers, will value this officer's ability to get things done, but will lament his/her lack of warmth.

A second officer seeks fun and excitement. This person is referred to as an <u>Influencer</u>. Predictably, this officer is highly optimistic, charismatic, and popular. Peers, subordinates, and even chief officers will value this officer's flexibility, friendliness, and intuition, but will lament his/her irresponsibility and inability to confront the tough issues.

The third officer strives for relationships and intimacy and may be thought of as <u>Steadfast</u>. Predictably, this officer is well disciplined, goal oriented, and plans well with good follow through. Peers, subordinates, and even chief officers will value this officer's dependability and ability to achieve and empathize, but will lament his or her perfectionism, inability to respond quickly, and rigidity with principles.

The fourth officer seeks quality and peace and is referred to as <u>Conventional</u>. Predictably, this officer is calm under pressure, receptive to suggestions, and listens superbly. Peers, subordinates, and even chief officers will value this officer's compatibility and tolerance, but will lament his/her interpersonal detachment, fear of confrontation, and need for direction from others (Extended DISC®, 2003).

These motivations determine a variety of fairly predictable behavioral and emotional factors including:

- Areas of strength/weakness

- The kinds of interpersonal connections that are developed with others

- The perception of other's motives

- Avoidance areas/comfort areas

- What happens during times of stress

- The views others hold

- Repetitive patterns of challenge (commonly occurring problems)

- Leadership strengths and weaknesses

- The most effective way to lead and supervise them

Let's take an in-depth look at each of these general personality styles Driver, Influencer, Steadfast and Conventional.

Drivers

Drivers are like a general. They are decisive, tough, strong-willed, competitive, demanding, independent, self-confident, aggressive, blunt, self-centered, overbearing, and sometimes exceed authority.

Drivers seek power. Simply put, Drivers want things their way. It is almost impossible for them to relinquish their power and freedom and if, by necessary circumstances they do, they become frustrated and angry. Sometimes people who hold positions of authority, i.e., teachers, bosses, police, clergy, and military officers present a particular challenge to Drivers who find it difficult to relinquish control to their superior.

These superiors often find that their subordinate Driver oversteps his boundaries, works outside the protective net of a team, and usually does not consider other's feelings or needs.

Drivers want to get things done. Drivers like to work. But don't expect them to attach the same importance to things other people care about, like other people's achievements, academic degrees, career positions, and marriages. But give them a reason to produce, and they are gung ho. Drivers are often workaholics and want to get the job done. They will resist being forced to do anything that doesn't interest them.

Drivers want to look good. Being loved is not important.

Drivers are bottom-line oriented. And while they like to be respected for their intelligence, insight, and ability to get things done, they don't crave a whole lot of love. They want to be admired for their logical, practical minds. When dealing with Drivers, be quick, precise and factual. What's in it for them is the key question to answer. Drivers are unmoved by tears and other displays of "weakness." Drivers don't care too much about the "touchy-feely" unless it has a bottom-line benefit.

Drivers fight for sport. Drivers don't start a conversation by saying, "In my opinion." Instead, they present opinions as indisputable fact. In fact, when engaged in discussion, other personality types tend to view Drivers as argumentative, angry, and dogmatic only to realize later that Drivers were merely enjoying a spirited debate. When Drivers do get angry, they tend to deal with it quickly by stating their position, yelling, or criticizing. Other personality types are left feeling hurt or angry for a much longer period of time and are often surprised to learn that Drivers are finished with it and have moved on.

Drivers cannot not lead. Drivers are sometimes called "control freaks" because they desire and seem successful in securing leadership positions. They like to be in the driver's seat and feel frustrated and bored when they are not in charge.

Driver strengths
As Fire Officers, Drivers are:

- Natural goal setters-appear comfortable and confident
- Highly disciplined and accomplish what they set out to accomplish
- Quick and easy decision makers
- Goal oriented
- Comfortable in power positions
- Excellent organizers
- Superb delegators
- Self-motivated
- Competitors
- Highly task oriented and efficient
- Difficult to discourage
- Forthright in telling others where they stand in a relationship

Driver weaknesses

As Fire Officers, Drivers:

- Appear self serving
- Are out of touch with feelings
- Deny personal failings
- Have to be right
- Cannot relax unless accomplishing something
- Appear arrogant
- Defy authority
- Won't admit faults for fear of losing power and control
- Seek power to control others
- Dislike being told what to do
- Require loyalty and obedience
- Criticize others and seldom praise

Influencers

Influencers seek to have fun. Sociable, talkative, openly enthusiastic, energetic, persuasive, flamboyant, frantic, careless, indiscreet, excitable, hasty, laid-back sense of time.

Influencers value play. I's think of life as a big party and they want to meet as many people at the party as possible. I's view work differently than do some others. It is not a series of tasks to accomplish. Rather, they prefer to view the workplace as a place to have fun and enjoy themselves.

Influencers need applause. I's need to be noticed and be praised for their effort. Although they may not always achieve results in the way, say, a Driver desires. But their effort is genuine. I's often behave as though they have the world by the tail, but they do have their fears and frustrations-which they may not confide until they know they are emotionally safe. Safety is most effectively evident to I's through praise.

Influencers need many connections with people. Because of their demeanor, I's appear nonchalant, uncaring, flippant, self-centered, and even arrogant. But nothing can be further from the truth. They need to be stroked and they enjoy physical contact. In fact, physical contact is usually the most direct, comfortable intimate connection.

Influencers want to be popular. I's like to be center stage. Social acceptance is very important to them. Friends are often the highest priority to an Influencer because popularity and social contact quenches their thirst for general approval. They love intimate conversation but can also engage in surface chitchat with the best of them.

Influencers like action. The action oriented nature of fire service appeals to I's. They are easily bored and seek adventure. Thus, many fires service personnel possess a measure of Influencer in their personality. Many fire service I's have a hard time sitting still for a long period of time. They choose friends who, like them, refuse to allow the "boring details" to get in the way of the most important thing in life—play.

Influencer strengths
As Fire Officers, Influencers:

- Are highly optimistic
- Like themselves and accept others easily
- Like to volunteer for opportunities
- View life as an experience to be enjoyed
- Are people oriented
- Are friendly
- Are able to take risks
- Are energetic
- Inspire people to cooperate and excel
- Like to tackle short-term projects with visible results
- Are enjoyable to work with

Influencer weaknesses
As Fire Officers, Influencers:

- Require that all activities be fun
- Can handle stress only for short periods of time
- Do not concentrate for any length of time
- Take few things seriously
- Need a lot of interaction with people
  Are sloppy and unpredictable
- Resent authority
- Sometimes a lot of talk with little action
- Are unreliable

Steadfasts

Steadfasts are like counselors. Calm, steady, careful, patient, good listeners, modest, trustworthy, resist new ideas, stubborn, resist change.

S's are motivated by altruism. S's do nice things for others. They look for opportunities to give up something in order to bring another person happiness. Selflessness rather than selfishness is their guiding philosophy. Many

S's are uncomfortable doing things solely for themselves. They hold doors open for people, offer rides when someone's car breaks down, contribute to charities, even devote their lives to helping others.

S's seek intimacy. More than anything, S's want intimacy in their lives. To love and be loved is their primary motivation, even at work. We are not talking about sexual intimacy here, but rather to deep, satisfying relationships. While most I's have many acquaintances, S's have fewer and these are probably "deeper." A pure S will sacrifice a career path in order to improve or hold on to an important relationship. Previously thought of as solely a female characteristic, nurturing and caring are now more accurately viewed as an S personality trait.

S's crave being understood. S's are at their best when they are listened to, when they feel understood and appreciated. S's tend to reveal their inadequacies unabashedly because they value being known and understood so much. In the eyes of an S, being vulnerable is a small price to pay for the chance to connect emotionally. S's probably have their hearts broken more than most people, but they also spend much more time in love. In fire service, the S person thrives on comfortable, familiar relationships that are characterized by respect and patience.

S's are complicated. With S's, a simple pat on the back is not enough. They expend great effort to change the world and often need to be told how wonderful they are. The complicated part, however, is that they will not ask for attention and will probably pout if they don't get it. They need to be thanked and specifically remembered for their good deeds. They need sincere gratitude. S's need a lot of tender loving care.

S's are directed by a strong moral conscience. S's are motivated to behave in a proper, appropriate manner. They have a moral code that guides them in their decision-making, their value judgments, even their leisure time. S's prefer to do what is right and to be "good." S's come with the strongest sense of integrity of all the groups. An S would rather lose than cheat. They do not prefer positions of authority like Drivers do, but they are highly ethical and should be in positions of decision-making more than they are.

Steadfast strengths

As Fire Officers, Steadfasts are:

- Highly disciplined
- Receptive to other suggestions
- Strong goal oriented
- Excellent planners and follow through superbly
- Oriented toward ethics and standards of conduct
- Stable and dependable

- Excellent behind-the-scenes workers

- Appreciative of beauty and detail

- Sensitive and enjoy deep conversations

Steadfast weaknesses

As Fire Officers, Steadfasts:

- Are verbally self-abusive

- Are smug and self-righteous

- Are perfectionists

- Set unrealistically high goals

- Are easily discouraged when unsuccessful in accomplishments

- Are frustrated by lack of team cooperation

- Expect others to understand their goals and make them a priority

- Feel others are not capable of doing things as well they

- Crave security in career

- Feel inadequate with natural talents and creativity

- Shy away from public exposure and performance

- Tend to over plan and over prepare

- Overextend themselves

Conventionals

Conventionals are like scientists. Precise, follow rules, logical, careful, formal, disciplined, withdrawn, shy, do not express opinions, get stuck in details, does not take risks.

C's are motivated by peace. C's will do almost anything to avoid confrontation. They like to flow through life without hassle or discomfort. Feeling good is more important to them than being good.

C's need kindness. C's respond with strong, silent stubbornness when they are treated unkindly. They resent being scolded and dislike harsh words. To a C, how something is said is far more important than what is said. On the other hand, they open up immediately to people who are kind. Driver style fire officers are often amazed to learn that their C style subordinate employees despise them for the manner in which Drivers dispense orders and handle mistakes.

C's prefer quiet strength. Like Clint Eastwood or John Wayne, C's prefer the strong, silent approach. They usually do not resist by any boisterous, vociferous means. If C's perceive another person to be demanding and bossy, they will become a quietly implacable foe to a leader's direction.

C's keep a low profile. C's are comfortable being the expert. As such, they like to be asked their opinions although they won't volunteer them. They value the respect of others, but they rarely go out of their way to seek it. They need to be coaxed to talk about their skills, hobbies, and interests.

C's are independent. Unlike Drivers who want to control others, C's want to avoid being controlled. They simply refuse to be under another person's thumb, especially when treated without the respect they feel they deserve. C's want to do things their own way, in their own time. They don't ask much of others, and resent it when others demand things from them. They often comply with unreasonable demands—just to keep peace. They will express their anger and frustration only when they can no longer stand being bossed around. C's don't like to be pushed, and they can be fearsome when they finally "blow up."

C's are motivated by other people's desires. C's prefer to supervise by group decision. Disliking to make risky decisions, C's value new supervisory ideas and are open to the recommendations of others on ways to resolve any and all situations. C's make agreeable dates. They are interested in making sure the other person has a good time, and are willing to do whatever the other person wants. C's want suggestions, not demands.

Conventional strengths

As Fire Officers, Conventionals are:

- Quiet, reflective, and peaceful

- Sincere and have a genuine

- Patient with self and others

- Compatible with others

- Good blenders in social situations

- Comfortable in accepting life

- Open to suggestions

- Appreciative of exposure to many possibilities

- Cognizant of the value of goal setting

- Trusting that they will succeed in many different environments

- Accommodating of others

- Good negotiators

- Calm under pressure

- Nonconformists

Conventional weaknesses

As Fire Officers, Conventionals are:

- Somewhat boring

- Passive in their approach to life

- Not openly excited about experiences

- Prone to avoiding intimacy

- Bashful and unsure of themselves

- Easily manipulated into changing plans

- Ambivalent about direction and goals to pursue

- Resistant toward making commitments

- Fearful of confrontation

- Compliant only to please others

- Hesitant to contribute openly

- Reluctant to take a stand on issues

- Apt to take a "wait and see" attitude toward life experiences

- Waiting for a sign or for someone else to make decisions for them

- Waiting for others to set goals and then prone to criticizing the goals set for him or her

Why Is All of This Important?

The fire chief looked up from his note taking, somewhat surprised that the coach had stopped with the lecture about the elements of the four personality styles.

"Okay, fine," the chief said, "but so what?"

The chief was rightfully a tough student. He knew that a bunch of action-oriented fire officers weren't going to be satisfied with merely memorizing the characteristics of each style.

"I'm just catching my breath," said the coach.

The chief shifted in his seat. "I've heard that in corporate America, people join organizations, but leave supervisors."

"Yes, by all accounts, that is true," the coach said.

> *"But turnover is relatively low in fire service," the chief suggested.*
>
> *"Your problem is not turnover as much as it is morale and conflict. Personnel don't tend to leave, but they do exhibit many other signs of dissatisfaction such as sick time, conflict, formal complaints, and diminished service," the coach explained.*
>
> *"How do we address this?" the chief asked.*
>
> *"Through the differences that exist as well as by knowing what motivates each personality style," the coach said.*
>
> *"I assume that having only one style of personality would not be a good thing."*
>
> *"Differences definitely have the potential for greater strength," the coach said.*
>
> *"That's what I want to know."*
>
> *"Then let's continue."*

Working With Differences

"This year 85 percent of the employees who lose their jobs will lose them because of personality conflicts. Only 15 percent will lose their jobs because they lack technical expertise" (Hartman, 1999, p. 15).

The military style, from whence fire service borrowed its leadership practices, is mostly transactional in nature. Orders are given and followed and little emphasis is placed on gaining input from each officer or firefighter. In the past, fire service was like an assembly line with the personnel acting as the parts—one was about like another and could be readily exchanged with no loss of efficiency.

Now, personality plays a more critical role. The increasing predominance of specialization in an information era means that each fire officer and firefighter possesses knowledge and expertise that is vital for optimal fire service performance. Thus, increasing pressure is being placed on fire officers to exploit the strengths of the different styles, predict the result of intermingling certain styles, and coach a particular subordinate officer for maximum service productivity within the parameters of his/her personality style. In the end, the most efficient fire service comes down to the relationships developed between each level of rank. Successful fire departments are always illustrated by successful relationships.

This next section is aimed at helping officers learn what happens when personalities collide and how to maximize the differences between styles in order to achieve service excellence. In addition, being aware of your own personality style will help you understand the potential strengths and pitfalls as you relate and coach subordinate officers each with his/her particular personality style.

Relationship Combinations in Coaching and Leadership

Driver-Driver

What happens when two Drivers work together? Some call it war! What happens when a Driver is the coach? If the coach has no awareness of his or her goal, the coaching takes on a task orientation to the exclusion of self-awareness. And what happens when the subordinate officer is a Driver? Most officers report that the subordinate gets things done with little need for supervision, but that he or she oversteps boundaries and may ignore rank.

Because of their need to be right and their aggressive, blunt, and competitive nature, Drivers do not tend to take turns listening to one another or attempting to understand each other's point of view. Even when the coach is a superior officer, a fire officer will often challenge (albeit silently) a superior officer's stance. Remember, Drivers are task oriented and do not typically concentrate on intimacy or the process of developing a relationship. Instead, they tend to compete for who is right, who will win. Drivers tend to control their own lives as well as the lives of anyone who will allow it. Oftentimes, it is this very attempt to control that is the performance problem.

Mutual respect is the key element for Driver-Driver relationships. It is as much the responsibility of the superior officer to demonstrate respect as it is for the fire officer. Practicing the skills of reflective listening and making tentative suggestions (as opposed to dogmatic demands) can help one Driver work with another.

Drivers do not like or value anyone who dictates their destiny. Yet they are quite comfortable dictating the destiny of others. Superior officers who coach subordinates should take the stance of a consultant by offering tentative suggestions, asking the subordinate for his/her opinion, asking the subordinate to outline his or her strategy, and asking the subordinate to evaluate their own performance. It's not that the coach can never offer suggestions, but the suggestions should have a tentative quality to them instead of an order. Remember, coaching is a formalized relationship in which two people acknowledge that the superior officer is working to improve a subordinate officer's or firefighter's performance. It is not an ongoing series of reprimands.

The problem with two Drivers working together in a coaching relationship is that the coach may have difficulty viewing the subordinate's issues with any objectivity. For example, I designed a coaching program for a large suburban fire department. Following an extensive 360 degree feedback process, we paired superior officers with their subordinate officers for supervised practice of some of the skills that we had been teaching. My interest was peaked by one particularly interesting pair, both of whom were Drivers. The subordinate began by presenting only the most positive portions of feedback (Driver's tendency to hide insecurities).

As soon as the superior officer was bored—which occurred in less than four minutes—he demanded that the subordinate officer reveal the negative stuff, most of which had to do with issues regarding "critical demeanor," "lack of encouragement," and "micro-management." But, instead of listening and developing a performance improvement plan or even practicing some of the identified "soft skills," the superior officer focused his attention on technical matters that were not marked nearly as low on the feedback form. Suddenly, the coaching focused on accomplishing tasks and technical issues and failed to address those factors more closely associated with relationship development and mentoring. The result of this type of coaching, if left unchecked, would likely have been a continuation of the problems that the subordinate officer had been cited for in the 360 degree feedback.

So what happened? The two men were victims of their blind spots. The coaching was a Driver style session from a staunchly Driver-style coach. Granted, if an identified performance problem is purely technical in nature, a Driver-style coaching approach may be effective, but a lack of technical expertise is the sole problem only about 15% of the time. The other 85% of employees who experience performance-related job problems do so because of personality related issues.

Driver coaches must be on the lookout for some of the more emotional factors related to job performance and not diminish the importance of warmth, listening, enthusiasm, fun, empathy, and receptivity to suggestions. There is little doubt that a Driver coach benefits from focusing on the positive aspects of the Driver personality style. Two healthy Drivers carry their own motivations within themselves. If they can achieve mutual respect, they can stimulate each other with strong expectations and become a highly organized front.

One Driver superior officer and a Driver fire officer were so motivated to work out their differences and improve the fire officer's performance that they practically set a record for short-term coaching. They had one goal—to escape my "meddlesome" consultation—as they good-naturedly termed it. I never saw two individuals learn diplomacy, acceptance, encouragement, and warmth more rapidly than this pair. Their motivation actually promoted good relations within the station until genuine attitudinal change could follow and further ensure positive superior-subordinate officer relations.

No emotional baggage

The lack of concern for "emotional" elements is often detrimental for Drivers, particularly when they supervise Influencer, Steadfast, and Conventional types. But a Driver coach who is conscious of his/her weaknesses and who makes a concerted effort to overcome these, possesses strength that cannot be overlooked.

Drivers benefit from how little emotional baggage they allow in their lives. They don't require an extensive emotional support system in order to perform well. And sometimes they are thrilled to share a task with another Driver because neither needs hugs and kisses or constant pats on the back. "Let's just get this done," is a common and characteristic phrase for a Driver.

Recently I had the privilege of working with two fire officers, one of whom had been a superior of the recently appointed chief. Both were pure Drivers and extremely competent. During a tumultuous period in the distant past, the now chief was severely reprimanded several times by his superior (at the time) and written up for all sorts of infractions. Although the chief loathed the fire officer, business was business, and his purpose in being the chief was to lead the best fire service department he could. He squared his shoulders and repeatedly dealt with his old boss in a professional manner. Likewise, the fire officer (now the subordinate) harbored long-held feelings of disgust for the chief. He viewed the chief as an incompetent, politically driven, self-centered, know-it-all. But he too, spent little time ruminating over his feelings and dealt with the chief in a business-like manner. The result at six months was nothing short of fascinating. Because they were compulsive goal setters, extremely competitive, and wanted nothing more than to show the other guy how competent they were, they accomplished some rather lofty departmental goals during a particularly difficult budgetary period. And while they never claimed that any sort of friendship existed between them, they jokingly acknowledged that their dislike for one another "is probably the source of some pretty damn good work." These two men reveal some of the other possibilities for two Drivers who work together in coaching.

The need for productivity

It is possible for Drivers to push each other to be ever more productive. They can both enjoy working together and accomplishing a great deal because they share a task orientation. They are both fast paced and tenacious. Drivers appreciate productivity and are likely to work best with those who share similar beliefs, even if what they produce together falls short of perfection.

Goal setting and extreme competition

At this writing, the fire officers we mention in the "no emotional baggage" section state that while they would not go out with each other for a cup of coffee—unless doing so could result in some incredible accomplishment—they are "pumped" about the cooperative competition they share to see who can produce the most. This is a positive result for two Drivers who have decided that, while they don't like each other, there is a much bigger issue at hand—community service. But the same two guys could fall into negative interactions in which quality is sacrificed for quantity. When two Drivers get caught up in winning, they take a narrow perspective of who can do more. As a result, these relationships are fraught with confrontations, hostility and aggression.

Drivers must keep the bigger picture, the purpose, in mind. As a Driver coach, you must constantly assess what is important, why the fire service exists, and how your actions can contribute to a cohesive, trusting environment.

Driver-Steadfast
Power versus intimacy

The main struggle between Drivers and Steadfasts is based on their differing motives. Drivers are motivated by power, while Steadfasts are motivated by intimacy. In addition, neither offers the other what he or she wants without first demanding that his or her own needs be met.

One of the greatest frustrations between Drivers and Steadfasts involves perceptions of intimacy. While talking about intimacy in a fire department sounds odd, it is nevertheless one of the most important issues to understand. Steadfasts harbor a deeply held need for appreciation that Drivers have a hard time grasping.

A fire officer meets with his command staff each week to get an update on new training programs and the preparations for ISO audits. The municipality is one of the fastest growing in the nation and many new, young firefighters have been hired. The fire officer (Driver) starts each meeting with a go-around to gather information on results. Results to the officer means number of personnel trained and the bottom line on reports in preparation for ISO certification. But results to the Steadfast fire trainer (there are many Steadfasts in fire service) means something entirely different. The Steadfast trainer is concerned with how the training impacted the recruits, which recruits show the earliest promise of dedication and skill, and their connection with the group.

Prior to the Steadfast trainer's knowledge of the Extended DISC®, their weekly meetings went like this.

> *The Steadfast type trainer said, "We had the eight new people in class along with those who were regularly scheduled. The best part was the new guy, Cook, who came up after the class and told me how the class was much clearer and pertinent than the overview he received at the academy. He wanted me to know-"*
>
> *"Thanks, Bret," interrupted the Driver type Chief. "I just need a brief, bottom-line report at this point. Let's continue going around."*

> *Both guys leave the meeting frustrated. The Driver chief hates hearing from Bret each week, but he's pivotal in terms of the outcome of the ISO inspections. Bret is frustrated every time the fire chief cuts him off from sharing what he believes is important and the things that really matter to him. After both guys learned about coaching and Extended DISC®, their dialogue went like this.*

> *"Yes, we put twelve more guys through the training and wrapped it up for now," the Steadfast trainer reported. "I finished the latest ISO report and put it in your box for editing."*
>
> *The Driver type fire chief smiled while listening to Bret's briefer message and made a mental note to contact Bret more often because he wants Bret to feel connected and appreciated.*
>
> *"Very good Bret," the chief said. "I'd like to meet with you when we finish to find out how you feel about this new batch of recruits."*

Risk versus security

Drivers take risks as easily as they breath. They tend to view those who don't, as scared and weak. If you are a driver style coach, you should be aware that Steadfasts don't like taking risks and can easily view those who do as loose cannons. Subordinate officers who are pushed too hard by superior officers are left with the impression that the superior officer does not care about them and is setting them up to fail. It's not that Steadfasts won't or can't change. They simply need to feel secure that they will be successful or have the support of those asking them to take the risk.

Selfish versus self-sacrificing

Drivers are basically selfish, while Steadfasts enjoy being self-sacrificing. But it is important for superior officers to recognize the sacrifice made by the Steadfasts. While the Steadfasts won't speak up, they may begin to keep score if appreciation is not communicated to them.

Hiding insecurities versus revealing insecurities

Drivers believe that they will lose power by revealing their insecurities, while Steadfasts believe that they can only be truly understood by revealing their insecurities and failings. Driver coaches should spend some time listening to the doubts of Steadfasts. In this way, they will help the Steadfast feel valued and develop a sense of trust.

On the other hand, if you are a Steadfast coach, you cannot expect a Driver subordinate to easily reveal faults and insecurities. In fact, you may perceive that the Driver engages in a fair amount of denial regarding his/her shortcomings. But it is more likely that the Driver does not see the value in self-revelation. Help the Driver see how avoidances usually result in the very things the Driver is afraid of. For example, when someone fears being controlled, they usually take on a dominating demeanor in self-defense. The natural response is for superior officers to squelch the overbearing behavior. The result is that the subordinate officer experiences being micromanaged and controlled.

Productivity versus perfectionism

Drivers want to accomplish a lot. Steadfasts want to make sure it's done right. Both are highly committed to productivity, but they disagree on the quality of the finished product or the necessary schedules. Both are weak without the other. Drivers get things done, but the quality may be poor. Steadfasts turn out a good product, but may take forever to do it. Together, they form a strong front for rapid, quality service. Both must keep the other's motive in mind as well as what each ultimately wants. By focusing on bottom-line job desires, each is more likely to get what they want by incorporating the salient strengths of the other.

Insensitive versus too sensitive

Because Drivers are mostly concerned with accomplishing tasks, they tend not to take other's feelings into consideration. They tend to be blunt in their communications and are relatively unaware that others don't like them. Drivers quickly get angry and just as quickly get over it.

On the other hand, Steadfasts carry hurt feelings around like out-of-date luggage, it's not very pretty, but they just can't get rid of it. The two styles clash immeasurably in fire service. If the Driver is the superior officer, he/she is likely to never know how the Steadfast subordinate officer really feels. All that is known is that the subordinate is withdrawn, sullen, and not forthcoming with creative input. Having these perceptions of the subordinate officer, the superior officer believes that the subordinate is a weak leader, indecisive, and too sensitive (an additional sign of weakness). The subordinate officer views the chief as cold, arrogant, and uncaring. "I'll go to hell and back for a chief that cares about us as people. But ethically speaking, I can't sacrifice myself or my people for someone I don't' trust."

Quick to anger but moving on versus unforgiving and resentful

Steadfasts remember everything that ever happened in a relationship. They scar deeply and do not forgive easily. Drivers do not forgive any more than Steadfasts. Intellectually, their heads simply help them to move on to cope more efficiently with life.

Rebellious versus acquiescent

"I work closely with a Driver and a Steadfast," said one fire officer. "The Driver shoots first and asks questions later. The Steadfast will only shoot after receiving permission.

Both are Responsible-Both personalities are highly dependable. They take commitment seriously and act accordingly. Neither tolerates irresponsibility well. Both are highly principled. Drivers are fiercely loyal to causes or tasks, while Steadfasts are loyal to people.

Both are achievers

Both are tremendous taskmasters. They work hard through their lives to succeed. Play is secondary to work for both groups. Drivers are delegators and therefore achieve through others while Steadfasts are doers and therefore achieve through themselves. They both do best when allowed to operate within the limits they set for themselves. They are always stretching themselves professionally, but often for different reasons.

Both are intimidating

Drivers and Steadfasts share the dubious honor of being perceived as intimidating. Each intimidates the other. Steadfasts are so good at what they do that they intimidate Drivers. Drivers are so logical and verbal that they intimidate Steadfasts. Both can either recognize and appreciate each others strengths or feel intimidated and behave in a destructively blaming fashion. Neither is particularly sympathetic to the other's personality. Both remain somewhat aloof and feel justified in their intimidating style.

Critical of others versus critical of self and others

Neither style is comfortable with mistakes. Steadfasts look for fault within themselves, although they may not overtly take responsibility for it in public. This is because they fear rejection. On the other hand, Drivers find fault with others and may only introspect in private. Both personalities are highly critical and blame-oriented.

Arrogant versus self-righteous

Both come off as "right." Both are quick to judge the other. Neither is quick to see his/her own shortcomings despite repeated remarks from the other. Drivers are perceived as arrogant and always right. Steadfasts maintain a kind of moral self-righteousness and piety. Drivers hate this.

Active versus negative

Both tend to "pollute" the environments of others with negativity. Drivers move through down times more easily than Steadfasts and neither know how to play well. They both tend to look to others to bring out the sunshine in their lives.

Drivers Need Steadfasts:	**Steadfasts Need Drivers:**
To teach them compassion	To teach them honest feedback
To soften their communication	To teach them assertiveness
To point out details	To get the job done
To encourage them	To give them specific direction
To encourage their risk taking	To foster a sense of security
To plan the action	To execute the plan
To confront them directly	To understand them
To listen without taking comments personally	To appreciate them
To approve of their style and direction	To include them in plans
To trust them	To be trustworthy

Driver-Conventional

Driver-Conventional relationships are the most common and, interestingly, the most complimentary relationships among the styles. They are both power oriented, self-serving, and need respect. Upon first glance, the two styles seem too opposite to be complimentary, but it is these very differences that mesh fairly well in fire service. For example, Drivers like to tell people what to do and Conventionals are more comfortable being told what to do. Drivers are very impatient and Conventionals are very patient. Some of the strongest, most well-oiled departments I know are those in which the fire officers are D/C combinations. Must the chief officer be a Driver? Not at all. In fact, I have found that Chief Conventionals who tend to listen best and take in information are often best paired with Driver Fire officers who appreciate the fact that the chief encourages their input. Driver fire officers also appreciate the fact that a Conventional chief stays out of the daily operations.

Power versus peace

Drivers will choose power and challenge over a peaceful existence any day. Arguments and tension in relationships don't bother Drivers whereas Conventionals tend to avoid conflict, not because they are afraid, but because conflict is messy and disrupts their desire for smooth sailing.

The issue of respect

Drivers and Conventionals seek respect in different ways. Drivers expect to be accommodated whereas Conventionals expect to be left alone. Because Conventionals often have diminished self-esteem, they are more vulnerable to feeling a lack of respect than are Drivers. Although Influencers (I) and Steadfasts (S) do not handle the way Drivers show respect very well, Conventionals often take Drivers with a grain of salt and even appear to understand that when Drivers appear disrespectful, it is not personal.

Adventure versus security

Drivers thrive on adventure and often seek the opportunity to risk physical danger. They tend to seek riskier and riskier adventures. Conventionals like adventure as well, but want the assurance of support systems and/or guidelines.

Leadership versus protection

Both seek leadership positions but carry out their duties in different ways. While Drivers delegate business in an impulsive, blunt, no nonsense manner, Conventionals tend to gather information before making a decision. Drivers are criticized for being too harsh. Conventionals are criticized for taking too long to make a decision.

Change versus stability

Drivers take risks as much to avoid being bored as to achieve something in particular. Conventionals take risks also but will do so only when the odds are predictable.

High profile versus low profile

Although there are many great Conventional leaders, they also make great sidekicks because they are willing to go along for the ride. They are easily entertained and prefer to leave center stage for the Drivers. In a transactional style of leadership, a great number of Conventionals are essential because they go along. As fire service changes from a transactional style to a Constructive® style, a greater mix of the styles is called for. Because the Constructive® style encourages more input from the bottom to the top, all personality types are preferred because service strength is improved through the intermixing of strengths among the differences.

Controlling versus refusing to be controlled

"I'll give you an example of this," said one chief officer after hearing an initial explanation. "The Driver officer I'm thinking about, promotes his ideas to the rest of the staff and is amazed when they don't just automatically run with it. If he gets a lukewarm reception to his notions, he just raises his voice and says more of the same. Pretty soon, it's like he's ramming something down our throats. What is interesting though is that Conventional officers are often the ones who most often balk at his demands, not because he has bad ideas but because he is attempting to force issues down everyone's throat. You can just see the Conventionals stubborn resolve not to be controlled in the way they shift and cross their arms when he gets revved up."

Delegator versus doer

Success for Drivers comes as a result of giving orders, allowing others to do their jobs once they have delegated them, and encouraging individuality as long as the work gets done. If work is delayed or too many mistakes made, Drivers continue delegating but do so in critical manner. On the other hand, Conventionals accomplish things on their own and many things others never know about because Conventionals are not self-promoters. They carry out assignments quietly as long as things go smoothly.

Verbally demanding versus nondemanding

Drivers are the most verbally demanding of all the types. Conventionals are the least verbally demanding. Drivers verbalize their position, while Conventionals express themselves nonverbally. Drivers have strong expectations of their employees and cannot operate without goals. They are so goal oriented that they expect everyone else to do the same. On the other hand, Conventionals are comfortable floating through life. While Drivers prefer predetermined action plans, Conventionals do not see the need to set goals and rarely follow through as tenaciously as the Drivers.

On advice

"My husband must be a Driver," said a female fire officer. "Whenever we are lost in a car, he refuses to stop and ask for advice." Whether her husband is a Driver or simply male, her point is well taken. Drivers don't seek advice or accept it when unsolicited. Drivers sometimes get frustrated with Conventionals who constantly seek advice and therefore tend to make decisions more slowly.

The Driver husband, in the example above, is also a fire officer and had this to say about his Conventional wife. "I love her to death, but one thing that drives me nuts is her constant questioning and need for reassurance. Sometimes I feel like saying 'just do it.'"

Poor listener versus excellent listener

Drivers prefer debate to just listening. On the other hand, Conventionals dislike debate and prefer to hear what others have to say. Drivers are so certain they know everything that they do not need to fully listen or gather details. Giving advice and getting results is their method of operation. Conventionals are so genuinely interested in others' feelings and concerns that they are sought after for their patience and gentle manner. Their centered demeanor has a calming effect on others.

While no one is limited from embracing the strengths of the other personality styles, none of us can really abandon our innate core personality.

Rather, the goal in the change process is to develop: (1) awareness of which traits you should develop from the other personalities, (2) awareness of the motives, needs, and wants of all four of the basic personality styles, (3) flexibility in choosing appropriate style-related behaviors for given situations.

<u>**Drivers Need Conventionals:**</u>	<u>**Conventionals Need Drivers:**</u>
To calm them in crises	To motivate them
To focus them on quality	To keep them task-oriented
To promote compromise	To organize them
To bounce ideas off	To lead them

Driver-Influencer

These two styles enjoy verbal banter and do not get bogged down in emotional baggage like Steadfasts and Conventionals. Both are excited about change and find little need to be concerned with stability. In fire service, this combination can be very difficult. The self-centeredness of the Influencer and the selfishness of the Driver presents certain fire service problems, namely that neither tend to give much that the other needs or wants. Only when each understand the needs and wants of the other and learns to appreciate what the other offers can they form a productive alliance.

Looking good (intellectually) versus looking good (socially)

Both Drivers and Influencers want to look good. There is probably nothing that allies them more than hiding their inadequacies and appearing good on the surface. Both struggle with intimacy although they do so differently. Drivers are more direct about guarding their feelings while Influencers openly invite people in but remain elusive. The element that is most lacking in this combination is emotional depth. Neither caters to the needs of others. In a fire department, Drivers and Influencers have a most difficult time admitting their inadequacies. As a result, both may resort to blaming the other for errors.

High profile

Both like visibility. They are not behind-the-scenes type people and prefer to be on stage. Drivers maintain their high profile through knowledge, hard work, and leadership skills. Is maintain their high profile through their innate love for people, charismatic style, and positive energy.

Controlling versus needing freedom

One of the greatest sources of tension between Drivers and Influencers centers around the Drivers need to control and the Influencers need to avoid being controlled.

Unemotional versus emotional

While Influencer does not live with the emotional depth of a Steadfast, they are certainly more demonstrative with their feelings. Drivers, on the other hand, are stoic and rarely display any sort of emotional range other than frustration or anger. Interestingly, Drivers like the emotional displays of the Influencer. The Influencer seems to provide added texture and color to the normally monochromatic existence of the Driver.

On logic

Both styles are capable of debating issues without necessarily resorting to emotional drama. Both possess strong verbal skills and enjoy the pleasure of boldly debating opposite points of view while remaining personally unscathed. Both are direct with their communication. This is the one aspect of their style that tends to mesh and is perhaps the saving grace in D/I relationships.

On delegating

Drivers are the masters of delegation. They are masters in their ability to see the big picture and select competent individuals to carry through on the details. The Influencer is a good delegator also but does so without the need to control. People tend to trust the Influencers and want to follow their leadership. In addition, firefighters follow the Influencer because he/she is loved. Firefighters follow the Driver leader because he/she demonstrates the confidence of a leader who knows the right path (whether or not he/she really does). Over the long haul, it is the Drivers who generally remain committed and successful in the position of leadership. They remain focused on the task. The Influencer often finds managing others too demanding, unpleasant, and mundane.

Intense versus carefree

Drivers seem to care about everything while the Influencer seems to care about nothing. Drivers are intense and approach every problem with attacking resolve whereas the Influencer takes the approach that things will work out anyway so why get too uptight about it. Actually, the traits of the two styles can be a powerful addition to the department. The intensity of the Driver is often softened by the spontaneity and humorous outlook of the Influencer.

<u>Ds Need the I:</u>	<u>The I needs Ds:</u>
To teach them charisma	To focus them
To accept their leadership	To notice them
To cheerlead for them	To risk with them
To understand that their criticism is not meant personally	To keep them on task

Steadfast-Steadfast

Steadfasts in relationship with one another are deeper and commit longer than any other style combination. On the positive side, Steadfasts share perfectionist tendencies and appreciate other Steadfasts dedication and commitment to quality work. Steadfasts are loyal people and respectful of authority. Steadfasts trust one another in general. Reliable and conscientious are accurate descriptors. There is seldom a power struggle between Steadfasts and they tend to enjoy warm and friendly relationships. On the more challenging side, Steadfasts get nasty when they feel left out or rejected. At that point, the relationship is characterized by bitter power plays, resentful comments, and behind the back maneuvering. Because Steadfasts tend to be rather passive, they may not confront their differences directly, preferring instead to be more passive in their disagreements. On the whole however, Steadfasts share many responsible traits important to successful relationships. They are usually seen as role models of self-sacrifice, understanding, listening, patience, generosity, encouragement, and relationship development. Yet curiously, even with all of these wonderful characteristics, Steadfasts tend not to always work well as a team, preferring instead to do the work themselves.

Nonconfrontational

A command staff of a large suburban fire department was composed of seven members. Six were strong introverted Steadfast personalities and one was an extroverted Driver. The Influencer chief was frustrated by the staff's lack of expressed passion or desire to work together. Each member saw himself/herself as an expert who had responsibilities over his/her own specialty and battalion. The chief hired consultants to come in to conduct team-building workshops in an effort to get the staff members to work more in unison. In turn, the command staff nicknamed the chief "Martha Stewart" since he constantly tried to engineer a close, "homey" environment. On several occasions he even had home cooked meals catered during in-house retreat meetings, replete with tablecloths. Finally, he asked the consultant if designing some exercises to force the staff to confront one another would help them behave in a more cohesive manner.

The chief's solutions were the problem. The Steadfasts didn't like being exposed or forced to confront one another. These fire officers wouldn't challenge another member of the team unless that person did something unethical. Instead of telling the chief that his methods were making the situation worse, they simply avoided him or answered "yes sir" to his orders to get him off their back. They then simply went about their business as they saw fit, and ignored his orders. Finally the chief was so frustrated that, in anger, he gave up and made one of the Steadfast chiefs responsible for a vital community project. To his surprise, the Steadfast chief laid out the various tasks on the table and simply allowed the other members to choose which section of the project they wanted. Each completed their piece and then put the separate pieces together like a puzzle. "I think it's a lonely and isolated way to work," said the chief in private. "But I'm going to have to let go of this idea of an energetic and passionate team. At least they got the work done and in record time."

Loyalty

Steadfasts care about people. This caring for others makes them extremely loyal to each other, to law and order, to verbal commitments and to society's expectations. The Steadfast style remains the last bastion of the belief that one's word means something. Steadfasts tend to carry through on their commitments even when the situation demands that they should renege.

Commitment and appreciation

Steadfasts are so focused and committed to what they do that they often run the risk of becoming myopic. Steadfast leaders are sometimes so myopic that they become micro-managers and thus take initiative away from their subordinate officers and firefighters. What some Steadfast leaders don't realize is that, although they appear calmer and more patient than do Drivers, they are just as apt to rob the initiative and energy of their subordinates through their perfectionist, resolve.

Perfectionism

Steadfasts do most everything above and beyond the call of duty. They believe in quality, not quantity, and find other Steadfasts who are equally concerned with detail, to be quite refreshing. The one thing that drives an Steadfast crazy is nonchalance and a messy, unstructured approach.

Passionate

Steadfasts live for passion. They want to feel life rather than merely exist and their work activities must count for something. This is why fire service tends to draw a lot of Steadfasts. They care deeply and share intimately.

Obedient

Steadfasts are the most obedient of all the styles. Steadfasts follow rules, respect authority, accept law and order as important and have a high regard for moral obligations.

Trust

Although Steadfasts are suspicious and lack trust in relationship with other styles, this is not true of S-S relationships. The primary reason is that neither Steadfast gives cause for the other to be suspicious. Both are concerned about the well-being of the other.

Steadfast-Conventional

Steadfasts and Conventionals are both inclined to be concerned with feelings and are low key in their approach to each other. In fire service, my experience suggests that Steadfasts complain most about Conventionals lack of initiative, stubbornness, and lack of passion for a job or task. Conventionals seem more likely to complain that Steadfasts are too controlling, emotional, and unforgiving. Steadfasts comment positively on the peaceful nature, kindness, willingness to listen, tolerance, and patience of Conventionals. Conventionals appreciate Steadfasts for their sincerity, leadership, tactful assertion, and loyalty.

To be good (morally) versus to feel good within oneself

Steadfasts and Conventionals both need to feel good inside, but for very different reasons. Steadfasts are driven by a moral conscience, while Conventionals are more concerned with avoiding distress. Steadfasts willingly take on an issue if a principle is involved. Conventionals are more inclined to ignore a problem, regardless of the principles, if they perceive discomfort or distress could result from the confrontations. Steadfasts often resent the lack of involvement and moral commitment of Conventional companions. Conventionals tend to resent the persistent lecturing and moral demands of Steadfasts.

Autonomy versus protection

Conventionals are basically followers. One chief recently hired us to help him with his promotions process. We administered the Extended DISC® to seven candidates. "I'm looking for someone like myself," he said. "I want someone who is full of initiative, tough, no nonsense, and willing to set himself apart from the shift. I'm tired of having a bunch of leaders who can't lead." When he saw the results, several colorful expletives were heard down the hallway. "These people are just like the ones I have now—sheep." All of the candidates were Conventionals. When we explained to the chief that these candidates generally accept being directed and protected by others, he instructed us to get ready for another round of assessment.

The concern of the Conventional is not just the direction they receive, but the style of the direction. *How* a leader directs them is more important than what the direction is. They are terribly resistant to demands or hostile control. Steadfasts, on the other hand, accept direction out of obligation and other appropriate expectations of relationships and societal pressures, but they prefer autonomy. Steadfasts are typically not good team players. They will not accommodate others the way Conventionals will. They do not want to lead anyone (including their C companions), which creates leadership problems for the personality combinations. Steadfasts are more committed to doing a job right, while Conventionals are more concerned with simply getting along. Neither personality prefers to lead, although Steadfasts end up doing so in the majority of S-C relationships.

Difficult to understand versus easier to understand

Typically Steadfasts are perceived to be more difficult to understand, although both have clear needs. The Steadfasts need to be understood and appreciated. The Conventionals need to feel in control of themselves and be respected. Conventionals operate on a power base but seek peaceful, accepting relationships. Steadfasts operate on an intimacy base but seek control and understanding.

On doing

Conventionals usually get the job done. They are not particularly concerned with the schedule or exactness of their work. They do quality work and concern themselves mostly with fulfilling the agreement of the contract. They are steady workers who enjoy both doing the job themselves and delegating it to others. They can be lazy and/or overwhelmed when they accept too much work at one time, or they can lack enthusiasm for their endeavors if they have to deal with rigid supervisors or unfulfilling tasks.

Steadfasts enjoy doing the job themselves rather than delegating it to others. They love having skills jobs that require their particular expertise. In fact, one may well find the artisans of our society are most represented by Steadfasts who enjoy the opportunity of creating and implementing their craft on their own. Therefore, they are more inclined to trust themselves, while Conventionals are better at delegating the responsibility to others.

On control

Both personality styles are controlling, but Steadfasts are more likely to try to control others, while Conventionals seek primarily to control only themselves. Steadfasts want to know everything that is going on in their co-workers' lives. Steadfast officers tend to be suspicious and keep their eyes on everyone's business.

Emotional versus emotional and logical

The strongest difference between the Conventionals and Steadfasts is their use of emotion or logic. Steadfasts thrive on emotional interaction. They tend to focus on feelings, while Conventionals focus on logical reasoning.

Irrationally unrealistic expectations versus irrationally timid and fearful

Steadfasts want everyone to read their minds. They expect everyone to just know how they are feeling. Steadfasts tend to fantasize a lot about how things should be, and then expect others to share the same fantasies and act accordingly. In fire service, this means the Steadfast does not speak up or act in an assertive manner to aggressively correct misdeeds. Peers are often frustrated at Steadfast officers who are nice to their face only to stab them in the back later.

Conventionals behave irrationally out of fear. Conventional officers often carry irrational ideas of others and what they are certain will happen if they confront someone or make a wrong decision. Conventionals are often paralyzed to act because they are certain that they can predict a catastrophic outcome. Out of such fear, many Conventional officers leave decision making up to their subordinates, claiming that they prefer to lead by democratic decision. In reality, they want no part of risky decisions. Conventional officers are often found holed up in their offices.

Achieve versus balance

Steadfasts are more inclined to stretch themselves in life toward increased productivity, while Conventionals are more content balancing their lives with work and play. Steadfasts are more determined to put whatever time and effort is required to be the best. Conventionals are more concerned with enjoying the total process of living, which includes a balanced support system of friends, family, self, and work.

Impatient versus patient

Conventionals tend to be more laid back about time constraints and are less often irritated about colleagues arriving late unless he/she has been taken advantage of in the past. Steadfasts, on the other hand, are usually prompt and expect others to be the same. Conventionals usually see little value in getting all worked up over something they can't really change anyway.

On criticism versus tolerance

Because the majority of fire service personnel are Conventionals and Steadfasts, the issue of criticism makes for an interesting discussion. My experience is that most fire departments are witness to a fair amount of conflict. This can be explained in large part by understanding the C-S dynamic.

For both Cs and Ss, getting mad is not enough. They wait to get even. They may hold the grudge as long as they feel the other person needs to be punished. The difficulty for other styles comes in understanding how someone can hang on to a grudge for so long. Drivers, for example, get over their anger fairly quickly and believe in moving on since the past cannot be changed anyway.

Conventionals and Steadfasts are the holders of those long-standing workplace grudges that we are all familiar with. One gets the image of the Hatfield/McCoy feud that lasted for several generations. In almost every case, there was a past incident where the C or S was hurt, felt under appreciated, or ignored. The way to address this issue is to inquire about the underlying hurt and then be willing to hear what will probably sound irrational.

On conflict

Neither style is interested in conflict but Steadfasts will rise to the occasion when they feel an injustice has occurred. Remember, the Steadfast is a highly principled person who does not tolerate wrong behavior. They will speak their minds and confront anyone when a situation flies in the face of truth and honesty. Like cornered bears, Steadfasts will lash out irrationally when they perceive that someone has wronged them in an unforgivable way.

Conventionals, on the other hand, are less inclined to create a scene and stir up trouble for themselves. To avoid conflict, Conventionals often say, "I don't care." Even in those matters that do not carry the potential for conflict, Conventionals say, "Whatever you want is fine with me."

On advice

Conventionals are inclined to allow others to set their own boundaries. They are less likely than Steadfasts to follow up on their advice to ensure compliance. Steadfasts, however make stronger disciplinarians. When they give advice or orders, they expect other people to follow them.

On listening

The primary difference between Steadfasts and Conventionals is their emotional attachment to the conversation. Both care deeply about people, but Cs are more apt to hear the issues objectively, while Ss are instinctively drawn to the individual. Both respond with sincere concern for the individual and the content.

Ss Need Cs:	Cs Need Ss:
To show them the good in others	To motivate them
To teach them relaxed attitudes	To be kind to them
To listen to them	To teach them creativity
To respect them	To encourage and believe in
To carry out specific assignments To be agreeable	To build their self-confidence
	To initiate activities

Steadfast-Influencer

In fire service, the Steadfast-Influencer relationship allows a great deal of closeness, more than any of the other personality combinations. The reason is because they represent the entire spectrum of emotions and together they can create the kind of synergy that fire service values, including genuine human connection, depth, sincerity, compassion for others, excitement, and optimism about people. The primary difficulty between these two styles comes in their vastly different perceptions of work and play. Steadfasts believe play comes after work is done. The Influencers believe that while work is necessary, play is more important, and tend to give it first priority.

Steadfasts are steady, the Influencer is somewhat flighty. Steadfasts prefer stability, the Influencer prefers change. They are opposites in many ways, but the opposites can definitely work. Perhaps each supplements what the other needs. Perhaps their differences afford them the opportunity to appreciate the other's strengths. Regardless of the reasons, Steadfasts and Influencer frequently seek and enjoy each other's companionship.

Appreciation or praise

Steadfasts thrive on appreciation. These fire service personnel willingly forego personal pleasure in order to meet the needs of others. It means a great deal when others, however briefly, forego personal pleasure to appreciate them. The tough thing is that Steadfasts give at such a committed level that superficial praise is generally not enough. A handwritten note from someone who genuinely appreciates them or to acknowledge them at an awards dinner is more apt to make the Steadfast feel appreciated.

On the other hand, an Influencer typically throws something together at the last minute and tends to come up smelling like a rose. A pat on the back is often sufficient to make them feel appreciated.

Steadfasts also perceive appreciation through the equipment provided to them by the employer. Many fire officers have commented on how unappreciated they feel because the workplace provides them with shoddy equipment.

To be good (morally) versus to look good (socially)

Steadfasts are concerned with moral obligations whereas the Influencer is concerned with social recognition. This is perhaps the most frequent and common difference between Steadfasts and Influencer. Steadfasts sometimes see the Influencer as shallow, whereas the Influencer sees Steadfasts as "worry warts." A Steadfast would suffer from moral guilt over a perceived mistake where as an Influencer would suffer from social guilt.

Security versus adventure

Steadfasts are often envious of Influencer self esteem. The Influencer is amazing in that they are born with a healthy dose of self-esteem. The Influencer does not seek validation from outside sources. They tend to like themselves and usually feel confident that things will work out. Their concern is one of image. This innate confidence allows them to seek adventure throughout their lives, while Steadfasts continually grasp for the elusive feeling of security. In fact, one of the reasons Steadfasts gravitate toward the Influencer is that the Influencer offers them, through their association, a feeling of confidence and security.

Conversely, the Influencer gains a lot from the Steadfast as well. Steadfasts provide a sense of grounded security to the Influencer who does not come by this naturally. The Influencer style is prevalent in fire service due to the emergency nature of the job and the opportunity to be admired. But sometimes the Influencer will become dissatisfied if the particular station does not offer enough change, risk, and adventure. Keep in mind that while the Influencer likes risk, they do not care that much for extreme competition. The risk is in trying something new.

Autonomy versus freedom

This is another area of frustration that occasionally crops up between Steadfasts and Influencer. Steadfasts want autonomy to pursue a task while the Influencer wants freedom from completing a task as well as freedom to work on their own. If the Steadfast is a superior officer and the Influencer a subordinate, the Steadfast can sometimes fret over what appears to be a lackadaisical attitude toward time and task completion. But both prefer the freedom to work on their own and find independent work situations comfortable. However, the Influencer requires fewer rules and prefers contact with people more than the Steadfast.

Strong perfectionism versus scattered productivity

Steadfasts go through life noticing the detail and maintaining a penetrating concentration. Steadfasts are devoted to perfection and willingly work at something until they are practice perfect. They admire others who possess the same level of commitment to perfection and are frustrated at the Influencer who sometimes skates through life with the talent to be excellent but who won't spend the time to practice and focus long enough to be great. The Influencer often shows moments of brilliance and skill, but rarely focuses only on one thing. What they display is natural, not practiced. What the Steadfast displays is practiced more than natural.

Responsible versus irresponsible

The Influencer is more concerned with the speed with which they turn the fire truck than with the technique with which they do it. Chief officers complain that their Influencer fire officers don't give adequate consideration to the long-term consequences of their behavior. They do not typically take good care of their belongings because they think only of the moment. Steadfasts usually resist loaning equipment or important possessions to the Influencers.

Sincere versus insincere

Steadfasts pride themselves on their sincere and loyal commitment to Influencers.

Deals with conflict based on principles versus avoid conflict

While Steadfasts will engage in a good fight over matters of principles concerning friendship, the treatment of others, social proprieties, and keeping promises, the Influencer is more inclined to avoid the inevitable confrontation by laughing it off or quickly refocusing the conversation to a less controversial subject. The I is sometimes viewed as disloyal or as ingenuous because of their tendency to avoid taking a firm stance.

Blames self versus blames others

Steadfasts first look inward to explain poor relationships, while the Influencer looks elsewhere to place blame because they fear rejection if they own up to their limitations. Sometimes this prevents the I from properly developing himself/herself. Unless they are careful, the Influencer can spend their entire life explaining away their failures by placing responsibility elsewhere. Only when they look within, and see the importance of responding to their limitations, will the Influencer ever know the real power that comes from accepting responsibility for one's own actions. On the other hand, the S can blame themselves so much that they fail to learn how to predict other's behaviors and tendencies and fail to learn how to say "no" to ridiculous requests and dares.

Ss Need the I:	The I needs the S:
To promote creative, playful moments	To teach compassion
To foster optimism	To notice details
To remind them of their worth	To help them finish tasks
To show them the lighter side	To praise and applaud
To facilitate social relationships	To provide moral leadership

Conventional-Conventional

Two Conventionals are identified by the peace that exists between them. They are usually relaxed and patient and do not tend to expend excess energy on trivial power struggles or concern with details. Cs tend to tolerate differences and are more comfortable ignoring irritating behavior than making it an issue. Therefore, what often creates conflict for other personality combinations hardly affects the C-C connection.

Conventionals are not often drawn to leadership. Two Cs often struggle with poorly defined leadership roles as both wait for the other to take the lead. You can predict that neither C will be driven to plan or create strong goals for the future and neither will likely be upset if one decides to plan something or commit the other to a future goal. Two Cs are usually tolerant of each other, they are flexible and accommodating, they do not fear each other's independent preferences, and they listen to each other's job-related concerns. Because peace is the salient feature of these relationships, little overt conflict is evidenced. However, the most troublesome struggles are with motivation and leadership.

On peace

Conventionals get along with each other because they are motivated by peace. They will, however, defend themselves against the more aggressive, controlling types.

Patient and tolerant

If Conventionals lead, they do so by example. And this style sets an incredible example of patience, tolerance, and the acceptance of differences. They simply role model their value system consistently and unobtrusively.

Complacency

Conventionals rarely complain about being able to get along with another C. In fact, they rarely even notice problems until other styles point them out. In one sense, this is a blessing, unless their lack of awareness means they lack awareness of reality. The Cs passivity and need to avoid too many changes means they allow themselves to become complacent and to ignore changing circumstances. Cs sometimes put things off until tomorrow that should be done today. They procrastinate and put off important tasks and then find themselves behind compared with their competition. Cs must learn to balance their relaxed and complacent style with assertive productivity in order to successfully endure the ever-changing demands of daily living.

Self-Doubt

A pair of Conventionals suffers the most from self-doubt. They too often second-guess themselves about past decisions and personal capabilities. Neither is convinced he or she has made the best choice. Cs are more likely to ask questions about decisions than to take a direct position in support of or in opposition to whatever decision was made. Each waits for the other to react in order to determine whether he/she was right or wrong. Usually, neither gives a strong reaction, so questions about decisions remain unanswered.

Timid and uninvolved

Conventionals can sometimes be boring because of their reluctant, timid, and uninvolved natures. Cs can comfortably do nothing for a long period of time, yet drive everyone else around them into frenzy.

Cs seek a peaceful coexistence. They prefer to walk around life's hassles rather than face them directly. Are they patient and tolerant or masterful avoiders of life's troubles? It depends on the viewpoint. At any rate, Cs timidly avoid risks and decision making. They prefer a quiet, secure, and unobtrusive existence to a flashy, dynamic, and demanding life.

Conventional-Influencers
Gentle fun

This relationship is about the "Nice" guys or girls. They are affable individuals, seeking an easy (as opposed to difficult) style of interaction with limited expectations. Neither hassles the other. Neither is particularly keen about directing the other either. They can be excellent as friends and colleagues, but rarely find themselves in an intimate relationship.

Conventionals and Influencers accommodate each other. They do not generally motivate each other. Perhaps they lack the ferocity or drive Drivers and Steadfasts have to light each other's fires. But they appreciate each other's accepting and easy style. There is a casual blending of two comfortably independent people.

Peace versus fun

Conventionals try very hard to uncomplicate their lives, while Influencer keeps committing, connecting, and conversing in order to make life fun. Cs go with the flow while I overbooks and/or drags them into one commitment and appointment after another.

Power and control of self versus intimacy

Influencer is like a cat, able to come and go comfortably. Conventionals are like dogs, wanting a comfortable place to reside with a need to be noticed. Cs are concerned with developing a safe environment, while I is into risk.

Respect versus praise

Conventionals need to have their wishes respected. They resent being pushed into decisions they find uncomfortable. On the outside, Cs appear to need constant praise and attention. In reality, they want you to respect their pace and preferences. Cs are a rather quiet group and resent always having to speak up in order to secure their right to be left alone, do what they want, be with certain friends, or whatever. Influencers could generally care less about respect. They want to be noticed and praised. This is perhaps the most difficult interactions for the C-I combination. Cs are not know for their skill at or interest in praising others. I is often disrespectful of others and typically oversteps the acceptable boundaries with Cs.

Protection versus freedom

Influencer officers can often be seen pushing their Conventional counterpart to take a risk or try something wild and crazy. C, on the other hand, usually refuse, seeking a safe and comfortable route. One primary difference between Cs and Is lies in their range of experimentation with life's available activities. While C is most worried about what might happen, I is most excited about what can happen. I desires freedom from life's restrictions. C uses these restrictions to gain a feeling of security.

Stability versus change

Because of their desire for stability and discomfort with change, Cs are comfortable experiencing the same things over and over even to the point of eating the same foods. It is not that Cs don't seek variety, they do, but upon close inspection one will find that Cs seek the same variety. It is as if they keep a "little black book" of familiar activities upon which they rely. Is, on the other hand, float through life in a spontaneous rush. They thrive on change and variety in activities, people, and food is a vital part. In the fire service, Influencer may be bored with some of the mundane rituals that don't change much. My experience is that many I styles choose to remain on shift in order to have a second life outside of the fire service. This is usually a second job or hobby that provides them with some of the variety they crave.

Boring versus exciting

Conventionals are much more likely to fall into a rut than Influencers, a fact that eventually causes Is to fade out of the Cs life. The following conversation with a fire officer and his former chief explains the difference.

> *"He just didn't want to try anything new," the fire officer said about his former chief, "Same equipment, same way of doing things. I thought I was going to explode. I had to get out of there. I was dying of boredom. Don't get me wrong, he is a nice guy, and he always talked about being the best, but I wasn't motivated."*
>
> *"He was bright and had a lot of good ideas," the fire chief said about the officer. "The problem was that he had too many ideas. He wasn't willing to stick with one and see it through to completion before moving on to the next one. And he frustrated a lot of the other officers by pushing his ideas off on them. He should have been a salesman."*

Reluctant versus engaging

Conventionals often get a lot from being around Influencers because they are so energetic and engaging. I likes being around C if he/she feels a need to remain firmly grounded. Both must remain conscious of their inherent weaknesses in order to gain strength from the relationship. I occasionally needs the detail orientation and the cautious approach to change that Cs offer. Cs need the freedom to take risks that the Influencer offers.

Tenacious versus easily distracted

One metaphorically prone chief said this about his I and C officers: "His hero must be Muhammad Ali because he floats like a butterfly. The slightest wind that comes along blows him off course. If I want to generate ideas of energy, I know who to go to. My C officer, however, is like a snapping turtle. Once he latches on, he doesn't let go until it thunders. This is both good and bad. He sees a project through but he's not very flexible." Cs and Is make a powerful team when they learn to use their inherent traits.

Feels deeply but finds expression difficult versus emotional and expressive

Fire service seems to attract a lot of Conventional styles; people who are particularly effusive, but who feel deeply. The C cares about people or causes and may spend a lot of time thinking about it, volunteering, or planning activities behind the scenes in support of the cause. Serving others lends itself to this type of person.

Influencers' are sometimes frustrated over Cs lack of expressiveness and claim that he/she is unemotional. Nothing could be further from the truth. C feels strongly, but the feeling remains inward since he/she does not tend to be outwardly expressive.

Influencers must learn to be outwardly patient with Conventionals. They are measured in their approach to things and speak only when they are certain that they are right.

Doer versus performer

Conventional is not interested in great fanfare, whereas Influencer thrives on recognition. Cs and Is usually work well with each other because their role preferences lie in different directions.

Patient versus good natured

These are the two styles that are perhaps the easiest to get along with. Rarely angry, Cs and Is share a rare capacity for tolerance and acceptance that no other mixed combination shares. While Cs are patient, they would rarely be called "light-hearted." They are often good teachers however, since they tend to think sequentially and can envision minute steps toward learning something. Fire chiefs should puts Cs in charge of teaching assignments. The I has often been called light-hearted. He/she is an incredible mood-setter for the department and every chief should strive to have at least one I on staff.

Excellent listener versus poor listener

Cs are calm while I is a poor listener. Listening requires patience and a willingness to put others first. I tends to do neither very well. Cs can sit with another person for long periods and listen to them discuss the details of how they feel. I constantly interrupts.

Cs Need I:	I Needs Cs:
To excite them	To calm them
To encourage them	To listen to them
To accept their low profile	To praise them
To be kind to them	To play with them
To teach them how to promote	To teach them how to focus

Influencer-Influencer

Fun

No other combination of styles creates more energy and fun than do Influencers. Two I style personalities draw people to them like magnets. Everyone wants what the I has: charisma, a light-heart, laughter, spontaneity, and popularity. The one drawback is that someone has to tell the I pair when work needs to be done. Together, they are often unfocused and scattered. Details are tossed out the window like so much needless trash.

Needs attention

Each requires a lot of the other's attention. Actually this works out well since both require instant, shallow praise more than deep appreciation. Because both are optimistic, both praise each other easily. Fun and occasional praise is enough to keep the I-I pair from feeling neglected. It is not rare for a fire officer to be an I, depending upon promotion standards in the department. They are often so popular and well-liked that they remain in the forefront of other's minds and are the first to be recommended for promotion possibilities. But an I must utilize his/her ability to motivate and "pump up" subordinates and peers in order to remain successful. Taking care of details is not the favorite pastime of the I. He/she must use delegation to get things accomplished.

Freedom

This pair regards freedom as the sacred principle in their relationship. Neither desires to commit much beyond the present and neither attaches strings. Influencer fire officers do well to surround themselves with Cs or Ss in order to make sure a solid pathway is followed replete with all necessary details.

Highly verbal

Influencers can talk about anything or nothing equally well. They appreciate superficial as well as serious discussions. They are helpful in brainstorming and long-range planning. But the I is not a good listener and can miss important details.

Irresponsible

The I expects others to handle the details and loose ends. As with life, neither takes their role too seriously. In a transactional (command-style) leadership environment in which task completion is both process and outcome, this drives fire chiefs nuts.

Optimistic

The Influencer is an internal dreamer. He/she believes that anything is possible. They always seek the silver lining that gives them a Pollyanna appearance. But the Is don't get depressed easily and if they do, they don't stay depressed for long because Is support each other with hope and positive reinforcement.

Building Successful Relationships

Since the beginning of time, humans have been trying to learn what it is that makes them tick. Greek myths abound with stories of men and women who were changed by their interactions with one or more of the gods. This early explanation suggested that the deities influenced personality. Thereafter, astrologers embraced the twelve signs of the zodiac as the determining factors in personality, substituting planetary power for the powers of the gods. Chinese tradition associated personality with the year a child was born.

Later theoreticians turned to the environment to explain personality differences. They categorized personalities according to four dominant aspects of nature—earth, fire, air, and water. This theory of the elements provides us with an interesting starting point from which to proceed in our understanding of personality. It is simple, it is memorable, and it is rooted in something we can observe.

Personality Is a Compass Pointing North

Sigmund Freud believed that personality was formed by early life experiences. Formulating what has been called a "drive" theory, he believed that we are "driven" by past events that exert their influence on each of us by pushing us along in an effort to reduce tension from the repressed memories of traumatic childhood experiences.

Behavior can be understood from a much simpler framework, one that takes into consideration the following two precepts: (1) motives determine needs and wants (2) needs and wants determine behavior.

Motives are our innermost reasons. They explain why we think and behave as we do. Motives are more like compasses aimed directly toward the north, or arrows pointed directly at a target.

Freud conceptualized behavior as stemming from uncontrollable impulses and, like a bulldozer, pushes us from behind. While this difference at first seems like so much academic mumbo-jumbo, aiming at a target implies conscious intent and means that we can choose how to behave or react. All of these attempts at understanding personality strive for one thing, predictability in knowing what natural strengths and limitations you will face in your relationships. In this way, you can begin to strive toward maximum service effectiveness.

Great departments did not get that way by accident. They are a result of hard work, an understanding of personality strengths and weaknesses, and equal partnerships mixing personality traits for success. Great officers have a deep understanding of their weaknesses and seek someone to balance them. In so doing, they recognize that that person will do things differently and will have a different perception of how things should be done. It is within these differences (differences, not necessarily disagreements) that genius is truly born. Bad officers and bad departments aren't just bad luck either. Officers are ignoring their own negative traits and are blaming others for why things are not smooth and productive. We must take 100 percent responsibility for our relationship choices or we can never feel empowered to experience the tremendous strength that comes as a result of differences handled in a productive manner. We understand that Drivers seek power and challenge. We accept the fun-loving nature of Influencers. We accept the sincerity of the Steadfasts, and we appreciate the gentle touch of the Conventionals. Furthermore, we know that because of their styles, Drivers are sometimes going to be harsh. Influencers are sometimes going to be irresponsible. Steadfasts are more easily hurt and will withdraw without communicating openly, and Conventionals will tend to balk at change. All of these are frustrating traits when viewed outside the "shoes" of the other person. But when viewed from the standpoint that differences can translate to strength, these differences are like the parts of a rocket capable of working in unison toward a targeted objective.

Coaching Intervention Style

Every officer in the role of coach has the opportunity to create change. In order to be most effective, the superior officer's/coach's approach should match the specific needs of the subordinate. As you will note, this is a dramatic departure from the fire departments of old where personality differences were not considered. Let it be understood from the outset that we are not talking here about leadership during emergency situations that are task oriented, time sensitive endeavors. We are talking about the other 95% of the time in which officers are interacting, planning, and serving in preparation for saving lives.

There is a high correlation between the subordinate officer's personality and the style of coaching that is most effective. Drivers and Steadfasts are more resistant to change, while Influencers and Conventionals are initially more receptive to the change process. Resistance is less direct and abrasive for Ss than Ds. The intensity of the resistance is, however, fairly equal. On the other hand, Is are more likely to say they are receptive to change than the Cs are. However, both generally appear receptive and willing to adapt their approach at work.

Just the reverse is true of these personalities when it comes to follow-through and completion of the change process. Ds and Ss are far more likely to successfully commit themselves to performance improvement strategies once their resistance is removed. Is and Cs are more inclined to slip back into old behavior patterns or feel unmotivated to complete the performance improvement process.

As a coach, you can expect Ss and Ds to want answers. They want specific methods, solutions, and direction once they decide to embark upon a performance improvement and change program. They will fare best with specific assignments and expectations. The most frustrating aspect of coaching for them is coming to the realization that the coach will not and cannot design a specific behavioral process with guaranteed long-term success. What they actually need most is an attitudinal adjustment.

Focused on inner change, attitudinal coaching forces subordinate officers and firefighters to examine their motives and clear up unhealthy perceptions. As a result, interactions improve and their behaviors are perceived as more encouraging.

Drivers suffer most often from inaccurate emotional messages such as hidden insecurities blocking communication, or layers and years of denied anger. Steadfasts suffer most often from irrational thinking. They have relied so heavily on their "emotional muscles" that their ability to think rationally is seriously impaired. As you might imagine, attitudinal adjustment takes longer than behavior change alone and requires more patience than the behavioral process. Consequently Drivers and Steadfasts become more frustrated with the coaching performance improvement process.

Conversely, the coaching approach for the Conventionals and Influencers is more direct and behavioral. It is the kind of coaching Drivers and Steadfasts would really prefer. Usually, Influencers and Conventionals have positive and receptive attitudes, but their discipline and motivation often leave a lot to be desired. They require frequent "kicks in the pants" and constant support with new techniques for effectively tackling life.

Influencers and Conventionals need to see themselves completing goals and disciplining themselves consistently over a long period of time in order to increase their self-esteem and to develop healthy lifestyles. Giving a Driver or Steadfast more hobbies or tasks will do little to increase self-esteem. They are already driven to achieve and produce and probably don't feel that what they do is good enough. Instead, they should increase their awareness of self-flagellating, or arrogant feelings and thoughts in order to be more accepting of themselves and others.

To sum it up, don't give these styles what they want. You'll be playing into their defenses and they will not grow or improve. Drivers and Steadfasts want immediate action and behavior modification. They should get a time-consuming attitudinal adjustment instead. Influencers and Conventionals want a relaxed, attitudinal approach. Instead, they should get a direct process, requiring commitment and behavior modification. Set specific goals and "hold their feet to the fire".

Peter Senge (1993) indicates that it is imperative in this information era that supervisors understand themselves and others. Knowing ourselves makes our journey through life much more meaningful. It also enhances our opportunities to improve our performance and the performance of others. Somewhere along the line we have gotten the notion that we are not responsible for each other. We heartily disagree and believe that logic and common sense has been lost somewhere a long the way.

We humans can only be understood in a social context. Without other people with whom to interact, our strengths could not be developed and our weaknesses would not be apparent. Humans do not operate in a vacuum. Each personality relies on the others. Learn about the personalities without judgment. Seek to appreciate the unique strengths and limitations in others. As officers, strive to recognize the natural bonding or resistance that various personalities experience and keep one important mantra in mind: "What I experience in others says as much about me as it does about them."

Purpose

Understanding that challenge acts as a springboard, Purpose refers to why the coaching conversation is occurring and what the goals and objectives are. (The terms goals and objectives will sometimes be used in place of Purpose.) When the coach fully understands the purpose of the coaching conversation, it is easier for him to decide such things as, (1) the direction that coaching should take, (2) what self-sabotaging patterns should be altered, (3) whether the focus should be inner change or outer change, (4) which stretch goals should be established in order to stimulate growth, and (5) which coaching methods and techniques can aid in the process of performance improvement.

The general purpose of all coaching is to help someone, or a group, get better at something so that their performance is improved. Therefore, all coaching strategies must aim toward a change in one's behavior. But that being established, a lot of fire officers make a critical mistake when coaching; they immediately jump to action without considering some of the more inner and hidden emotional factors involved in poor or ineffective performance. Like the husband who responds to his wife's complaint about a co-worker by suggesting "just stay away from her," action-oriented fire service personnel sometimes fail to explore emotional factors that translate to ineffective performance as well as the available inner resources for coping.

The purpose of coaching serves as a map for the coach. The client (usually a subordinate officer) and coach (usually a superior officer) must be clear about both the general purpose of the coaching and the specific purpose of each conversation. The general, ultimate purpose is usually obvious and includes improving leadership skills, communicating vision, creating an encouraging atmosphere, or improving morale. But these goals are broad and general and must be operationalized in manageable steps. Knowing the purpose of the coaching conversation keeps the coach and client on course by suggesting relevant stretch goals, asking relevant questions, and cutting off irrelevant discussions. This is particularly important in group coaching where a number of firefighters (usually a particular station shift) have separate and different personalities, agendas, and skill sets. Keeping these shift meetings focused is more difficult than when having a coaching conversation with one person.

The purpose of coaching conversations pivots on what the challenge is. The first step is to understand or diagnose the challenge and why the person before you is unable to meet that challenge.

Chapter 5

Start by Asking
the Right Questions

Start by Asking the Right Questions

Introduction

The coaching process can be broken down into five steps. The exact determination of the dividing lines between the individual steps is less important than the approach that is taken to address the issues that arise during the process as a whole.

1. Careful Contracting

It takes skill to create a trusting environment in which open dialogue can occur and underlying issues can be brought to light. A great deal of honest communication and feedback will set the parameters of the coaching process.

A contracting meeting for the purposes of defining expectations should take place before the individual coaching begins. Those who should attend include the appropriate chief, Human Resources representative, and the person receiving the coaching (officer or firefighter). The objectives of the contracting dialogue include:

- Identification of success factors for a specific officer or team's current and potential role

- Agreement regarding confidentiality boundaries

- Identification of specific results expected

- Confirmation that the chemistry is right (if the coach is not the superior officer of the person receiving the coaching)

- Clarity regarding roles and responsibilities

- Agreement regarding milestones and timelines

- Agreement regarding financial terms

Addressing these issues will help to define the organizational and individual expectations and support the business objectives.

2. Comprehensive Assessment

The second step in the officer coaching process is the assessment of each individual officer. There are many types of assessments available (i.e., 360 degree feedback). My experience has been that face-to-face interviews are one of the best approaches to understanding the challenges facing the officer being coached. Another excellent approach is "shadowing" the officer (i.e., spending a day or two with the officer in her/his daily life on the job). The main advantage of these approaches is that they enable the coach to probe, see things first hand, and thus provide both quantitative and qualitative feedback that is real-time, powerful, and linked to service events.

The ultimate value of the assessment process is that the results clearly illustrate areas of strength as well as those requiring attention. This paints a clear picture for the officer and thus focuses and informs the coaching process.

3. Feedback and Action Planning

The first order of business in an effective feedback session is to revisit the agreed-upon objectives and to review the ground rules. Properly preparing officers for feedback is key to ensuring their willingness to listen, accept, open up, and move into action planning. Sessions should occur outside the normal station environment to ensure a more relaxed experience, free of interruptions or ready escape routes.

The coach must facilitate the feedback flow process, help the officer understand the data, and moderate any negative reactions to it. During the feedback dialogue session, the coach will continue to refer to operations requirements, leader attributes, and expected service results, then compare them to current performance. The aim is to work within a framework that directs feedback toward the key objectives of the business. The feedback session typically follows these stages:

- Reaffirm ground rules and establish rapport
- Review coaching objectives and service context
- Describe how to interpret results
- Give the officer opportunity to review results
- Discuss surprises or frustrations
- Highlight strengths
- Identify development needs
- Agree on areas of improvement
- Begin development-planning process

The action plan must focus on behaviors that contribute to specific business outcomes. A typical action plan includes:

- Strengths, and why they are important in the person's current role

- Development areas

- Action steps required, or interventions needed in areas requiring improvement or further development

- The type of coaching style that will best suit the development process

- Suggestions for active learning or experiential development suggestions

- Ways in which direct reports, boss, peers, and others can help

- A process for following up with key stakeholders

- Key milestones

Once the action plan is complete, key stakeholders will be invited to endorse it. These stakeholders typically comprise the same group of people involved in the initial assessment interviews. By sharing the action plan with those who were initially interviewed, the fire/officer can be assured that the planned improvements are consistent with expectation.

The other benefit of close-loop validation is that it involves those most likely to be influenced by the change in the fire/officer's behavior. As a result, this process fosters their commitment to help the officer develop.

4. Active Learning

Once the key stakeholders agree with the action plan, the coach guides and reinforces the development strategies, which can include techniques such as action learning, role-play, case study, simulation, video feedback, shadowing, and journaling. Special developmental courses and action learning are often recommended to support the coaching process.

This step is usually supported by a series of monthly meetings involving the coach, fire/officer, and key stakeholders. These dialogues help to ensure the milestones are being met and the ground rules are being followed, and the coaching process continues to be focused on the organization's business needs.

5. Reviewing and Sustaining Success

Approximately six months after the feedback session, an abridged version of the initial assessment is conducted to determine the impact of the process on the individual and the organization. The results of the assessment give credit for progress and address areas in which changes are still required, or bring attention to necessary mid-course corrections. The results of the abridged assessment are shared with key stakeholders to further the development of the officer and ensure alignment.

Our research shows that follow-up is a critical factor in the success of the entire coaching process. Additionally, to ensure overall quality, assessment of the coach is essential.

Good coaching begins with an understanding of the challenge. Many fire officers don't get a clear picture of the challenge because they fail to ask the right questions. Because many of you have been trained in a transactional style of leadership (largely characterized by commands and orders), you have not been trained to pay particular attention to the "systemic" nature of relationships and reactions. The right questions can help.

This chapter provides the specific questions for successfully accomplishing some important initial steps in coaching:

- Contracting the work

- Joining with subordinates

- Familiarizing yourself with the subordinate's challenges

- Testing subordinate's ability to own their part of the issue or objective

- Encouraging subordinates to set measurable goals

Was It Art or Science?

When I was in high school, a bunch of my friends and I left no stone unturned in search of "gimme" courses. We were a group of highly skilled slackers who simply wanted to avoid classes that smacked of reading, writing, or anything academic. Through sweat of brow, we located the perfect course to assuage our allergy to work—auto mechanics. Each day, we opened a hood, leaned over it like animals at a watering hole, occasionally tapped a wrench against something metal in order to appear busy, strategically smeared grease on our coveralls, and waited for an "A" to arrive in the mail. Of course, the actual extent of our ability included screwing up a simple change of spark plugs and failing to replace the oil pan plug when refilling the superintendent's car with oil. Needless to say, the letter "A" was not the letter listed on the grade reports as we had hoped.

But there was one guy named Joe Hemphill who was magic, a true artist. Invariably each day an impoverished student would drive their rattle-trap into one of the bays for free car repair. Like a heart surgeon emerging from scrub, Joe would approach the car with the focus of a man who had a life depending upon him. I remember how, with raised hands, he hushed the class and with a single nod, the car was started by one of Joe's lackeys. To us, it sounded like any other old car.

"Timing chain is bad," someone would say.

"No way, that clack is a bad rocker-arm."

"You're both crazy; the motor mounts are shot."

But Joe knew better. Without variance, he'd cock his head toward the origin of the sound, close his eyes, and within a few minutes, announce his diagnosis, all with amazing accuracy. He was one with the car. After his announced diagnosis, the teacher would hook up the test machine and basically verify what Joe already knew. "It's a spiritual thing," he would boast before sequestering himself in the corner and burying his head in a car magazine or a specifications manual.

I studied Joe as he studied cars. Although he will never know it unless he somehow reads this book, I learned a lot from him, a secret, and his method. Most of the guys were too busy goofing off to notice that when someone pulled up with a car problem, Joe interviewed him or her extensively. He asked seemingly inane questions about driving habits, accident history, upkeep record, what the problem was, and perhaps oddest of all, what the person wanted from the repair—a question that was significantly different than the "what's the matter?" question the rest of us asked.

Initially, I remember thinking what a geek Joe was for asking his questions. You simply fix the problem, I thought. Nevertheless, I saw something interesting emerge from his questions and his treatment of the customer. They became involved, an integral part of the repair process. Joe's odd questions were really quite brilliant because they served a bigger purpose and created other outcomes such as customer input, customer empowerment, the development of trust, and the fact that when that customer co-created the solution, they became a valuable resource as Joe's ally. Perhaps Joe already knew this, but what I learned was that even the most naïve driver knew more about the car than even they gave themselves credit for.

Perhaps most interesting of all, however, was that the customer left having learned something in addition to getting their problem solved. What was my lesson from Joe? That co-creating a solution is the key to increasing confidence in one's ability to think, understand, learn, choose, and make decisions; in other words, self-trust and self-reliance. The next time the customer came into our shop, they had more confidence to make suggestions, to be a contributor, and they increased the chances for an effective solution.

There is more to coaching than just solving the problem. The process for addressing a problem is ultimately what gives the client the confidence to solve other problems as well. Joe knew that while he could change out an alternator, it was what the customer learned through being a part of the repair process that really solved the bigger problem and even defined the customer's perception of success.

This process of co-creating problem solutions became Joe's real art. He wasn't born with "it," but somewhere along the way he learned that the right questions could serve him well.

Start With Good Questions

We ask questions all the time. But for the most part, we don't give our questions or the process of asking our questions much thought. Why should we? It is such a part of our every day communication that we fail to notice the wealth of information available from well-placed, well-timed, properly conceived questions.

As a result of the unexamined nature of the question process, most of us have developed some fairly ineffective question asking habits. The biggest problem is that we tend to think that questions are merely requests for information. But questions have so many more potential uses including:

- Relationship building (joining) with the subordinate or peer

- Empowerment of the subordinate or peer

- Diagnoses of the challenge

- Increasing the subordinate's or peer's awareness of his/her role in the challenge

- Increasing the subordinate's or peer's ownership of the challenge

- Goal setting

- Planning for performance improvement

- Increasing the subordinate's or peer's awareness of ineffective patterns of interaction

People do not relate and talk, but rather relate in talk. In other words, their exchange of messages is their relationship. Questions, and the manner in which they are asked, can communicate respect, confidence, and curiosity, or doubt and criticism.

Remember those times when, as a teenager, you came home past curfew. There stood your mother or father who asked, "Where have you been?" Was that merely a request for information or was there a powerful underlying message that really communicated anger and frustration in the relationship? Your tendency was probably to avoid trouble with a carefully crafted excuse and a bit of cover up. Not the kind of thing that is useful in the workplace, but a tactic that is all too prevalent.

How one introduces the coaching sets the expectations, tone, and context for future coaching conversations. Given initial research into what subordinate firefighters and officers want from a coaching relationship, the fire officer, in the role of coach, needs to begin applying himself or herself to the task of developing a collaborative, constructive context for coaching. The purely transactional nature of fire leadership that was characterized by orders and commands is diminishing. The act of joining, which we will discuss in this chapter, seeks to establish and optimize a cooperative relationship.

Contracting

Contracting is arguably the most important phase in the coaching process. Both people—coach and leader—build a relationship and set the coaching direction. While this relationship is ideally built as soon as the supervisor takes the supervisory position or as soon as the subordinate person is hired or moved into the position, it can, nevertheless be developed even after a lengthy working relationship.

The coach considers whether the subordinate is open to feedback, to suggestions, to career development. Together the coach and the subordinate draw the goals and parameters for the coaching relationship and set up expectations that drive the rest of the phases. In the initial coaching conversations, the coach might ask:

- What would you like to improve upon?

- If we develop a coaching relationship, which performance improvement goals are you targeting?

- Which supervisory skills would you like to work on?

- Would it be helpful to you if I served as your coach for performance improvement?

- Would you like to discuss that?

- Would you like to work on that for a few minutes?

- Would you like to understand that better?

- Tell me how I can be of help to you on this matter?

- If we discuss this for a few minutes, what do you hope the outcome will be?

Asking these questions is important in order to avoid resistance on the part of the subordinate. When coaches take a direction without the consent of the subordinate, resistance to the coach's help is the likely result.

But contracting serves another important purpose as well, empowerment for performance improvement. Engaging subordinates in the co-creation of the coaching contract gives them a sense of control over their future and their performance goals. They're no longer at the whim of factors outside their control.

The following are some questions for establishing a coaching contract for performance improvement:

- What departmental or supervisory challenges are you facing?
- Have you met this challenge successfully before?
- What is your best thinking about this challenge?
- What is preventing you from meeting the same kind of challenge this time?
- What is keeping you from getting the results you want?
- How do you account for not being able to accomplish this?
- How have you risen to the occasion this time?
- How urgent are you?
- How much time do you have to achieve this?
- What do you find personally challenging about leading this effort, given the results you have to date?
- How do you think I can be useful to you?

During this initial coaching stage, the coach and subordinate are attempting to design a working relationship. The coach offers the subordinate a taste of what working together (in coaching as well as in the larger context of departmental business) will be like.

Joining

There is no getting around good old-fashioned joining skills on the front end of contracting, such as neighborliness, friendliness, approachability, basic humanness, a sense of humor, and sincere interest in the other person. It is the initial and basic ease, flow, and even fun in your conversations that builds strength for the tougher times that will later pull on the fabric of your relationship.

Your subordinate, particularly a new one, needs answers to the following questions:

- How quickly can you get on board with me?
- Do you get what I'm talking about?
- Are you practical, effective?
- Do you have some depth to your experience?
- Do you care about me as a person?

Subordinates want to know whether you will really be able to help them, but they seldom voice these questions. You have to pass the subordinate's "smell" test.

You must be conducting your own assessment as well. Coaching requires the willingness of the leaders to explore their own strengths and weaknesses. Wise officers are aware that they are not only part of the picture but deeply embedded in the successes and disappointments of all departmental efforts. Officers are almost always part and parcel of the problems as well as the successes. When you are honestly willing to look at yourself, energy-draining conflict and poor performance are more easily overcome.

One way to begin joining is to start joining right in the contracting conversation. Then subordinates have a taste of how you coach and supervise them. You can immediately begin a productive partnership and build elements into it that will keep the other phases on track.

The following are some questions for joining:

- What do you do best and how do you envision doing this each day?

- What is it that you want me to understand about you?

- How do you envision that we will work together?

- How do you prefer to receive feedback from me in the future?

Familiarizing Yourself with the Subordinate's Challenge

A partnership begins when the subordinate talks about the specific issue where he or she is currently stuck. Although occasionally fire service personnel are confronted with a lack of equipment or budgetary issues, for the most part, fire service personnel become stuck with *people problems*. Sometimes just listening, following your curiosity about the issue, and constantly restating for clarity, helps the subordinate in defining the central issue, unseen opportunities, and challenges.

Specific listening skills

A number of listening skills can enhance the early part of the coaching conversation. I will highlight four of them here that I use most often at this stage.

Concreteness means inviting the subordinate to get more specific about the challenging issue. Although fire service personnel are usually fairly specific about technical or equipment-oriented matters, they are often vague about human relations issues. But this is where specificity is vitally important. You are not asking for details for details' sake. You are inviting the subordinate to describe actual behaviors and circumstances in order to clarify what he or she is really talking about. By pushing for specificity, you are doing an enormous favor for the organization, because these fire officers are often not clear with their chiefs about their expectations.

Some questions that elicit a concrete response include the following:

- What specifically frustrates you about the situation?
- Can you give me an example?
- What do you mean?
- When did this happen?
- What specifically do you expect from him or her?
- How often has this happened?
- Under what conditions does this occur?

Empathy is your effort to show you understand the subordinate's concerns. The more you can express, in your own words, the subordinate's message, the more he or she will think, "OK, somebody knows what I'm talking about!" When you are on track with the subordinate's concerns, you will be addressing his real issue—not the issue you think the subordinate means. This is very important and deserves a short discussion.

When we complain, we focus on what someone said, what someone did or didn't do, and how someone or something else should change. The focus is outside of us. And that is where our focus will remain in the absence of another person's understanding and empathy. This is not to imply that we are completely responsible 100% of the time. It does imply that we play a role in every challenge and that learning comes from the realization of our mistakes and our ineffective patterns. The following are some examples of the use of empathy in a coaching conversation:

- You seem most concerned about the morale of the shift and whether you have the capability to create a more encouraging atmosphere.

- You seem to feel caught between being loyal to those peers who have been here a long time and who liked the outgoing chief and at the same time, wanting to validate the younger peers and the new chief.

- It appears that you are struggling with having to give hard feedback to a couple of the long-term, older firefighters, and they may be oblivious to the fact that their performance no longer meets expectations.

- You say that you are angry with the other command staff members for the recent decisions they made. Are you also hurt that they did not give your opinion consideration?

- You often sound frustrated. My sense is that you feel pulled between the demands of the chief and the inexperience of the new recruits.

Showing empathy can help your subordinate sift and weigh her concerns. She can either say, "Yeah, I guess this is a big issue for me." Or she can say, "You know, when I hear you put it that way, I'm actually more troubled about something else."

Confrontation does not mean chopping off someone's career noggin. There are plenty of opportunities for real conflict in organizations. In this context, confrontation means pointing out discrepancies between what the subordinate is saying and what she actually does. For the most part, discrepancies exist outside of our awareness and there are numerous personal and departmental examples of these discrepancies.

For example, a large discrepancy exists when organizations throw out the phrase that *people are our most important asset*, but then fail to demonstrate this in action; or when an officer claims to support the shift, but then gossips about individuals' personal lives in a destructive manner; or when the officer invites people to share their work related problems, but responds only with frustration when they do.

In all my years of coaching, it is this discrepancy between words and actions that prove the most troublesome for fire officers. The reason is quite simple. When under the supervision of an incongruent officer, subordinates learn to tune out the words and trust only the actions. Encouraging words mean little when the corresponding actions don't follow.

How do you bring it up in a coaching conversation? You bring forth the discrepancy in a neutral tone, not with a "gotcha" attitude. You simply hold up a mirror so the subordinates can make their own judgments about the fire officer's incongruence. The more neutral you are about showing the mismatch, the more powerful this intervention can be for the subordinate. By neutral, I mean being descriptive about the behavior the fire officer is doing rather than being critical or judgmental. Here are some ways of using confrontation in a coaching conversation:

- You say that improved service is your number one concern, yet you say that you haven't communicated specific guidelines or expectations.

- In the last ten minutes that we have talked, you have given arguments both for and against reprimanding the driver.

- This is the first time I have heard you question the chief's direction and lay out a thorough alternative strategy.

- You say that you want the firefighters to trust you and share their concerns about the way you lead them, but my observations are that when they have gathered the courage to do so, you have openly rejected their input.

Spending time on a subordinate's discrepancies in behavior can help her finally deal with some contradictions that may have been living in her for months or even years. It helps her get closer to a decision point about them, rather than continually bringing them up to half-consciousness and then ignoring them.

Respect goes beyond holding the subordinate in high regard or admiring personal qualities. It has to do with having a deep belief that he or she has the capacity and the resources to handle and resolve the situation. You believe and show that ultimately the fire officer has the resilience necessary to address the issue. Do not rescue the client by providing answers too quickly. This is not to say that providing answers is never allowed, but doing so too quickly can remove the fire officer's problem-solving accountability. You can illustrate respect in a coaching conversation in these ways:

- You have successfully dealt with challenges like this before.

- You actually show more knowledge in this area than you give yourself credit.

- The combination of traits you bring to the issue—practical savvy along with holding the larger goal in mind—is what the situation calls for.

- There are specific traits that you possess that will help you solve this challenge. What are these and how will you put them to use?

Once you have engaged the subordinate officer by using the four listening skills (concreteness, empathy, confrontation, and respect), he has well articulated his situation. The two of you know more what is at stake, and you share a background from which you will work.

Testing the Fire Officer's Ability to Take Responsibility

When having a contracting conversation with a fire officer for the purpose of developing a coaching relationship, I always try to determine whether the officer is willing to take responsibility for contributing to the present problem. Fire officers, and firefighters can use coaching as an effective tool only when they are willing to focus on their own functioning. Early on, I test for this necessary condition, since it is not worth making a coaching contract to coach if this willingness is not present.

From the very beginning, subordinates must learn that, as coach, you do not probe only at the external sources of blame, but also for the ways in which the leader has contributed to the current problem.

A distinguishing characteristic of Constructive Coaching is that the focus of conversations is on the [client] fire officer's personal responsibility for the present problem. Too often, fire officers either deny or are unaware of how they contribute to the present challenge. Thus, the alternative is to place responsibility on someone or something else, thus failing to explore inner resources for solving the present challenge.

For example, in a performance evaluation a lieutenant was urged by a battalion chief to take a firmer approach with firefighters. A recent three-vehicle accident that involved a gravel truck and gasoline fire was poorly handled. In addition, the lieutenant's shift consistently failed to complete routine station duties prior to shift change. Even though the lieutenant tries to place blame elsewhere, notice how the battalion chief holds the focus on the lieutenant.

> "The Assistant Chief and I have identified some areas in need of improvement in your shift," Battalion Chief Gaines said. "We were especially concerned with the way that multiple-vehicle accident was handled last week by the engine company and paramedics on your shift. I also want to visit with you about how the station is running during your shift. How do you think we can best address these concerns?"
>
> "Well," Lieutenant Baker said," I guess I should have a talk with the firefighters. But I know what they are going to say. They'll bring up the fact that we have three new and inexperienced people and that the more experienced firefighters are having to take time out to teach them how we operate."
>
> "Would I be right in assuming that whenever you have talks with your shift, they tend to place blame elsewhere?" Chief Gaines asked.
>
> "Yes sir, that's probably right."
>
> "How have you responded to them whenever they do this?"
>
> Lt. Baker scratched his head, "Whenever they…"
>
> "You know, whenever they indicate that something is outside their control," Chief Gaines added.
>
> "I'm not really sure. I usually just restate what I want them to do."
>
> "You don't sound very sure of yourself, Lieutenant."
>
> "No sir. I guess I don't," Lt. Baker said. "Except for the three rookies, my crews are all very experienced and they're all older than me."
>
> "Meaning?" the Chief asked.
>
> "Meaning that they're set in their ways."
>
> "And do you encourage them acting set in their ways?"
>
> "I'm not sure. I mean they know what they are supposed to do."

"Exactly!" Chief Gaines said. "What do you do when they ignore your orders to do something differently?"

"I usually back off and let them do their jobs."

"Do you feel uncomfortable supervising them?"

Lt. Baker thought a minute and said, "Yes sir, I guess I still do."

"I see," the Chief said. "Can you imagine a different pattern of behavior? Instead of letting your discomfort cause you to back off, what can you do differently?"

"I'm not sure."

"What would you like to do?"

"Maybe it's more the way I approach them rather than what I say. Sometimes, maybe I'm too accepting."

"Could be we're on to something here," Chief Gaines said.

This example is like many between a chief officer in the role of coach and a subordinate fire officer. This is not therapy or esoteric wisdom. It is the realization that the officer or firefighter's greatest leverage for change is his own response to the issue. Your contribution is to assist officers in identifying their part of the co-created problem or, in the case of non-problem-centered proactive coaching, how they can co-create a positive, high performance service department. One way to test the subordinate officers' willingness to look at their role is to ask questions like the ones below. If they welcome this kind of self-reflection, you have a good potential partner to coach.

- What recurring patterns are present in this situation?

- Which patterns work well and which detract from the effort?

- How are you a part of these patterns?

- How have you responded to this issue?

- What is your knee-jerk contribution? For example, are you often the overachiever, the blamer, the pursuer, the victim, the helper, the avoider, or the parent?

- Can you imagine a different pattern?

- How willing are you to develop the stamina required to stop your part of the pattern that is no longer effective?

- How will this help you get to your goal?

- How can I be of help to you?

Giving Immediate Feedback

It is during the initial phase of coaching that you give your own feedback and observations to the subordinate. Most of you will have known each other for a very long time, but even if you have just begun your coaching relationship, you have your own experience of the fire officer up to this point. From a systems view, this brief experience gives you a picture of the officer's or firefighters' functioning within the challenge at hand. In other words, what you view and experience with them is probably what others view and experience with them as well. You will be asking yourself these initial questions:

- How do I feel with this person?

- Do I feel energized or drained by him or her?

- Which of my feelings are about the officer and which are my own peculiar issues?

- What are my initial expectations for this person?

- Am I experiencing initial knee-jerk reactions?

- Do I understand why this person behaves as he or she does?

- Which part of my reactions to the officer must I take responsibility for?

- How would this person's behavior affect other people or the shift?

As will be discussed in the techniques chapter, the use of immediacy is one of the most powerful coaching skills. Your own interaction with the subordinate is a window into characteristic patterns that either enhance or detract from his or her, the shift's, or the battalion's performance. Particularly in the initial contracting phase, it is important to feed back your own experience, here and now, of your subordinate that is, what is happening between you. Keep in mind, you will be acting on the belief that what happens in the immediacy of this moment is what happens out there in the subordinate's work world. The feedback should be frank, specific, not protective, and yet collaborative.

For example, the city manager of a large suburban municipality called me to work with the fire chief. The chief told me that there had been a lot of dissension within the fire department since he took over. As the chief and I talked, it became apparent that he was frustrated and resorted to blame. He was upset that he had stepped into a situation where he did not have the support of the command staff. They preferred another candidate, but were overruled by the mayor and city manager. Since taking the job, the chief said he had received nothing but passive-aggressive responses and a lack of follow-through on his requests. My initial reaction was one of empathy that the chief had walked into a bad situation. I found myself agreeing with him and then felt stuck because I had no idea how he was going to overcome the resistance of the entire command staff.

Then the issue slowly began to emerge. As he spoke, the chief revealed absolutely no attempt to view the situation from their viewpoint. Even in the midst of disagreement, centered and objective people are able to understand, rightly or wrongly, how another person or group can feel the way they do. Furthermore, the longer we talked, the more the chief spewed blame, and blame, and blame, and blame instead of attempting to accept the situation as is and take some responsibility by finding solutions. I began to feel tired and, after a while, found that I wanted to tune him out. I even noticed a feeling of frustration beginning to well up. I knew I either had to give him my immediate experience and potentially lose him as a client, or pay for my silence by being a victim of his blame. Besides, I sensed that he would blame me as easily as he did everyone else if I didn't work magic for him in coaching.

I interrupted him after thirty minutes, and said, "You know, as I'm listening to you, I find it hard to concentrate on what you're saying. You seem angry and relentless. I feel physically tired, frustrated, and slightly on the defense in response to your anger. I wonder if that is how the command staff experiences you? Frankly, I wonder if you are contributing to an already difficult situation."

The chief stopped for a moment and considered my response. I thought there was a chance that he would dismiss me for not understanding his point of view. Instead, he looked away and, in a lower tone, said, "That's probably true. I'm trying too hard to meet the expectations of the mayor and city manager. I know what the command staff is saying about me being a political appointment and that I'm not the most qualified. I'm not used to being second in anything. I'm trying to prove them wrong, you know." It was in that moment that he knew he would get the real stuff from me, and I knew that he was open and resilient enough to see me as an ally in the coaching process.

While fire chiefs receive their fair share of disagreement, they get this kind of immediate feedback so rarely that it gets their attention. It tests the cliché they sometimes use but do not live out, *I don't want just another yes-man*. I like to think of immediacy as a kind of "stick-your-finger-in-their-chest" moment, which can be delivered at once boldly and respectfully, directly engaging the presence of the person you are coaching. The fire officer may step into the moment, seeking more information about self-defeating patterns. When this happens the officer will say something to the effect, "This is the kind of feedback I can do something about." Or he or she might retreat from the frankness.

The act of retreating communicates a clear and powerful message. The fire officer is saying one of several possible things:

- "I can't hear this right now. It's too painful or embarrassing."

- "I don't trust you enough to get into it."

- "I disagree with your assessment of me/my situation."

- "I'm not used to conversing this way. I don't understand the rules here."

Retreating takes several forms. In some cases, it is as though the officer or firefighter hasn't even heard you and continues on like nothing was ever said. At other times, the fire officer might simply say, "I don't want to talk about that right now." Still other times, the person you are coaching might appear defiant and defensive.

When your subordinate retreats, what should you do? It is sometimes helpful to address the act of retreating directly through the use of immediacy. For example, you might choose the following:

- "I am aware that you appear uncomfortable right now. Would you mind talking about that?"

- When I shared my observations with you just now, you had no response. What is your reaction to what I said?"

- "I noticed a shift in your demeanor as I shared my observations with you. Would you mind sharing your reaction?"

I'm not advocating pushing your subordinates when they don't want to talk, but I have trained too many coaches who too quickly let their clients off the hook and miss the critical moments in coaching that can later result in tremendous performance improvements. Even if you decide that it is best to back off, you might do so by asking, "When will you be ready to talk about it?"

Of course, if you are the supervising officer, you can always pull rank and state that he has no option but to talk and talk now. Constructive coaching takes an exploratory stance whereby a superior officer teaches subordinate officers or firefighters to recognize self-defeating patterns and to learn how to use their inner resources for personal growth and enhanced performance. It is a leadership approach that veers from the transactional style that diminishes the importance of self-awareness, personal growth, motivation in decision-making, and the systemic nature of shift behavior.

If you find that the primary leadership approach of your fire officers is primarily transactional, then it may be a good idea to examine why and to initiate an ongoing regular coaching program for them.

Encouraging the Subordinate to Set Measurable Goals

Once you and the subordinate officer have settled on a coaching contract, you need to clarify goals for the contract. Coaching with fire officers involves working on their personal as well as their leadership skills and issues. Because many of the issues revolve around how they work with others, less experienced coaches can let actual departmental service goals get lost in the process.

By the time chief officers begin the coaching process, fire officers may have been mired in a problem for a long time. Sometimes both they and their shift start focusing only on the interpersonal issues or personality traits of one another and lose sight of the service issues. Chief officers must remain focused on measurable results and not allow the subordinate officers to become distracted by focusing only on themselves. Out of desperation, the fire officer may say, "I need to get along with my team better," or "I need to be more patient," or "I need to be more decisive and firm." All of the things officers say they need to do differently may be true, or may not be true. It depends on what they want to accomplish, what is not working, and why.

Focusing on specific outcomes is essential. How will the department benefit if the officer becomes more collaborative, more approachable, more decisive, or clearer? That these changes would help service delivery may seem obvious at the time. However, by helping officers articulate the actual fire service changes they want, you assist them. In some ways, becoming more collaborative, more approachable, more decisive, or clearer are the officer's personal goals for achieving specific service goals. It is important that chief officers not confuse personal goals with the department's outcomes, because fire officers and firefighters do it all the time.

There are, therefore, two kinds of goals fire officers need to work on: service goals—getting external results; and personal goals—what the officers have to do differently in how they conduct themselves in order to get the service results for themselves and their shift or battalion. The officers' personal goals, the challenges they face in pulling off the service goals, must follow the external department's goals. For example, say a fire officer wants to improve his decision-making skills, he or she needs to know for what purpose and what value this will have to the department. Granted, better decision-making provides a stronger presence with firefighters, but what is the "so what" value for the organization? The entire department gains credibility when the recipients of coaching link personal goals to department service achievements.

Having an outcome focus can make the difference between officers continuing or giving up when they hit daunting obstacles. Officers have told me they have a hard time separating personal goals from service goals. There is a simple way to think about it. I have them make a list of all of their personal goals and then have them answer, "why?" to each.

Personal Goals	**Why?**
Be a better listener	To diminish conflict over my appointment so that the command staff can focus on departmental objectives rather than their hurt and frustration.
Be more patient	
Gain adherence to my vision	
Gain respect of command staff	
	To establish an ongoing training regimen for increasing service delivery and reducing on the job injuries.
	Reduce grievances filed.
	Reduce unnecessary sick time.
	Embark upon new community fire and safety education programs.
	Gain support for a new coaching program for performance improvement and succession planning.

Service goals and their measures can be organized into three areas:

1. Bottom line

2. Work process

3. Human relations goals

Bottom line goals are the reason the department exists, to serve, educate, and maintain a sense of community safety. Work process goals address how the work is accomplished, from the beginning to the end of procedures, projects, and processes, in order to achieve the bottom line goals. Human relations goals focus on how people collaborate to accomplish both the bottom line and the work process goals.

Measures need to be established for these outcomes that are as behaviorally specific as possible and relevant to the goal itself. As a coach, you need to strongly encourage the officer subordinate to identify a measure for each department goal.

Department Goals and Measures

Arena of Goal	Goal Category	Measure of Goal Outcome
Bottom Line	Response Time	Reduce by 7%
(Why the department exists)	Education	Increase community service projects by 20%
Work Process (How the	Timeframes for projects	50% reduction in project time
work gets accomplished, from	Quality levels of service	95% reduction in community complaints
plished, from input to output)	Reduction in sick time	70% reduction
Human Relations	Reduction in grievances	80% reduction in employee grievances
(How people collaborate to accomplish the work)	Participation in voluntary coaching/mentoring program	100% participation

It is important that both chief officers and fire officers keep the ownership for deciding which goals and measures to pursue. Both must have investment in them and it is everyone's job to be specific about personal goals and work hard to ensure that they are the right goals for the department.

Therefore, it is the coach's responsibility to ensure that the goal-setting conversation is sequenced for best results, starting with the department's issues and sequencing to the officer's personal challenge to achieve results.

- Encourage the officer to name the service results needed.

- Find out what shift behaviors need to be different to accomplish the results.

- Explore what personal leadership challenges the officer faces in improving these results and team behaviors.

- Identify specific behaviors officers need to enhance or change in themselves.

This sequence links service results with shift behaviors and with behavior changes in officers. It is not typical for fire officers to link these three areas, yet, in this age of fiscal accountability and public demand for services, they are vital for departmental success.

The connection builds between those three areas in officers' awareness so they know what to attend to and where to look for gaps. Throughout the coaching process, you can inquire about all three: the department's results, the unit's results, and the officer's changes. Building these links into your conversations is important because it increases his understanding of the connections, shows him how indispensable it is to keep the three areas together, and points out how valuable your interventions are to his effort.

Example

Let's go back to my work with the chief. Allow my work with him to serve as an example for you in your work with subordinate officers or firefighters as the case may be. See how goals can be built from the presenting issues. The chief wanted to win the confidence of the command staff in order to achieve established objectives for the department. As you will see, the chief realizes that the objectives and the manner in which he attempted to achieve them were a part of the problem.

(Recall that the coach used immediacy to point out that the chief sounded angry, blaming, and talked incessantly. He seemed to awaken to this circumstance).

The coach said, "That sounds like good insight, and I can see how, in your desire to prove yourself, you are pushing hard."

"I've got goals," the chief replied. "I want us to be the best department in the metro area. For sure, the best command staff this department has ever seen."

"Do you think your desire to be the best comes across as dissatisfaction?"

"I can see that," the chief said, "and it's not the first time I've been told this. But, all organizations, and especially fire departments, need to have a valued and workable master plan. This is critical to future funding for new facilities, apparatus, programs, and staffing. Without a plan, justification for future projects simply will not happen. The success and image of this organization depends on planning. My experience has proven that a well thought out master plan generates tremendous support from elected officials and citizens, and provides credibility as they support us. "

"In the 1970's and 1980's," he continued, "we got apparatus and equipment just because we needed them. This is not the way of things today in the current budgeting world. Now we have to provide accurate and precise data for everything (i.e. new stations, apparatus, firefighters, educators, and inspectors). Gathering these data involves call volume and response time studies, detailed staffing requirements, and projected growth of the community. As an example, call volume data and positive response time statistics provides documentation to the City Council so that they can approve the construction of a new fire station in a developing area. Construction is only approved because

accurate reporting and preparation were given to justify the proposal. Our planning and the collection of precise data builds confidence and trust with city officials."

"You know, Chief, even now as you speak, I hear frustration," the coach said. "If you can stand outside yourself and watch and listen to yourself, what do you see?"

"Well, if you want to know the truth, someone who is relentless," the chief admitted. "But I just get so frustrated. I guess I've just got to take a different tack to accomplish what I want."

"I wonder how clear your goals are to everyone else?" the coach said. "What does the best mean—in what area and at what level? If you say, the best, how is the command staff going to know how good and in what way?"

"Well, it's two things: image with the city council and community and our response time."

"I assume that these two things are interconnected," the coach said. "Be more specific."

"Of all things, an article came out in the newspaper that a woman almost died as a result of poor response time even though the substation was close enough to be visible to the onlookers at the scene. There was a big screw up. It was embarrassing to say the least. Dangerously negligent is more like it. I won't stand for it. We've got to be at the scene in the least amount of time possible."

"By how much?" the coach asked. (bottom line goal and measure)

"In that case by 90%, but overall we need to reduce response time by 17%."

"What does the command staff have to do to make this goal more achievable?"

The chief looked perplexed and said, "Well, it's bizarre to me that we are in the business of saving lives and the command staff members are not assigning ongoing training modules for their shifts and subordinate staff. They're still operating from the old days and not thinking about public scrutiny and how our image can translate into new equipment." (work process issue)

"Clearly this is critical, but how would you know if training made a difference? Do you see what I mean?" the coach asked. "You can implore them to train more, but until they see how it makes a difference, they merely view the request as your own agenda and not one that is beneficial to them."

"Okay, you're suggesting that I need to tie two things together, you know, what I think we need to do or be in order to get what we want."

"Yes."

"If I look at it that way, I have to remove myself somewhat," the chief said. "Maybe in a series of retreats where we conduct some strategic planning. Where the entire command staff establishes departmental goals and then they create accountability to each other in how they will train the personnel to get there." (work process goal)

"Great! Now think about them working well," the coach said. "What would be happening if your command staff moved out of the past and had better vision? Think of what they would be doing that would help decrease response time by 17%."

"For one thing, we need weekly average measures instead of quarterly measures. That would allow us to address adjustments and make improvements more quickly." (work process measure)

"Okay, that's a start," the coach said, "and the idea of a retreat that invites the input of everyone seems like a good one. As you continue to work on this, you may discover even deeper work process issues. One item on the agenda for such retreats should probably pertain to command staff behaviors, how individuals need to act differently to turn response time and image around."

"Yes, they need to raise their game and overcome their petty jealousies. I'm the chief. The decision is made."

"By "raising their game," what do you mean, Chief?"

"Do I have to spell out everything? These are seasoned fire officers. Shouldn't they know to put aside back-stabbing and bickering?"

"If that were the case," the coach replied, "you wouldn't be sitting here right now."

"So I have to tell them how to be team players?" the chief asked.

"You telling them might be part of the problem."

"Right, right, I know. So—"

The coach continued, "So you need to set it as an agenda and give them an opportunity to have input. They are more likely to be invested in that which they have offered input. But at some point, you should present your own passionate vision of how you hope people will relate. You need to leave the series of retreats with a team relationship commitment." (human relations goal—expectations of team behaviors)

"How am I going to do that?" the chief asked.

"Exactly. That's the right question. How are you going to get it? Now you're talking about what you are going to have to do differently to have a more committed, team oriented command staff. In other words, what should you be doing differently?" (necessary change in leader behavior)

"Well, for one thing," the chief said, *"I could talk about the reactive nature of the city council and how they reward hard facts -- like response time. There is the real possibility that we will get funding for a new station if response times improve and we quietly published it for public consumption. I should also more directly address their concerns about the way I was appointed."*

"That would be great. It might help to cut through some of the animosity. I think a humble, understanding approach is right. By the way, what would be a measure of a better relationship with them?" the coach asked.

"They would be coming to me proactively with ideas on how they are going to train and lower response times. And firefighters would stop going to the union with complaints. It trickles down from my own command staff." (human relations goal—team behavior measures)

"If that's how you're going to measure it, you're going to have to track it," the coach suggested. *"Be aware of when it's happening and when it's not, and whether you're doing what you said you needed to do to get there."*

"I think if we improve our relationship, our decision-making will improve too. Then we could be more responsive to problems like image and response time." (human relations goal—team behavior expectations)

"Now we're cooking," the coach said. *"What's the problem?"*

"In command staff meetings, the bickering and backstabbing is incredible," the chief replied. *"We can't decide on anything."*

"You run those meetings, Chief. What do you need to do to improve that?" (change in leader behavior)

"How should I know? If I knew, I would be doing it."

"There are often two problems. Either you are contributing to the issue by being too controlling or the staff has no idea what kind of decision you're after."

"What do you mean they don't know what I want?" the chief asked.

"Well, are you seeking a consensus or do you want consultative input in order to help you make the decision? Sometimes communicating this up front can help people decide how to conduct themselves during the meeting."

> *"Oh, I see what you mean," the chief said. "That's helpful. Frankly, I think I'm too overbearing. You picked up on it at the beginning. I tend to bowl people over when I want something."*
>
> *"So what will you do and how will you know when things have improved?"*
>
> *"I think the easiest thing would be to honestly explain what I want, but respect their input. I should summarize at the end of each meeting to gauge their understanding and their commitment to the vision and the plan for decreasing response time."*

These conversations are lengthy but worth the time the chief and the coach put into them. These are the same basic kinds of conversations you will have with your subordinate officers. In this situation, the chief was able to identify goals and measures in each of the areas—bottom line, work process, and human relations. He made a connection between decreasing response time and improving the relationships between himself and the command staff. What is more, he knows his obligation to change his demeanor and approach when he relates to staff members.

Some of the measures in the conversation with the chief identify successful progress toward human relations goals. These are always the toughest to measure. The point of identifying measures is to provide a way for the chief and the command staff to know whether they are making progress toward these goals.

The ultimate goal is whether they make their bottom line result of decreasing response time and gaining the confidence of the city council. But it is the command staff behavior and work processes that will get them there. The measures for these goals provide the chief and the staff with growing knowledge of the specific actions that directly affect service delivery outcomes. They will be more likely to commit to change their habitual actions when they see that new individual and team behavior directly affect results.

Slow Down and Be Specific

Fire officers are often impatient to *get on with it* during the initial phase. Once they feel confident that they can work with a supervisor/coach, they want to start action. However, without clear goals and measures for those goals, neither the supervisor or subordinate officer is focused enough to choose the most effective course of action. Fire officers are often impatient and irritated with thorough goal conversations. They act as though the time it takes is a real problem for them.

What is really happening? In the scenario described above, the chief was becoming rigid because he could not figure out how to get his command staff to do what he wanted. Setting specific goals never occurred to him and he assumed that everyone understood what he was talking about and were simply being stubborn. When he interpreted their lack of action as one of stubbornness, he became even angrier.

It is too uncomfortable to experience the void in the conversation that stems from the chief's lack of clarity at the time. He would rather pop out of his discomfort and head for the action. He has been living, as have most officers in fire departments, in a fire-ready-aim mode; act first, ask questions later, analyze things even later than that. It is astonishing how often officers ignore the goal—setting process. I have come to the conclusion that the task of getting specific-like many that involve people processes with hard-line results—is simple, but not easy. Goals are simple and obvious to understand, but difficult to pull off well and consistently.

Though it may seem like swimming against the current, you need to slow your fire officers down long enough to establish clear goals, so they can be productive during the implementation. With no clear guidelines, the action phase of a change effort slows down because of hurried, misdirected efforts. You need to keep fire officers from side stepping a clear goal-setting process. You must bring backbone and confidence to your conviction that there is efficiency in doing it. If you have to, be a broken record about your conviction.

Fire officer hesitancy in seeking specific goals and outcomes often has very little to do with respect for you or your effectiveness. It has more to do with their own reactions to doing the hard work of aiming themselves and their shift, of honing in on specifics. Stay with them and frequently review the goals. You will get a reputation for being a focused chief officer and coach—not a bad rap!

Of course, there is no reason to be Attila the Hun about this. Sometimes a fire department situation is so ambiguous that it is difficult to clarify what work process or human relations goals would support achieving the bottom line result. A way to proceed is to encourage fire officers to establish, as best they can, work processes and human relations goals that begin to aim at the bottom line result.

When officers connect improvements in their leadership to specific work goals, they also build in their own feedback system. They realize how their own efforts have helped or hindered goal achievement and how they can sustain success. This kind of emphasis on goals can also give fire officers the incentive to become chief officers.

By the end of the first meeting, a coaching contract should take shape and have specific goals and objectives. I will use the situation between the chief and me as an example.

As you recall, my immediate feedback to the chief opened his eyes about why he was coming across in a negative manner. He realized that he was not holding his blaming at bay like he thought; it was coming through in his interactions with others. I asked him several of the questions that I have listed for you above including:

- If we discuss this for a few minutes, what do you hope the outcome will be?

- What do you think you need to improve upon?

- What kind of relationship do you envision between the command staff and you?

- If we develop a coaching relationship, which performance improvement goals are you targeting?

- Which specific leadership skills would you like to work on?

- Tell me how I can be of help to you in this matter?

Facilitating the chief's answers to these questions served the purpose of giving him a sense of control. I was acutely aware from his initial answers that he used a knee-jerk pattern of frustration and blame when he was unable to control outcomes. Engaging the chief in the co-creation of the coaching contract with the goal being to improve his relationship with the command staff, gave him a sense of control over his future and served to dampen his blaming. Because he was no longer at the whim of factors outside his control, he felt much more optimistic and tended to portray a more pleasant manner.

As a result of this conversation, the following contract was established:

1. Receive five coaching sessions focusing on improving leadership delivery, i.e., demeanor, listening skills, eliciting input, empowering fire officers, increasing encouragement skills.

2. Hold series of command-staff retreats for strategic planning of departmental training goals for reducing response time.

3. Develop an ongoing process for the "up flow" of information from fire officers.

4. Take weekly response time measures. Have these measures reported in local newspapers, fire department newsletters, and municipal newsletters.

5. Conduct 360 degree feedback for chief and command staff

6. Conduct employee opinion surveys every six months for eighteen months to assess morale and perception of leadership.

To work with difficult personnel, grasp the GREAT6 concept.

- Get a contract to coach

- Relationship before reprimand

- Expect great performance

- Analyze self as a possible part of the problem

- Treat everyone as valuable

- 6 things a Coach/Leader can do about resistance to change

Get a Contract to Coach

I will never forget one of my first coaching jobs. Following some leadership training I delivered to a fire department, a firefighter asked to see me one on one for some coaching to help him "improve his leadership skills." The chief consented. The mere fact that the firefighter asked to see me instead of being referred to me was a good sign that he was motivated. What I didn't know back then was what he was motivated for.

We sat down across from each other in a small office. When I asked him how I could be of help, it was as though a verbal starter gun had gone off. He launched into a diatribe about his immediate supervisor and every other supervisor within his sphere of influence. Like a locomotive headed down the track, rehashed incident after incident of all the wrongdoing ever perpetrated upon him in his professional life.

It was clear to me that he needed anger management and thus, that became my number one objective; to help him see how his own anger contributed to the downfall of his relationships. I was completely impressed with my diagnosis and plan of action. But that was not his plan, at least at first.

Getting a contract to work doesn't refer to anything written. Rather it is a verbal agreement between coach and client about what the client needs in order to improve. The tricky part is that what the client needs is not automatically evident, even to the client. Sometimes the coach and client must verbally mill about with each other before the issue becomes clear.

Belonging/Separating—Make Up Your Mind!

Perhaps you thought "bad" personnel possessed fixed, unalterable character flaws. When frustrated, most of us think so. Because in almost every work environment, "problem" personnel are viewed as the source of consternation, these are individuals who are perceived to be pursuing an intentionally difficult course and purposefully attempting to make life miserable for anyone in his/her path. In fact, nothing could be further from the truth. As strange as it may sound, most "problem" personnel are merely attempting to counter-balance two life forces: the need to be a unique individual and the need to belong, to be accepted. Let's explore this a bit further.

Tom was promoted to lieutenant five years ago. As a firefighter, he possessed many admired characteristics. He was dedicated to the department, maintained good relationships with his peers, came to work on time, and was generally in good spirits. His reasons for promoting were not uncommon. He stated that he wanted more responsibility in leadership and more money. He remained on shift, which allowed him to conduct a small side business during his days off.

As a firefighter, all was well as he received consistently good performance evaluations. But within a year of his promotion to lieutenant, the battalion chief was disillusioned. My experience suggests that this is an all too common problem. A seemingly skilled firefighter is promoted and has little, if any, leadership skills.

It is not an oversimplification to assume that whenever our need to belong is threatened or whenever individuation is thwarted, we attempt to swing the pendulum to regain balance. It is this attempt to balance that results in problematic workplace behavior. Furthermore, the organization's attempt to correct the problematic individual often results in increasing the problematic behavior.

This section is intended for coaches and leaders who want a theoretical and skills based approach for improving the performance of problematic employees. It provides an in depth look at how some employees under perform and get labeled as problems. In most cases, while problem employees are a contributor to the larger, under functioning work system, they are also a symptom of the system that is, in essence, the real client.

Although problematic employees are identified in every workplace, the sources of these problems are not. I wrote this chapter because the real workplace symptoms are often unrecognized, usually undiagnosed and therefore, never addressed. Organizations are perplexed as to what to do. One thing is for sure; the cost of poor performance and the need to retain good employees is a major impetus for improvement.

It is true that people join organizations, but leave under performing, mean spirited, unethical, and uncaring supervisors. Organizational costs to rehire and train a single employee range anywhere from $50,000 to well over $250,000 depending upon the person's position and expertise.

When organizations hire coaches to work with a "problem," they often believe, or at least hope, that the problem resides with one person only. They dust off their hands once the referral is made and the coach begins her work. Case closed! Then they are amazed and frustrated when the complaints again surface about the same employee or leader and back to coaching they trot for more of the same attempted solutions. Usually, if performance does not improve after the second coaching attempt, the employee is terminated, reassigned, or the whole matter is just ignored — often the latter.

Meanwhile, other employees who have been or are currently being affected by one person's bad behavior are themselves suffering with diminished morale and performance.

In most organizations, fixing a problem employee seems simple enough. Reprimand him, set him straight, present logic or the consequences, and he will see the light. Right? Not usually, at least not for long. There are unseen forces at work that makes behavior repetitive and tough to change, even in the face of dire consequences.

Change is tricky business. Anyone who has ever had a problem employee knows this. Initiate a change procedure and either someone else pops up with a problem or things get worse with the same person.

While I cannot make you a change expert within these pages, I do offer you a more thorough description of how some problematic employees are a symptom or sign of a larger issue. I do give you specific skills that can help you with your frustration. This is not a book that offers magical solutions for evil or dangerous employees. These people should be terminated and, in some cases, prosecuted. Furthermore, it is not my intent to portray coaching as a way to shield anyone from accountability or to use coaching as a way to "baby sit" people so that they avoid liability. Rather, this book is an approach for helping good people overcome poor performance or inappropriate behavior so that maximum productivity and good will is restored.

This book offers practical knowledge and useful techniques for diagnosing the reasons for poor performance and behavior as well as for intervening. This book is for coaches, managers and leaders who, whether it is labeled as such, coach others toward improved performance. The active approach to coaching in this book reflects the belief that the coach is equally responsible for performance outcome. As a result, coaches must understand these two vital and complex issues:

- Why some people do not perform up to their capabilities.

- How to create an encouraging environment that allows people to create and achieve according to their innate desires.

It is no overstatement to say that coaching for performance improvement, particularly those who underachieve or misbehave, is the most challenging task faced by coaches and leaders today. The goal of this book is to bridge the gap between theory and practice with a sophisticated how-to approach for both beginning coaches and new leaders to experienced practitioners. In addition, we have included coaching strategies with people from diverse backgrounds because the U.S. workplace is becoming increasingly multicultural.

It should be understood from the outset that the term "problem employee" is not a judgment but merely a descriptive term and does not always mean the employee should be terminated. Oftentimes there is the desire to retain these employees because they have qualities and talents that offset their problems. Perhaps they have been loyal and effective but have merely made an error in judgment. Perhaps their area of expertise is such that terminating them and training someone else is too expensive. For whatever reason, the organization desires to retain them and improve their behavior and/or their performance.

Six Things a Coach/Leader Can Do About Resistance to Change

It is really difficult to change. Changing ingrained habits and behaviors can be like giving up your identity or your best friend. Sometimes, the more you want it, the more resistant you become, succumbing to an internal battle that feels like good vs. evil, right vs. wrong, one part of me vs. the other part of me.

Fritz Perls, co-author of *Gestalt Therapy; Excitement and Growth in the Human Personality*, referred to the dichotomy between the two parts of one's personality as the topdog/underdog conflict. The topdog, a "demander of perfection," claims to always know what's right and good for you, often echoed in the words, "You should…" or, "You better…" Coming across as a self-righteous and judgmental "bully," the topdog's main objective is to get you to change, even if it's out of fear.

The underdog, whose job is to protect feelings from getting trampled on, reacts to this bullying and "holier-than-thou" manner by sabotaging the change effort. Anxious over not measuring up to such high standards, the underdog assumes a victim mentality and creates reasons and excuses for failure and inaction. The underdog perceives every demand to change as a personal attack of one form or another.

Here are the six things a supervisor can do to encourage an employee to change, while averting a stalemate with his or her underdog:

1) Lay out the desired behavior change in a calm, objective way.

Simply discuss the business need and the impact that the change will have on the person's development and leave out the judgmental voice. If you get too critical or dogmatic, you set yourself up for a negative reaction.

2) Acknowledge the employee's ambivalence about making the change.

Let them know you recognize how hard it can be to make this change and you appreciate the difficulty of this challenge. Volunteer any strategies you might have used in the past to overcome your own barriers or offer to brainstorm together how to defeat the obstacles. After that, give them space to figure out how they will solve their problem and make the necessary adjustments and set a timetable for following up.

3) Continue to hold the person accountable for their job performance.

Despite any manipulations or sidetracks the person may throw your way, continue to hold your ground that this is a vital aspect of their job performance and their work will need to be up to standard. If you accept mediocre or inconsistent results, you will be lowering the bar for that employee, the department, and yourself.

4) Confront the person on their resistance when you see it or hear it.

If you observe the person "acting out," don't sweep it under the rug. Privately call them over, let them know what you observed and give them an opportunity to share what's going on. When people feel they can talk through their discomforts in a safe environment, they are more likely to give up some of their "armor" and bring themselves to a less emotional, more rational way of viewing their situation.

5) Put the ball in their court.

Let the person know you care about them and their development, but that you cannot do this for them. Clearly lay out the goal, offer support, coach them through the transition, but ultimately, it will be up to them to do it or not. If they believe that this is all your agenda, the focus will become about you. If they like you, they might do it; if not, they might resist more. Take yourself and your personal agenda out of the middle and leave the decision and the responsibility in the person's own hands.

6) Celebrate success.

Ken Blanchard, of *One Minute Manager* fame, says to catch people doing things right. In the beginning, even when people approximate the correct behavior, they should be positively reinforced. If you see acceptable progress, don't give up on the employee and you'll teach them not to give up on themselves, either.

The long-term answer lies in maintaining the delicate balance between *respecting* your employee's resistance while still *expecting* them to make the change. The respect/expect juggling act allows you to support the human face of change without compromising the rigorous business demands of the organization.

Contracting in Coaching

- The Importance Of A Contract In The Change Process
- Elements Of A Coaching Contract
- Contracting With The Difficult Client

The coach must take a leadership position from the beginning. Theoretically, coach and client enter coaching with the same goals. The client's presence is either an acknowledgment that he/she wants help and that he/she is inviting the coach, an expert, to help the client change a situation that is maintaining or producing stress or discomfort; or they are essentially being forced to attend by someone in authority. In practice, however, the client(s) and the coach may, and usually do, differ in their understanding of the location of the performance problem(s), the cause(s), and the process of "raising the game."

Organizations have generally identified one member as the location of the problem. They think the cause is the identified person's deficits. The organization usually expects the coach to concentrate on that individual, working to change him/her. To the coach, however, the identified problem is only a signal light whereas the cause of the problem is the "dysfunctional" workplace transactions. The coach's job then is to move the identified problem client toward more functional, need satisfying modes of interaction by helping the entire workplace system toward a more complex form of organization—one that copes better with the current societal and workplace circumstances.

As a result, the coach's input may activate the mechanisms within the workplace system that preserve its homeostasis and thus, the real problem and reason the coach has been contracted.

Interestingly, when shadow coaching self-directed teams, we sometimes give certain members the instruction to behave in ways that trigger the team's homeostatic mechanism. At a break point we then halt the action and, with no judgment, debrief the process by pointing out what just transpired. This helps team members recognize, if not the source, the ongoing transactions that maintain the problem. For example:

During the team or organization's common history, rules that define the relationships of employees to one another have developed. These will always be out of the realm of consciousness and will have occurred at a surprisingly rapid pace. Any challenge to these rules will be countered automatically. The coach must find this through observation. Furthermore, an individual or team coming for coaching has previously struggled to resolve the problems that brought them. Their attempts to cope and resolve the problem may have narrowed their life experience. They will tend to over utilize familiar responses. As a result, both individual employees as well as teams have less freedom than usual, and their capacity for exploration has been reduced.

So coach and clients form a partnership, with an ultimate goal that is more or less formulated, which is to improve performance. Other goals, however, that contribute to better performance includes reducing conflict and stress for the team and organization, and learning new ways of coping with the various personalities.

Bibliography and Recommended Readings

Perls, Fritz, 1977. <u>Gestalt Therapy: Excitement And Growth in Human Personality</u>. Crown Publishing Company, 1977.

Chapter 6

The First and Second Meetings

The First and Second Meetings

Chapter 6

Introduction

First of all, we must understand that fire service is in the midst of change. The days of leadership by orders, whereby chief officers give orders to fire officers, who give orders to fire service personnel, who put out fires, is largely over except during emergencies. Our role has greatly expanded as have expectations and we are under greater scrutiny than ever before. Municipalities, fire service districts, and citizens expect a return on their investment so, as odd as it may be, we have to do more than just show up and save lives. People want to live in the safest environment possible. They want to go to work and not worry about whether their child is going to get hurt in a school fire or whether the neighborhood restaurant is going to burn down because it didn't pass fire safety standards.

As a result, what we do internally, day to day, has a direct bearing on the service people receive and on their perception that this community is a desirable one. In the long run, a desirable community means that people maintain pride in their property. That translates to strong property values and strong property values means tax dollars are funneled to us for jobs and equipment.

"Yes sir. But what does this have to do with coaching?" a fire officer might ask.

And the fire chief might answer, "Increasing specialization among fire service personnel and the recruitment and retention of the best people means that we have to maintain the highest level of performance in all of our service endeavors. To do that, we must embrace a new approach to setting objectives; one that incorporates a team approach whereby communication goes both ways and the special talents of each person are utilized toward the common goal. In order to boost our service performance and meet community expectations, we are going to begin a more formal process that entails conversations that are designed to accomplish specific objectives such as goal setting, performance review, overcoming obstacles, or self reflection. As a result, you will notice that I will be asking you questions that I may have never asked before and doing so in a way that seems different. I want you to understand that this is part of the coaching process."

At the risk of being redundant, we are going to stay with a discussion of the initial phase of coaching for one more chapter. The reason for this is because we realize that, for some of you, *coaching* is a new concept, one that goes beyond the traditional transactional style. With anything new, and particularly so in leadership, it is important to set the proper tone from the start and you will be able to do so if we cover the initial phase adequately.

The first meeting between a *superior* officer and the subordinate is often the most important and usually the most difficult. When we say *first meeting*, we are not necessarily talking about the first time a superior officer lays eyes on a subordinate. For the most part, superior officers will be embarking upon a coaching process with people whom they have known for quite some time. Rather, we are talking about the initial meeting whereby a superior officer begins the formal coaching process.

The first meeting or two is difficult because the officer must address or, at least deal with some things that have not traditionally been formally addressed by fire departments, including personality dynamics, individual perceptions of department vision and mission, personal goals, job fit, leader and organizational expectations, and the previous history between the superior officer and the subordinate (if any).

Beginning the Coaching Relationship

One of the most important considerations for the first conversation is how to make the transition from the traditional leadership style to one that initiates a coaching relationship. How the superior officer opens the meeting has an important bearing on the tone of the remaining coaching conversations and the performance of the participating individual or team. Coaches should convey confidence, warmth, positive regard, helpfulness, trust and trustworthiness, objectivity, knowledge, and firm yet flexible boundaries, between themselves and their subordinates. This is the time when coaching participants form their impressions of the leader and assess whether or not they think the coaching is going to be helpful to them.

Unfortunately, participants sometimes dismiss coaching that could be helpful because the initial conversation was either boring or intimidating. Others may be put off if the coach takes on a persona that seems fake or contrived compared to their previous style. Therefore, it is important for all leaders, when embracing coaching as a leadership strategy, to address the obvious change in their style before doing anything else.

For example, a chief officer begins the coaching process with a lieutenant. The two men have known each other for several years.

> *"I want to take just a moment to explain what coaching is more specifically, and to tell you what you can expect from me," the chief said.*
>
> *"Sounds good to me, Chief," Lt. Smith replied. "You mentioned that coaching is a new style of leadership."*
>
> *"That's right. And it means that the way I've been doing things will change somewhat."*
>
> *"Yes sir. How so?"*
>
> *"My conversations with you may seem a bit more formal," the chief explained.*
>
> *"Okay."*
>
> *"I may ask you specific questions designed to get you to look specifically at your performance or my questions may be aimed at getting you to set specific goals. Much of the time I'm going to get you to examine your own role in getting better performance out of yourself as well as your people."*

This is just one way to begin a coaching relationship. The following are five additional ways. First, start with a brief statement about what coaching is and why it is important. This is the simplest, most logical way to start. The coach gives a brief (1 to 2 minute), opening statement. When initiating a coaching relationship with familiar people, it is not only important to notify them of a change in the relationship, but what the purpose and benefits of coaching are as well.

For example, the coach might say, "I'm glad to have this opportunity to work with you in this capacity. Let me take a moment and explain what coaching is. This may help you understand more specifically what we will be doing here. Coaching is an ongoing process whereby I help you improve in some specific way. Whether the targeted improvement is in the form of skills, knowledge, or insight, my job will be to work with you in order to help you gain the resources necessary to be better. I will do my best to serve several functions including, disseminator of information, career counselor, psychologist, advocate, political advisor, training consultant, and teacher. As much as anything else, I will work to help you gain not only the confidence but a process for learning how to learn so that even unfamiliar situations are not insurmountable for you. In this way, you will be successful and excellent as you promote through the ranks. And individual excellence translates into greater departmental service."

Second, the chief could begin with a brief statement about coaching and then begin contracting. This is a good way to start because the focus of the conversation is immediately placed on the person being coached—the "client."

> *A chief might begin a coaching relationship with a fire officer by saying, "Thanks for meeting with me. My goal is for this coaching to be ongoing and a resource for your continual improvement. Before we finish talking here, we should determine how often we should meet. My preference is to schedule regular meetings so that other issues don't take precedence."*
>
> *"I've been looking forward to this," Lt. Smith said. "Typically we promote by assessment scores, but you can't learn leadership by testing for it."*
>
> *"I agree," the chief said. "Let me start by asking you what leadership challenges you are facing?"*
>
> *"That's a good question. I think my biggest challenge is separating myself from the rest of the shift. I've known these guys for a long time and I think I started out trying to be their friend. I still don't think I have enough separation."*
>
> *"And how does that affect you?" the chief asked.*
>
> *"Well, when it comes time to get tough on someone, I feel uncomfortable…"*

A third way to start is with a brief, broad statement about coaching and then asking the client what his or her goals are. Beginning the coaching relationship in this way gives the client control and serves to empower him or her toward maximum involvement in the coaching process.

For example, the chief might begin like this:

> *"My role in this coaching relationship is to serve as your resource, but it is the responsibility of both of us to create what happens here. Your primary role is to identify what you need to improve upon. Then we work together to get there."*
>
> *"I understand," Lt. Smith said.*
>
> *"What do you want to accomplish here and what outcomes do you want?" the chief asked.*
>
> *"No question about it, I need to learn how to deal with difficult people. I've got some Generation X people who just don't seem to have the work ethic that I do. I've heard them called slackers and I can understand why."*
>
> *"And what outcome would you like?"*
>
> *Lt. Smith said, "I find myself getting angry and then I lose objectivity. I want to remain objective and professional."*
>
> *"Okay, we'll leave it at that for now. But we will have to get more*
>
> *continued*

> *specific about this goal as we go along. Be thinking about what being objective means, what it looks like, how you want to respond, and most importantly, how will you know that things have improved when, in fact, they have improved?"*

A fourth way is to start with a brief statement about coaching and then get a sense of the client's awareness of his or her role in the challenge. This is a bold way to start and should be used only if the coach is familiar with the client, the challenge, and has a clear indication that the client is contributing to the challenge.

> *"The purpose of coaching is to help accentuate your strengths and minimize your weaknesses. Awareness is one of the most helpful skills to strengthen. Please understand that my questions are designed to get you to focus on those things within your control. In no way are they meant to place any blame on you. For example, I would like you to consider whether you might be encouraging others to keep doing the things you don't like?"*
>
> *"Actually," Lt. Smith said, "I've thought about this a lot. I tend to isolate myself from conflict."*
>
> *"And what effect does this have?" the chief asked.*
>
> *"I get the sense that people just avoid me, like, what's the use?" Lt. Smith said.*

The fifth and final possible beginning is to start in an unusual way, a way that grabs the client's attention. There are times when the coach may want to use a creative beginning to get the client's attention, especially if the coach believes that the client may not be committed to coaching. This type of opening can be interesting and can set a good tone for the conversation. One type of unusual opening includes role-playing a leadership challenge.

> *The chief said, "I understand you've been having particular difficulty with one of your firefighters."*
>
> *"That's putting it mildly," Lt. Smith replied.*
>
> *"I would like for you to briefly describe the conflict and then I want to role play. I'll portray the firefighter and let's see where you get stuck."*

Role-play is a bit unusual and uncomfortable for people who have never done it before. But with a little prodding, it is an invaluable tool. There is essentially one goal when role-playing and that is to solve the client's present problem. When helping fire officers get unstuck in leadership challenges, it is imperative that coaches ascertain the source of each challenge. In some cases, the problem is a self-destructive behavior outside the client's awareness, a behavior that other's find offensive, frustrating, or discouraging.

While discussing the challenge, the coach notices that the client appears unsure of himself. His voice lacks power and he appears to feel bad about his disciplinary role.

> *"I guess I come down on the guys pretty hard when I have to," Lt. Smith said. "But they don't seem to take me too seriously. I knew it was going to be difficult to supervise people who were my friends, but I never thought it would be this hard."*
>
> *"Okay," the chief said, "I have an observation for you. It's your voice. Are you aware of how you sound?"*
>
> *"I guess I never gave it much thought."*
>
> *"I hear equivocation," the chief said.*
>
> *"Pardon me?"*
>
> *"You sound uncertain, Lieutenant. Let me ask you something. Do you deserve to be a leader here?"*
>
> *"I don't know," Lt. Smith said. "Sometimes I wonder. I don't think the firefighters fear me much."*
>
> *"I'm not sure that fear should be the goal," the chief suggested. "But as we talk, I'm aware that while you say one thing with your words, your voice says something else. It's almost apologetic."*
>
> *"You think the firefighters are picking up on this, Chief, and blowing me off?"*
>
> *"If I was a firefighter, I wouldn't worry much about slacking off around you."*

In other cases, the problem is a simple lack of skills. In this scenario, the coach works to help the client, a lieutenant, prepare for a performance evaluation with firefighters.

> *"The firefighters don't take the evaluations seriously," Lt. Smith said. "They just want to know whether or not they will get a raise this year."*
>
> *"I'm fully aware of that sentiment and we are going to change things around here," the coach replied. "I'll tell you why they don't work. First, feedback given only once per year does not motivate people to improve. They can slack off until a few weeks before their evaluation. Secondly, when merit pay is strictly related to the yearly evaluation, it is the score on the last page that matters most, not the ongoing feedback. Thirdly, annual evaluations are set up to keep score, not to educate or improve. As a result, there is tremendous anxiety surrounding the evaluation. It is not viewed as a helpful tool. Evaluating personnel performance should be ongoing and personal, not in the form of an e-mail. The goal will be to change performance evaluations to performance coaching."*

Have the client take a personality assessment and begin the conversation by discussing the results. We highly recommend utilizing a personality assessment prior to beginning any coaching relationship. A good evaluation can greatly reduce the time in discovering the source of leadership or performance problems. As we discussed previously, most leadership struggles stem from two sources: personality style differences and what we call blind spots whereby people are not aware of the negative effects of their interaction on others. In this opening, the coach, begins the meeting by discussing the results and focusing on both strengths to build upon as well as areas the client needs to improve upon.

> The coach began by reviewing the personality assessment findings.
>
> "Your results offer specific revelations in six areas," the coach said, "including (1) personal attributes, (2) motivators, (3) situations you tend to avoid, (4) your ideal supervisor, (5) your communication style, and (6) your decision making style. Let's start with your attributes that reveal some important strengths. How does that sound?"
>
> "I was wondering how that came out," Lt. Smith said.
>
> "Then I would like to discuss your reaction to the suggested improvements and tie them into any performance or leadership challenges you are having," the coach continued.
>
> "That sounds good to me," Lt. Smith replied. "I already see some things I agree with and some things that I think may be having an effect on the way my shift responds to me."
>
> "Excellent! While this assessment is usually very accurate, it is more important that you see a connection between the results and the behavior you would like to change. And there's something else I would like to understand. What your ideal supervisor should do to bring out the best in you. This will help me to improve so that we can improve together."

Have the client give you (the coach) feedback about your own leadership behavior that may be having an effect on him or her. This is a very courageous thing for a coach to do. It is only effective if the coach is and has been the client's supervisor. Otherwise, beginning the coaching relationship in this manner makes no sense. But it is excellent modeling for the coach to begin by asking for open and honest feedback. Of course, it is vitally important that coaches be trustworthy.

These examples illustrate that there are a variety of appropriate ways to open the initial conversation. The right kind of opening, combined with the desire to help the client will have a strong positive effect on how coaching starts.

Setting a Positive Tone

An important task for the coach during the first and second meetings is to establish a positive tone for the meeting. The tone is the prevailing atmosphere and it stems from a couple of sources, including the coach's enthusiasm and the client's comfort and trust. The coach can establish a positive tone by being enthusiastic, focusing on performance improvement (instead of using coaching as a disciplinary tool), focusing the meeting time on relevant performance issues for the client, and on helping the client have successes by setting reachable, small, incremental goals.

It is very important that the coach not let the client focus on griping, deflecting, avoiding, blaming, or on negative issues that are outside the client's control, for a majority of the first two (or any) meetings. Allowing client's to do these things would set a completely ineffective, non-working tone. In addition, a client who is allowed to complain incessantly will not come to respect or trust the coach. An interesting phenomenon occurs when coaches skillfully place pressure on clients to take responsibility - their anxiety rises. When anxious, people search for ways to diminish their feeling. They either run from the source of the anxiety or confront it. The latter produces growth. When coaches create anxiety, yet serve as a resource for growth, clients will seek growth producing, performance enhancing solutions for diminishing anxiety.

Clarifying the Purpose

Coaches must be sure that the purpose of the coaching is clarified during the first meeting. Clarification is particularly important if there has been no voluntary selection of coach and client. In other words, if the coach is the superior officer and is requiring that his/her subordinates participate in coaching, then a thorough clarification of the coaching meetings is imperative. Clients may fear that coaching is just another word for discipline or that they are being singled out as someone who lacks ability and skill. In essence, the purpose of coaching includes:

- Preparation for a new position

- Succeeding a ranking officer who is retiring

- Correcting poor performance

- Ongoing leadership training

- Preparing for leadership following an operations position

Even if clients know why they are participating in coaching, clarifying the purpose is a good idea.

> *"Thanks for coming," the coach began. "Let me explain what this is and what we will be doing. At that point I would like your reactions. This is a meeting referred to as coaching. Much like in sports, coaching*
> *continued*

> *is a process whereby the coach (me) helps you improve to be your best. Within a short time, we will decide how often and how much we will meet. The overall purpose of these meetings is to help you succeed the outgoing chief. You've been in operations your entire career and this position involves a variety of skill requirements, some with people and some political. It is a vital role that you will play and I want to see you not only succeed, but be great. Therefore, we will be examining different segments of your position during these meetings and exploring and practicing how you can improve. How does this sound?"*

Coaches should clarify the purpose of the meeting at the beginning of each meeting. For example, although the overall purpose of coaching in the above scenario is to help this client successfully succeed an outgoing chief, there may be a slightly separate focus for any single meeting.

> *"As always, our goal is to help you prepare for this position. But today,"* the coach explained, *"I think we should focus on resolving the conflicts you may experience with shift changes. It is my understanding that you have a pretty stubborn crew, Lieutenant, and it may require all of your faculties...."*

Explaining the Coach's Role

During the first meeting, the coach should explain what his or her role will be throughout the life of the meetings. Offering an explanation helps clients form a picture of what to expect from the coach.

> *"Let me explain my role to you because I'm not sure what your expectations are,"* the coach began. *"Although I haven't gotten your input yet, I suggest that we meet weekly for the next eight weeks. My role in these meetings will be to facilitate your improvement by pushing you to explore how you can improve. On some occasions, the situation may call for me to be a facilitator and merely ask questions to stimulate your thoughts. On other occasions, the situation may call for me to become more active and offer up suggestions. On still other occasions, I may push hard if I sense that you are falling into old habits or patterns that are sure to prove ineffective. In essence, I will serve as a resource, a teacher, an advocate for your progress, a counselor, and a sledgehammer. Of course, the latter may have a velvet covering."*

Explaining How the Meeting Will Be Conducted

Closely allied to explaining the purpose and the coach's role is explaining what will happen during a meeting. Coaches should clarify during the first meeting how they plan to do things. The coach can help ease tension, ensure the smooth functioning of the meeting, and set a working tone (as opposed to a social tone) if the kinds of discussions and coaching focus are covered.

> *"Each meeting, we should spend the first few minutes going over any relevant experiences since our last meeting," the coach explained. "Specific ways that you have improved, critical incidents whereby you used the skills and methods we have discussed, and even internal reactions you experienced should be the focus at first. Then we'll focus on anything that you want to discuss. If you don't have anything in particular to talk about, we'll focus on a new leadership issue of my choosing. We'll always spend the last few minutes talking about what is coming up for the week and how you can use the skills and techniques we have covered."*

Helping Clients Verbalize Their Expectations

Asking clients to state their expectations for the coaching is a simple skill. "I want you to think about what you hope to get from coaching," is so simple as to hardly be worth discussing. But asking the question is not enough. We have coached many fire service personnel and oftentimes they state few, if any, expectations in the initial stages of the coaching relationship, particularly if they feel that they are being forced to attend. They seem to just want to endure it. Under such conditions, coaching is probably worse than doing nothing at all. So, the decision is to do nothing and let things continue as is, or somehow get the client to be involved. The technique may be to broach the issue of their hesitancy.

> *"What do you hope to get from coaching?" the chief asked.*
>
> *"I don't know, Chief," Lt. White said. "Whatever you think I need."*
>
> *"The purpose of coaching is not to simply impart my wishes on you. That just makes me a boss," the chief added. "Coaching must involve a desire on your part to be better, even excellent at something. My part is to help you by facilitating your growth. For this to work, you will have to need what I can teach and facilitate."*
>
> *"It's not that I don't want to do this thing, Chief. I just haven't given it much thought."*
>
> *"I appreciate what you are saying, Lieutenant. And I'd guess that you are somewhat uncomfortable."*
>
> *"Yes, I guess so. But I'm sure I'll get used to it."*
>
> *"Good!" the chief said. "It shouldn't take but a moment to think about how you would like to improve."*
>
> *"Hmmm," Lt. White said. "All right. The one thing I would hope to get out of this coaching is more confidence around the personnel who are older than me. Sometimes they seem to look at me like I'm too young."*

Sometimes fire service personnel attend a first meeting having expectations that are not in line with the purpose of the meeting. When this happens, the coach must reiterate the purpose. The more common example of this is the client who dominates the meeting through incessant complaining.

> After rambling for several minutes, Lt. White said, "Like I've said, they're a bunch of slackers. Time and time and time again I've tried to motivate them, but it's no use. They'll never possess the work ethic of my generation. And I can't stand it when new, young firefighters come along who have promise, only to have their motivation diminished because of the lackadaisical, lackluster performance of their peers. You know what else I can't stand..."
>
> "Lieutenant, let me jump in here. The purpose of our meeting is to find solutions for how you will best supervise this group. Your frustration is clear but we need to move toward giving you strategies for working with these people. I don't want you to waste your time complaining when we could find solutions that might limit your frustration."

The Attractive Coach

The *attractiveness* of the coach is an important issue that should be discussed at this juncture. Attractiveness does not refer to physical features, but rather to the level of respect and trust given to the coach by the client. Although admittedly vague, the coach's attractiveness has as much to do with the client's receptivity to the coach's efforts—and therefore to coaching success—than perhaps any technique, strategy or suggestion the coach might use. Therefore, a tyrant chief officer who decides that coaching could be a useful leadership strategy will likely experience resistance or apathy to his/her efforts. The strategies and skills covered in this book can make an adequate leader better, a good leader great, but it cannot bring immediate respect to a tyrant. That takes time and only if the coach follows the approach consistently.

Checking Out the Comfort Level

In the typical boss/subordinate relationship, there is usually minimum focus on the inner experience of the subordinate and maximum focus on task accomplishment. In coaching, however, equal attention is given to the client's inner experience. This is because in coaching consideration is given to the client's inner experience as it has an effect on performance. Therefore, the client's emotional state is just as valid a focus for coaching as is goal setting, improving leadership skills, establishing vision, or communicating with different generations.

A common *inner* experience that has an effect on the coaching outcome is apprehension and discomfort, particularly during the first meeting. Apprehension can be problematic, particularly if the coach is unattractive to the client. To begin reducing this discomfort, the coach might spend a few minutes focused on the topic of comfort level.

Examples:

- "Tell me how you feel about coaching with me?"

- "I have decided to change my leadership approach somewhat through this method called coaching. You will, no doubt, become aware of this change in the way I interact. This may cause you to experience discomfort."

- Give me one word that captures the way you are feeling about being here."

Content and Process

There is an important distinction to be made between content and process. In this book, *content* means the topic being discussed during the meeting. All meetings have a content area that could include topics like specific leadership skills, understanding personality types, or positive discipline to name just a few. But some meetings have less of a content focus than others. In fact, some meetings may focus solely on *process*, those less visible qualities possessed by the client that include, voice tone, trustworthiness, ethics, demeanor, congruence between spoken words and actions, warmth, the practice of encouragement, and boundaries with lower ranking personnel. Focusing partially on process issues is a portion of almost all coaching relationships and coaches must be ever conscious about whether the current focus should be on a topic or on a process. Devoting too much time in the first meeting to explaining rules or explaining the leadership role causes boredom. By the same token, focusing too much time on process can create an aura of psychotherapy and make the client uneasy.

It is very important that the coach explain to the client what content and process are, the differences between the two, and how time will be devoted to each area.

> "As we get started here," the coach said, "I want to explain something about what we will be talking about. Normally the talk around the fire department is task oriented, that is, we discuss how something should be done or not done. Less often do we talk about leadership qualities or aspects of personality that either empower or impede your leadership. What we will be discussing is often difficult to predict. Although I may ask you to focus on a particular skill, there may be some other, less obvious qualities that we should focus on. Using fishing as an analogy, content is like what type of rod or lure you use, while process is akin to how the cast is made."

Other First Meeting Considerations

This book assumes that most coaching takes place between a superior officer and his/her subordinate. As you have already imagined, this pairing is fraught with anxiety. Our experience suggests that subordinate officers sometimes make the following assumptions:

- That coaching is just a form of discipline

- That confidential information will be shared with others

- That coaching is a forced process and that refusing to participate can result in negative consequences

- That coaching is simply another word for the same old leadership style

We urge those of you who read this book to be crystal clear about your coaching motivation. It is our experience that superior officers who misuse coaching or who lack awareness of their motives do tremendous harm to their overall leadership reputation. Additionally, it is vital that coaches understand their own personal style when interacting with their subordinates. Lack of awareness contributes to incongruence between what is said (the words) and what is meant (the real meaning behind the words). Miscommunication occurs when the receiver perceives the message differently than was intended by the sender or perceives the meaning accurately when the sender lacks awareness of their intent.

Confidentiality is, by far, the most important issue for establishing trust. Even though coaching is not psychotherapy, subordinates must trust that the superior officer has their best interests and growth in mind.

Closing the First Meeting

Perhaps this subheading sounds silly and inconsequential, but wrapping up the meeting sets the tone for the following meeting and can send the message that the client's learning is collaborative. Instead of just ending the meeting abruptly, the coach may want to get some feedback from the client in the form of the following questions:

- How was the meeting for you?

- How was it different from what you thought was going to happen?

- What stood out to you?

- Was there anything we discussed that you didn't understand?

- Do you have any questions about the meeting, its purpose, or what is going to happen?

- What did you learn from the meeting today?

During the close of the first meeting, the leader may benefit from summarizing the meeting and commenting again on the purpose of the upcoming meetings and what the possibilities are for the future.

The Second Meeting

Before entering the second meeting there are several important questions the coach should ponder:

- What is the purpose of this meeting?

- How should I follow up on the client's thoughts from the first meeting?

- Is the client feeling free to work or is he/she there because they feel ordered to do so?

- Is our relationship conducive to work?

- How should I open the meeting in order to set a working tone?

The Purpose of the Meeting

Coaches continue to set the tone during the second meeting, being aware that some clients will still be uncomfortable and suspicious. In addition, the coach needs to give thought to opening the second session.

Perhaps the most common error new coaches make is assuming that coaching meetings must accomplish a task. Like learning a new apparatus function or new life-saving technique, the assumption is that the coaching challenge is beyond the participants, out there somewhere in the environment. While this may often be the case, such an assumption excludes the possibility that the challenge is personal, within the individual, or inter-personal, between the coach and the client. Coaches must determine prior to each meeting what the challenge is and then decide if, when, or how it will be broached during the meeting. You may choose to start the meeting in a broad sense by allowing the client choose the direction.

> ""Bob, thanks for choosing to meet again," the coach said. "We covered some interesting and hopefully helpful ground last time, but I feel that it's most important to allow you to take the direction that you feel is most helpful for you at this meeting. What are your expectations for this meeting and how would you like to start?"

Or the coach might have said, "Okay, let's talk about what's been going on since the last meeting." This opening is appropriate if the client is the type of person who tends to get down to business and does not blame others. As you can see, this opening has the tendency to facilitate a discussion of events, not of the client's efforts to improve. While there are no right or wrong ways to open, it is important for the coach to understand that the way a meeting is opened has much to do with what is discussed. At other times, because you feel strongly about an issue, you may choose to begin by suggesting a direction.

> *"Bob, thanks for choosing to meet again. We covered some interesting and hopefully helpful ground last time, but there is something I would like to check out. You seemed hesitant last week and I wasn't sure if you were suspicious of the coaching or what. Can you explain?"*

In the first example, the purpose of the meeting may be to help the client get comfortable in selecting a direction, one of the primary characteristics of leadership. In the second example, the purpose may be to help the client learn how his/her reactions deter relationship development.

Oftentimes you may wish to establish a positive tone from the beginning of the meeting. For example, the coach could say, "Let's review what we discussed last time and how you have begun to make changes." This opening sets a positive tone. The client is asked to talk, not about problems, but about changes that he/she has initiated.

Chapter 7

Basic Skills
for Coaching

Basic Skills for Coaching

Throughout the first chapters, we have referred to various coaching skills but have not discussed them in great detail. In the next few chapters, we describe specific skills that we feel are essential for good coaching. Some of those are basic human-relations skills that you may have learned in other places or in various fire leadership courses. You may recognize the names of some of these skills.

- Active Listening
- Reflection
- Silence
- Clarification
- Summarizing
- Mini-Lecturing and Information Giving
- Modeling and Self-Disclosure
- Delegation

Active Listening

Active listening entails assessing and understanding not only the content of the spoken words of the speaker, but the voice and body language as well. It also involves communicating to the person speaking that you are really listening.

Most people have been trained to listen to only the speaker's voice or his/her words, but there is much more. Voice tone and inflection, facial expressions, body posture, eye movements, and energy level, communicate, in many instances, deeper, unspoken messages. Even though most of us have been trained to listen mostly to words, we are often acutely aware of the unspoken, nonverbal aspects of communication. Nowhere is this more important than in coaching.

Skilled coaches try to listen to all sources of a client's communication, not just to the words. To the extent this is possible, coaches should be aware of what clients are feeling and thinking at all times. We urge you to practice this skill whenever you are with a group of friends, family, or colleagues. See if you can take in more than just the spoken word. What are people really feeling? What are they really trying to communicate? Why might they be holding back from what they really experience? The more incongruent a person is between verbal and nonverbal communication, the more problems this will create in communication, leadership, self-understanding, trust development, and relationship maintenance.

Sometimes nonverbal acts are consistent with verbal messages; for example, a person pounds the desk while expressing anger toward someone. But often, this is not the case. Furthermore, in the initial stages of relationship building, it is generally ineffective to confront the person with any inconsistencies. Confrontations, poorly timed, can produce defensiveness and discourage further exploration. However, it is important to be aware of these inconsistencies. There might be a time when they can be appropriately discussed in the relationship.

In fire service as well as in coaching there are several reasons why someone might not communicate congruently, including fear of being honest with a superior officer, lack of familiarity with the coaching process, and fear of being perceived as incompetent, to name just a few. Skilled coaches have the ability to recognize what is unspoken and listen in such a way as to facilitate the client's awareness.

> *"Let me note something if I may,"* the coach said. *"As we have talked, I've sensed that you are uncomfortable."*
>
> *"Well yes, I suppose I am,"* Lt. White said.
>
> *"That's understandable."*

There are some definite cardinal sins to avoid at this point. The first is to attempt to provide a quick fix by attempting to assuage the client's discomfort. Saying something like "don't be uncomfortable," or "it's all right, I'm in my coaching mode," sounds like something a parent might say in an attempt to get a child to quit worrying. It does nothing but create further discomfort and mistrust on the part of the client. The second cardinal sin is to force the client to state the source of the problem definitively. The problem in the eyes of the client may be you, the superior officer and coach. Forcing the client to be honest probably does nothing but force the client to lie.

The best approach is to note what you observe and move on. Striving to understand the client's point of view, whether agreeing with it or not, is one of the most important leadership and coaching techniques available. Merely attempting to walk in the client's shoes is the prime element in the development of trust between client and coach.

Reflection

In coaching, to reflect a comment is to restate it, conveying that you understand the content, the feeling behind it, or both. As a coach, you will find it helpful and necessary to use the skill of reflecting both the client's spoken and unspoken messages. The purpose of reflecting is: (1) to help clients become more aware of what they are saying, and (2) to help clients understand themselves and their behavior, (3) to help clients understand the connection between their behavior and their work performance, and (4) to help clients understand the impact of their behavior on others.

Example #1

> "I guess you could say that I wasn't completely prepared for the position," Lt. White said. "What I mean is, I wanted the challenge of the new position, and I even knew what other people have said about the promotion, but you don't really know until you're there for yourself. It's not the technical stuff. I know that backwards and forwards. It's managing the people. That's the hard part."
>
> "You're saying that certain aspects of the job took you by surprise and that managing people is the most difficult challenge," the coach said.

Example #2

> Chief Gaines said, "I've had it with the Gen Xers. Do you realize that in twenty years of fire service, I've never taken a sick day. Then these Gen X slackers come along and think that sick time is just another word for vacation. They don't seem to grasp what it is really for. Most of all, what I say seems to bear no weight whatsoever. They just roll their eyes when I turn my back."
>
> "You're frustrated that the younger personnel appear to have no work ethic and little respect for authority," the coach said.
>
> If done effectively, these reflections serve the purpose of stimulating additional conversation and helping the client move toward the eventual goal of improving leadership skills. Continuing, example #2 illustrates this.
>
> "You hit the nail on the head," Chief Gaines agreed. "This group doesn't seem to value their jobs. When I got into the fire department, I was thankful just to have a job. Times were different then."
>
> "The differences in work ethic are clear cut. And the times are different as well."
>
> continued

> Chief Gaines said, "Yes, hmmm. This was all I had. My options were a lot more limited then. Things are probably a lot more different now. These guys probably get into the fire service thinking that if they don't like it, then they'll just go do something else."
>
> "You're aware that differences in the times produces differences in what people want and how they behave," the coach suggested. "More freedom means refusing to do something that is not rewarding."
>
> "Oh," Chief Gaines said, "they're probably just as much of a product of their times as I was. I'm going have to find a way to deal with them."

Responses determine the development of a relationship. When coaches and leaders use responses that dominate, moralize, or sympathize, they discourage the other person and block self-exploration and increased awareness. The other person learns to respond by defending, attacking, giving up, or feeling worthless.

When coaches respond in a way that facilitates a relationship, the other person feels safer, more open, and less defensive and is more willing to talk about his or her concerns. After you know what those concerns are, you may be better able to encourage that person.

The most effective responses that lead to this exploration are those that focus on the other person, invite further exploration, and understand rather than judge. Effective responses include focusing on the other person. To develop focusing on the other person:

- Stay on the topic presented.

- Attend closely to what is said.

- Recognize silence as part of the communication.

- When responding, use the word "you" or the person's name.

- Always focus on what the person is saying means to them instead of how it affects you.

- Be a clear and accurate mirror. What is said is what you respond to.

- Don't react out of your interpretation of your needs.

- Listen. Don't conclude where the person is going before they get there.

- Be aware of how your response will be received.

- Invite exploration.

Stay on the client's topic. Keeping focused on the topic requires considerable effort. You may need more information in order to acquire a better understanding of the feelings and beliefs that are being expressed. Questioning the person may produce defensiveness, create barriers or doubt, and indicate you are more interested in questioning than in understanding.

Some additional suggestions for improving reflection skills include asking the following questions about what you say:

1. How does what I said fit in with what the other person said?

2. How does it relate to how the other person sees the world?

3. Is it of any interest to the other person?

4. How did what I said show the other person that he or she contributed to what I said?

5. How did what I said contribute to continuing rather than ending the conversation?

6. In what possible ways might what I said be interpreted?

7. Did I discourage the other person by what I said?

8. How did I demonstrate that I listened to the other person?

9. How did I sound? Was I enthusiastic?

10. Was the other person more encouraged or more discouraged by what I said?

In summary, the use of reflection clarifies and deepens the client's understanding and communicates that the coach is in tune with what the client is attempting to say. It is important to use reflection with another, rather odd, skill known as the use of silence. Silence is the next skill we will explore.

Silence

There is a quirky phenomenon existing in face-to-face interaction that involves silence. Nothingness forces most people to talk. Try this some time. When talking with someone over dinner, maintain good eye contact, a pleasant face, but say nothing when they finish their portion of the conversation, and see what happens.

One of two things will occur. They will either ask you if perhaps a stroke has removed your ability to respond or they will fill the dead spaces with verbiage. In a coaching situation in which you are the coach, 99% of the time the client will fill the dead space. Why? Because silence in conversation makes people feel uncomfortable. This is a useful tool in coaching because you can use the client's discomfort to place responsibility on them to talk.

This is a useful skill to use strategically in those situations where the client is quiet, reticent, or resistant.

The technique of silence is simple. The difficulty is that it runs counter to convention and is therefore uncomfortable for the coach. The rule is simple—do nothing. The timing of silence is crucial. The coach cannot be silent too much and cannot use silence as a way to control the client. It should be used sparingly. An example of what not to do goes like this.

> *"So, we've pretty much covered what the purpose of coaching is and what our respective roles are," the coach said, "and you've had some time to think about what you want to target. What is it that we will work toward?"*
>
> *"I'm not really sure," Chief Gaines replied.*
>
> *"Okay, then what did your personality style assessment reveal?" the coach asked.*
>
> *"What do you mean?"*
>
> *"When you looked at your assessment results, what stood out to you?" the coach prompted.*
>
> *"Those personality things are fun. I took one once before, but honestly, I'm not sure it told me anything I didn't already know."*
>
> *The coach asked, "Well, have you been thinking about working on anything else pertaining to your leadership?"*
>
> *"Not too much. Whatever you think...."*

This could go on forever! Playing twenty questions is more akin to interrogation or investigation, not coaching. Little progress can be made until the client is doing at least 50% of the work. This is the benefit of silence—to gently force clients to work. Before we delve into the skill let's briefly discuss why clients appear resistant. A more thorough discussion of resistance is included in a later chapter.

What appears to be resistance may not be the conscious refusal to participate. For example, some clients may truly have no idea what they need to improve upon. This is the reason for including the extensive chapter on personality styles in chapter three. Gaining personal awareness in the form of strengths and weaknesses usually facilitates clients to identify what they need to improve upon. It is more rare for clients to be unable to identify goals following the personality style assessment. Therefore, the second reason for the client's inability to identify coaching goals is fear of the coach or the fear that coaching is merely a cloak for a micro-managing superior officer to wield power. In such instances, coaches should not initially press the client in goal setting if it appears that the potential goals are of a more personal (personality based) nature. Lack of trust on the part of the client is the reason. Instead, choose a less personal, smaller goal to target for improvement until trust can be established. The third reason underlying the lack of goal setting is akin to the second reason above, but much easier to deal with.

It is our experience that a good number of fire service personnel are unaccustomed to the one-on-one, ongoing and formalized attention from a superior officer. As a result, they may play out the *subordinate does whatever ordered to do* role, particularly if the traditional transactional style of leadership has ruled supreme in the department. This style essentially communicates a do as I say message that prevents subordinates (in this case clients) from feeling comfortable with a coaching process that allows clients to set their own personal agendas even though these agendas should fit within the service and leadership goals of the department. In these cases, gently press the client for responses and then remain silent.

> *"Tell me what you've been thinking about your coaching goals, Lieutenant," the chief said.*
>
> *"Well, I haven't really thought much about it," Lt. White replied.*
>
> *(silence)*
>
> *After an uncomfortable twenty seconds, Lt. White said, "Well, uh, maybe I could stand to work on my ability to handle conflict."*
>
> *"Tell me more about that," the chief said.*
>
> *"It's a long standing concern for me. I would just like to be able to deal with anger better."*
>
> *"What do you mean, Lieutenant?"*
>
> *Lt. White said, "My DISC® assessment showed me something that I'm already aware of, but need to address once and for all…"*

The chief's initial use of silence was effective in that it sent a message to the lieutenant that the work was up to him. The beauty of the skillful use of silence is that it tells clients that they are responsible for being at least half of the equation in the process of performance improvement.

Clarification

To clarify means to pinpoint the key issues in the client's statements. It is done for the benefit of the client, the coach, or both. This skill is important to use when the client's discussion is meaningless or rambling or when the client is confused.

> *"It's just frustrating sometimes, you know," Chief Gaines said. "When we're operating on a limited budget and we're working on equipment that needs to be updated and then they come down on us when something breaks down. I mean nobody knows better than we do that this stuff needs to remain operable. What do they think? We don't take rescue seriously? We're just the whipping boy sometimes, that's all. I just wish they would be honest about it. I mean, every single one of us got into this to do good things. We're no different from them. They just like to wield their power. We're easy to pick on sometimes…"*
>
> *"Let me see if I understand, Chief," the coach said. "It seems to me that you are both frustrated that the equipment is older and in need of constant repair and upset that other personnel place the blame on you."*
>
> *"That's exactly right. I feel personally responsible for the way things work around here and I don't need a bunch of people to jump down my throat. I wish they would somehow get this message."*
>
> *"You're saying that being responsible is not the issue," the coach said. "No one feels more responsible than you. You're wondering how they can be encouraged to understand what the real issue is."*
>
> *"No question about it. Maybe I should take the bull by the horns."*

In this example, rather than questioning the client further, the coach took jumbled information presented by the client and used a statement to reorder it in an attempt to clarify the key issues. You will notice that the coach is not attempting to solve the problem or to appear like an expert on the dilemma. According to the old proverb, the goal here is to "teach a man to fish," rather than giving him one. Clarifying statements allows clients to examine what they are saying so that they can focus deeper on the pertinent issue(s). In this way, the self-directed client moves toward the real solution, which, in this case, may have been reluctant to take action.

We cannot emphasize enough the importance of clarification. If client's thoughts are vague, confusing, or incomplete, as they often are in moments of stress, they have difficulty foreseeing solutions.

Summarizing

The skill of summarizing is another skill that "leads horses to water," yet doesn't "force them to drink". It is a must for all coaches and involves pulling together the myriad of things that clients talk about into a coherent, cogent statement that serves to focus clients' attention toward solutions. Thus, it is a good problem-solving tool.

There are several instances where summarizing can or should be used. A summary may be helpful when coaches allow overly talkative clients to speak uninterrupted for several minutes. Without a summary, clients may focus on irrelevant points that have little to do with a problem solution. A summary tightens the focus and allows the client to focus only on those issues that are relevant to the challenge at hand. A concise summary is also useful in making a transition from one topic to another. The summary can highlight key points in a discussion and can serve as a bridge to the next discussion. A summary is especially important if the discussion has been diffuse or has involved overlapping points of ideas. A good summary will pull together the major points and can serve to deepen or sharpen the focus of conversation.

For example, the coach could say, "So far you've been talking in general about changes you would like to make in the department. You began by discussing how the new station would affect personnel as some people choose to transfer. After that you talked about your own promotion and how this would take you away from some of the things that drew you to fire service in the first place. Finally, you brought up your concern over the disciplinary aspects that will confront you in your new position. You are mostly talking about changes. I want you to think about what you are really trying to explore. What concerns you most about the changes that are coming?"

In this example, the summary serves to highlight the client's concern over change and set the stage for the coach to sharpen the focus. The client answered in the following manner.

"I think I'm mostly concerned about my ability to be a leader of the people with whom I've been a peer for the past thirteen years. Frankly, I'm asking myself if I can garner their support and encouragement."

Note that the summary does not stimulate a rehashing of what has already been said but is rather a stimulus for further exploration.

Another good time to use summarizing is at the end of a meeting. Because many ideas will have been discussed during the course of the meeting, a skillful summary can be helpful. In our discussion of ending a coaching meeting later in this book, we address the different ways to summarize.

Mini-Lecturing and Information Giving

Sometimes coaches must provide information to clients. One of the primary roles of the coach is to occasionally be the expert and to offer expertise on subjects such as leadership, team-building, creating followership, and discipline, to name just a few. Sometimes, mini-lecturing morphs into the full-blown teaching of group seminars where the coach lectures extensively. When giving mini-lectures in a one-to-one format, keep the following rules of thumb in mind:

- Make it interesting

- Make it relevant to the client's goals

- Make sure you consider cultural and gender differences

- Make it short (usually no more than 5-8 minutes)

- Make it energizing

- Make sure you have current, correct, and objective information

Giving information enables people to learn from you and from the discussion that follows. By keeping your comments relatively short, you can provide good information without turning the face-to-face coaching into a class. The key to successful mini-lecturing is to briefly provide new and interesting ideas. Very often, beginning coaches are reticent to give any information or will give boring mini-lectures. A good coach has to have good things to say and be well informed about the subject. Therefore, coaches should undergo a continual process of leadership education, learning group facilitation, learning team building, understanding personality differences, understanding the influence of systems on decision making and organizational performance, and understanding generational differences. We have provided much of this information within this book but coaches would be well served to continue learning about these topics from other sources.

> The coach said, "You've been talking about your confusion regarding why your firefighters do some of the things they do. It is extremely important that you do in fact, understand personality differences. For example, let's take a few minutes to look at the strengths and challenges of each style. The Driver or "D" style is someone who is decisive, tough, strong-willed, competitive, demanding, and self-confident. The "D" style is not geared toward relationship development and is usually not particularly patient. This is a person who frequently oversteps their boundaries and who often thinks teamwork is a waste of time. Therefore, when you attempt to lead "D" style people, you will notice that they appear to lack warmth or enthusiasm. They are oriented toward one thing: goal attainment, and they will forge ahead with great force to get what they want. Others say D's are cold, aloof, hard hearted, critical, one-track minded and never wrong. Now, knowing this about "Driver" style people, how does this help you?"
>
> "Yes, it offers a good explanation for why things happen as they do. For instance, one of my guys continually upsets his peers with his argumentative style," Lt White replied. "You're saying that this is mostly personality style related. Does this really explain why he does these things?"

> *"Absolutely!," the coach said. "Another word for personality is habit. People are very predictable. We tend to react in a stereotypical manner within a variety of different circumstances. Furthermore, your own personal style will interact with his in a fairly predictable manner as well."*
>
> *"What do you mean?"*
>
> *"Your style is Steadfast or "S", am I right?" the coach asked.*
>
> *"Yes."*
>
> *"S's and D's often experience conflict. Tell me if this is what happens. If he hasn't said this to you directly, you may have gotten the sense that he perceives you as indecisive and too slow to make decisions. On the other hand, you perceive him to be arrogant and unwilling to consider the well-being and feelings of others. You see him as a poor listener. He sees you as resistant to change. You see him as having a short fuse. He sees you as lacking backbone. Am I right?"*
>
> *"Exactly right," the lieutenant answered.*
>
> *"Okay, let's shift here and talk about what changes you should target in order to approach a fix in the future."*

This is an example of how mini-lecturing can, in a short time, provide information that is useful to the client. In almost any coaching session, there will be times during a session when a two or three minute mini-lecture on some subject will help to sharpen the focus of clients or simply help clients understand something about which they are confused.

Modeling and Self-Disclosure

Self-disclosure is one of the most important skills for leaders in a command-and-control environment. It is useful for getting clients to open up and helps to develop trust. One of the best ways to teach desired behaviors is by modeling those behaviors to clients. The coach's style of effective communication, ability to listen, and the encouragement of others, serves as a model for clients to emulate. Modeling involves energy, and enthusiasm, as well as verbal skills.

Perhaps the most important reason for using self-disclosure lies in its tendency to reveal the coach as a human who has dealt with many of the same issues in life as has the client.

The coach could say, "I want to tell you about my own struggle in learning to lead a bunch of people who were my former peers. The assessment you took reveals some characteristics that are similar to me—mild mannered, desiring to avoid conflict, exact, punctual, organized, thorough, steady, and undemanding. The first year was quite a struggle for me. I had chief officers breathing down my neck to get my people to be more responsible. On the other hand, the firefighters wouldn't view me in a leadership position and became the world's preeminent slackers. I tried to please everyone and the result was that I did a horrible job. I finally came to grips with the fact that my job is to treat people fairly, try to gain their respect, and..."

It is not necessary for the coach to self-disclose on every issue or topic that is discussed in coaching. Too frequent disclosure may even be distracting and confusing to the client. The self-disclosure should not be of such intensity that the coach becomes the focus of the coaching meeting.

Delegation

Delegation is a skill of which we have all heard, but which few understand. It can be used either as an excuse for dumping failure onto the shoulders of subordinates, or as a dynamic tool for motivating and training your team to realize their full potential. Everyone knows about delegation.

Most managers hear about it in the cradle as mother talks earnestly to the babysitter: "Just enjoy the television ... this is what you do if ... if there is any trouble, call me at..."; people have been writing about it for nearly half a millennium, yet few actually understand it.

Delegation underpins a style of management that allows your staff to use and develop their skills and knowledge to the full potential. Without delegation, you lose their full value. Delegation is primarily about entrusting your authority to others. This means that they can act and initiate independently and that they assume responsibility with you for certain tasks. If something goes wrong, you remain responsible since you are the manager. The trick is to delegate in such a way that things get done but do not go (badly) wrong.

The objective of delegation is to get the job done by someone else. Not just the simple tasks of reading instructions and turning a lever, but also the decision making and changes which depend upon new information. With delegation, your staff has the authority to react to situations without referring back to you.

If you tell the janitor to empty the bins on Tuesdays and Fridays, the bins will be emptied on Tuesdays and Fridays. If the bins overflow on Wednesday, they will be emptied on Friday. If instead you said to empty the bins as often as necessary, the janitor would decide how often and adapt to special circumstances. You might suggest a regular schedule (teach the janitor a little personal time management), but by leaving the decision up to the janitor you will apply his/her local knowledge to the problem. Consider this frankly. Do you want to be an expert on bin emptying and can you construct an instruction to cover all possible contingencies? If not, delegate to someone who gets paid for it.

To enable someone else to do the job for you, you must ensure that:

- They know what you want.

- They have the authority to achieve it.

- They know how to do it.

These all depend upon communicating clearly the nature of the task, the extent of their discretion, and the sources of relevant information and knowledge.

Such a system can only operate successfully if the decision makers (your staff) have full and rapid access to the relevant information. This means that you must establish a system to enable the flow of information. This must at least include regular exchanges between your staff so that each is aware of what the others are doing. It should also include briefings by you on the information which you have received in your role as manager, since, if you need to know this information to do your job, your staff will need to know also if they are to do your (delegated) job for you.

One of the main claims being made for computerized information distribution is that it facilitates the rapid dissemination of information. Some protagonists even suggest that such systems will instigate changes in managerial power sharing rather than merely support them - that the "knowledgeable" workforce will rise up, assume control and innovate spontaneously. You may not believe this vision, but you should understand the premise. If a manager restricts access to information, then only he/she is able to make decisions that rely upon that information. Once that access is opened to many others, they too can make decisions and challenge those of the manager according to additional criteria. The manager who fears this challenge will never delegate effectively. The manager who recognizes that the staff may have additional experience and knowledge (and so may enhance the decision making process) will welcome their input. Delegation ensures that the staff will practice decision-making and will feel that their views are welcome.

One of the main phobias about delegation is that by giving others authority, a manager loses control. This need not be the case. If you train your staff to apply the same criteria as you would yourself (by example and full explanations) then they will be exercising your control on your behalf. And since they will witness many more situations over which control may be exercised (you can't be in several places at once) then that control is exercised more diversely and more rapidly than you could exercise it by yourself. In engineering terms, if maintaining control is truly your concern, then you should distribute the control mechanisms to enable parallel and autonomous processing.

To understand delegation, you really have to think about people. Delegation cannot be viewed as an abstract technique. It depends upon individuals and individual needs. Let us take a member of the staff who has little or no knowledge about the job that needs to be done.

Do you say, "Jerry, I want a draft of the new truck specs on my desk by Friday"? No. Do you say, "Jerry, Robert used to do the specs for me. Spend about an hour with him going over how he did them and try compiling the specs for the new truck. He will help you for this one, but come to me if he is too busy with calls. I want a draft by Friday so that I can look over it with you." Possibly.

The key is to delegate gradually. If you present someone with a task which is daunting, one with which he or she does not feel able to cope, then the task will not be done and your staff will be severely *demotivated*. Instead you should build up gradually. First a small task leading to a little development, then another small task which builds upon the first. When that is achieved, add another stage, and so on. This is the difference between asking people to scale a sheer wall, and providing them with a staircase. Each task delegated should have enough complexity to stretch that member of the staff, but only a little.

Jerry needs to feel confident. He needs to believe that he will actually be able to achieve the task that has been given to him. This means that either he must have the sufficient knowledge, or he must know where to get it, or where to get help. So, you must *enable access to the necessary knowledge*. If you hold that knowledge, make sure that Jerry feels able to come to you. If someone else holds the knowledge, make sure that they are prepared for Jerry to come to them. Only if Jerry is sure that support is available will he feel confident enough to undertake a new job.

You need to feel confident in Jerry. This means keeping an eye on him. It would be fatal to cast Jerry adrift and expect him to make it to the shore. Keep an eye on him, and a lifebelt handy. It is also a mistake to keep wandering up to Jerry at odd moments and asking for progress reports. He will soon feel persecuted. Instead you must agree beforehand how often and when you actually need information and *decide the reporting schedule at the onset*. Jerry will then expect these encounters and even feel encouraged by your continuing support. You will be able to check upon progress and even spur it on a little.

When you do talk to Jerry about the project, you should avoid making decisions of which Jerry is capable himself. The whole idea is for Jerry to learn to take over and so he must be encouraged to do so. Of course, with you there to check his decisions, Jerry will feel freer to do so. If Jerry is wrong, tell him, and explain very carefully why. If Jerry is nearly right, congratulate him, and suggest possible modifications but, of course, leave Jerry to decide. Finally, unless your solution has *significant* merits over Jerry's, take his. It costs you little, yet rewards him much.

There is a danger with "open access" that you become too involved with the task you had hoped to delegate. One successful strategy to avoid this is to formalize the manner in which these conversations take place. One formalism is to allow only fixed, regular encounters (except for emergencies) so that Jerry has to think about issues and questions before raising them. You might even insist that he draw up an agenda. A second formalism is to refuse to make a decision unless Jerry has provided you with a clear statement of alternatives, pros and cons, and *his recommendation*. This is my favorite. It allows Jerry to rehearse the full authority of decision making while secure in the knowledge that you will be there to check the outcome. Further, the insistence upon evaluation of alternatives promotes good decision making practices. If Jerry is right, then Jerry's confidence increases. If you disagree with Jerry, he learns something new (provided you explain your criteria) and so his knowledge increases. Whichever way, he benefits and the analysis is provided for you.

Let us consider your undoubtedly high standards. When you delegate a job, it does not have to be done as well as you could do it, but only as well as necessary. Never judge the outcome by what you expect you would do (it is difficult to be objective about that), but rather by fitness for purpose. When you delegate a task, agree then upon the criteria and standards by which the outcome will be judged.

You must enable failure. With appropriate monitoring, you should be able to catch mistakes before they are catastrophic. If not, then the failure is yours. You are the manager, you decided that Jerry could cope, you gave him enough "rope to hang himself," you are at fault. Now that that is cleared up, let us return to Jerry. Suppose Jerry gets something wrong. What do you want to happen?

First, you want it fixed. Since Jerry made the mistake, it is likely that he will need some input to develop a solution. Jerry must feel safe in approaching you with the problem. Thus you must deal primarily with the solution rather than the cause (look forward, not backwards). The most desirable outcome is that Jerry provides the solution.

Once that is dealt with, you can analyze the cause. Do not fudge the issue. If Jerry did something wrong, say so, but only in very specific terms. Look to the actual event or circumstance, which led to the error, "you did not take account of X in your decision." Your objectives are to ensure that Jerry:

- Understands the problem.

- Feels confident enough to resume.

- Implements some procedure to prevent recurrence.

The safest attitude to cultivate is one where Jerry actually looks for and anticipates mistakes. If you wish to promote such behavior, you should always praise Jerry for his prompt and wise action in spotting and dealing with the errors rather than castigate him for causing them. Here the emphasis is placed upon checking/testing/monitoring of ideas. Thus you never criticize Jerry for finding an error, only for not having safeguards in place.

There is always the question of what to delegate and what to do yourself, and you must take a long-term view on this. You want to delegate as much as possible to develop your staff to be as good as you are now.

The starting point is to consider the activities you used to do before you were promoted. You used to do them when you were more junior, so someone junior can do them now. Tasks in which you have experience are the easiest for you to explain to others and so to train them to take over. You thus use your experience to ensure that the task is done well, rather than to actually perform the task yourself. In this way you gain time for your other duties and someone else becomes as good as you once were (increasing the strength of the group).

Tasks in which your staff has more experience must be delegated to them. This does not mean that you relinquish responsibility because they are expert, but it does mean that the default decision should be theirs. To be a good manager though, you should ensure that they spend some time in explaining these decisions to you so that you learn their criteria.

Decisions are a normal managerial function. These, too, should be delegated, especially if they are important to the staff. In practice, you will need to establish the boundaries of these decisions so that you can live with the outcome, but this will only take you a little time while the delegation of the remainder of the task will save you much more.

In terms of motivation for your staff, you should distribute the more mundane tasks as evenly as possible and sprinkle the more exciting ones as widely. In general, but especially with the boring tasks, you should be careful to delegate not only the performance of the task but also its ownership. Task delegation, rather than task assignment, enables innovation. The point you need to get across is that the task may be changed, developed, upgraded, if necessary or desirable. So someone who collates the monthly figures should not feel obliged to blindly type them in every first Monday, but should feel empowered to introduce a more effective reporting format, to use computer software to enhance the data processing, to suggest and implement changes to the task itself.

Since delegation is about handing over authority, you cannot dictate what is delegated nor how that delegation is to be managed. To control the delegation, you need to establish at the beginning the task itself, the reporting schedule, the sources of information, your availability, and the criteria of success. These you must negotiate with your staff. Only by obtaining both their input and their agreement can you hope to arrive at a workable procedure.

Once you have delegated everything, what do you do then? You still need to monitor the tasks you have delegated and to continue the development of your staff to help them exercise their authority well.

There are managerial functions that you should never delegate. These are the personal/personnel ones which are often the most obvious additions to your responsibilities as you assume a managerial role. Specifically, they include motivation, training, team building, organization, praising, reprimanding, performance reviews, and promotion.

As a manager, you have a responsibility to represent and to develop the effectiveness of your group within the company. These are tasks you can expand to fill your available time and delegation is a mechanism for creating that opportunity.

Chapter 8

The Coach's Use
of Self for Change

The Coach's Use of Self for Change

Storying and Restorying

When my precocious son was five years old, I took him on his first backpacking trip to the Rockies. I packed all the essentials for survival in a harsh environment: cigars, a wee bit of hair of the dog, and a paperback novel. My son packed his favorite trucks. What did he know about backpacking? I had our house, toilet, stove, and bed on my back. It was heaven at 10,000 feet. If only I hadn't forgotten my backpacker's ax and the Swiss army knife. Luckily, I had my trusty fingernails and teeth. When we returned home, his mother had allowed the ax and knife to remain right where I left it. A cruel jab, I thought.

"How did you do without your tools?" she asked.

Rather indignantly, as though he himself had been the subject of the poke, he said, "Show her your muscles dad."

I fired up my last cigar…outside of course.

The coach is in the same boat with the client or team, but must be the helmsman. What are the characteristics of that helmsman? What qualifications must a coach have? What inherent tools can be used to guide the craft?

You may not initially know the idiosyncrasies of a client's or even a department's dance, but after reading this book, you will be more aware of your developing style of coaching, and a theoretical set for change. The client will have to accommodate to this style to some extent or in one fashion or another, and then you will have to accommodate to them.

In some cases the individual or team will not automatically accept you, the coach, as the leader of this partnership, choosing instead to challenge your coaching expertise and authority. One can assume that these challenges stem from, (a) the client's discomfort associated with change, (b) the client's inability to see themselves as part of the current problem, or (c) a client's need to discredit you, the coach, in order to relieve themselves of responsibility for change. No matter what approach you bring to the change process, from a personally involved member of the "family" to a removed, objective analyst, you must develop some skill in using yourself as an instrument of change. You also have a growing body of knowledge and experience with individuals, teams, departments, and the process of change.

Coach's Use of Self

Coaches who views themselves as a primary tool for change, and who hone this skill to perfection, stand a greater likelihood of success from one coaching engagement to another. What does "using oneself as a tool" mean? It means employing those most desirable human characteristics for the purpose of helping another person grow.

If one were to think of coaching as somewhere along a continuum between art and science, which side would you be closer to? The "art and science" of coaching assumes a dual role, that of artist and of scientist. On the surface, this seems trite. All of us in coaching agree that a practitioner is first required to master the general principles and proven techniques in the practice of coaching. Later these principles and techniques must be applied skillfully in a way that is appropriate to each case and in a manner that is congruent with each coach's personality. There is, however, much room for disagreement about the degree to which the coach is more like an artist or more like a scientist.

Techniques do not make a coach. The coach's personal qualities, respect for clients, and the desire to see people perform at their highest level are also important. Techniques are the tools, but human qualities are the supreme qualification of the good coach. <u>Compassion</u>—a deeply felt understanding of other people's struggles—<u>sensitivity</u>—an appreciation of people's inner world—<u>encouragement</u>—the ability to stimulate lasting change by increasing self efficacy, can be lost in preoccupation with skills and techniques surrounding change. Without understanding and respect for individuals, coaching remains a technical operation, instead of becoming a living human experience.

Those who perceive coaching as primarily involving skills acquisition may emphasize the technical role of the coach, while those who perceive coaching as primarily involving role acquisition, i.e., leadership role, may emphasize a more artistic role for the coach. Perhaps the best way to become an effective coach is to first learn to be a "scientist" and then become an "artist." A beginner should concentrate on theories of change, and participate in a tutorial program of supervision or mentoring. During this training it is reasonable, even wise, to adopt the technique, style, and even language from one's mentors. Furthermore, it may be necessary to identify and modify or subdue certain types of responses that come naturally.

Assistant Chief Barnes was a manager and volunteer coach within his department. He had a good reputation as someone who possessed empathy with clients. When he worked with fire service personnel, it was immediately apparent that he had a natural gift for understanding and communicating his acceptance of people. Firefighters liked him and they spoke highly of him as a likable person.

Unfortunately, his natural warmth and compassion for people made him respond to performance problems by over utilizing compassion and under utilizing objectivity. He tended to take the side of the client and the client's often limited version of the cause of the problem and their tendency to blame someone or something outside themselves. Although many of his clients were happy to become dependent upon him, they failed to learn how to solve their own performance, leadership, or work relationship problems. Moreover, since they experienced no pressure to resolve their own problems, the coach was left with little leverage to influence them in significant ways. Client problems continued to re-surface. Recognizing this, he sought his own coach/mentor.

In his own coaching-the-coach sessions, Assistant Chief Barnes was helped to recognize and restrain his well meaning but counterproductive tendency to rescue his clients.

> *"Here's an admittedly odd question, Chief Barnes," the coach said. "When you become responsible for a client, how do you know?"*
>
> *"Hmmm…I think I know what you're asking," Chief Barnes said. "I sort of become uncomfortable, anxious."*
>
> *"How so? How do you know you are anxious?"*
>
> *"It's a feeling," the chief said, "a feeling that wells in my chest."*
>
> *"And then what do you do?" the coach asked.*
>
> *"It just sort of takes me over and I jump in with both feet."*
>
> *"What have you imagined would happen if you didn't jump in?"*
>
> *"You know," the chief answered, "I think it's my own anxiety, my own need to fix it. It's like I take on their problem as my own."*
>
> *"Very good! Now imagine the next situation where that feeling comes upon you. What will you do?" the coach asked.*
>
> *"I think at first I should listen or ask probing questions to get them to stretch to find their own solutions."*

Most new coaches, whether young or older come equipped not only with some innately helpful qualities but also with a number of unhelpful impulses. Common among these are, assuming an overly central and controlling position with clients, paying more attention to clients' feelings (or behavior, or thinking) than to other aspects of their experience, taking on the clients' dilemmas as problems to be solved and failing to boost self responsibility, or the converse (fearing rescue and giving too much responsibility to the client without offering support and encouragement), getting angry at resistant clients, and buying into the client's blame of an outside source as the origin of the problem. Because most of these tendencies are automatic reflexes of one's personality style, it is unlikely that newer coaches will be able to identify them without feedback or their own coaching. The only other way to detect troublesome lack of objectivity in a coach is to recognize repeated failures or stalemates with certain types of clients or teams. Once these clues to problem in the coach are identified, supervision, her own coaching, or feedback, will help to determine if the problem stems from inadequate skill or from unrecognized emotional reactivity.

Today, as fire service personnel join organizations but leave their supervisors, as departments constantly push for a competitive advantage, the art or science question is very much with us. Coaches cannot be laissez faire, nor can they be overly controlling, targeting only performance improvement with no regard to self-efficacy, enthusiasm, courage, relationship building, personal style development, diversity utilization, spontaneity, kindness, and respect, to name just a few. Going too far in one direction and the coach displays an inadequate respect for the client's own wisdom and cultural traditions. Too far in the other direction and the coach becomes merely a favorite aunt or uncle. Is the science of coaching tending toward an inadequate respect for clients' own wisdom and cultural traditions? Does an overemphasis on performance improvement diminish such human qualities as intuition, compassion, and emotional intelligence?

My position on the coach's use of self is that he or she must become comfortable with different levels of involvement. Like developing a feel for when to shift gears in a standard automobile, the art of coaching is knowing when to support, when to challenge, when to disagree, when to teach, when to lay back, when to question, when to push, and when to provide answers. There are limitations on the use of self, determined by personal characteristics and the characteristics of the client. But within these limits, the coach can learn to use techniques that require different levels of involvement, such as Connecting, Confirming and "Storying."

Connecting

Connecting is more an attitude than a technique, and it is the umbrella under which much coaching occurs. Without connecting, coaching is merely teaching. Connecting is an assimilation of a number of different skills that can result in the courage to take the risks on the pathway to change.

Connecting includes letting the client know that the coach understands and is working with the client's best interests in mind. Within connecting, the client has the security to explore alternatives and take risks. Connecting is the glue that holds the change process together.

Connecting involves accepting the client where he or she is but, at the same time, encouraging the client to explore her personal responsibility for her current circumstances. The following first example is an interchange between coach and client that demonstrates connecting.

"Thanks for meeting with me," the coach said. "What would you like to tell me about why you are seeking coaching?"

"Of course, the chief asked me to come," Lt. West said. "My last performance evaluation was pretty bad."

"You look discouraged."

"Yes. It wasn't my best year. Although I don't agree with some of the comments, I can see where they would view my performance as sub par. The thing they don't take into consideration is what I had to overcome."

"It sounds like you were beset by new or unforeseen circumstances," the coach said.

"Yes. That's right," the lieutenant said.

"And this affected your performance?"

"It sure did."

"How would you compare your past performances with this latest period?" the coach asked.

"I've always been on top of my game," Lt. West said. "My earlier evaluations were excellent."

"Then my guess is that you were unprepared for these unusual demands. Am I right? Reacting in old ways to new circumstances sometimes isn't effective. In other words, your usual ways of coping just didn't cut it."

"I guess that's right."

"Very well!" the coach said. "I want to help you stretch and discover new ways of responding. External circumstances aside for a moment, tell me, what are you doing that is keeping you from getting what you want?"

Connecting should be an ever present undercurrent. Connecting communicates respect and professional, if not personal, caring. Interestingly, connecting does not always mean agreeing with the client. In fact connecting means caring enough to disagree, correct, or even reprimand. In this vein, reprimands are offered in a respectful, caring manner, not out of power, anger, or an attempt to "one-up" the client.

In this second example, the coach is shadow coaching (observing and debriefing) a client named Bobby during a team meeting. Bobby has complained that his employees do not share information with him. The coach watches Bobby's demeanor to determine whether Bobby unknowingly puts up a roadblock.

The coach said, "Bobby, I cannot stand by and watch you do this without telling you that what you are doing is self defeating. It may get you the immediate results you want but in the long run, people will begin to avoid you."

Like all human creations, connecting is not necessarily a reasoned, deliberate process. Much of the connecting process occurs beneath the surface, in the normal processes of people relating to people. It is also true that the coach's own style will be compatible with some clients or teams, with whom she will find she can be very much herself. But with other clients she may find herself acting more boisterous than usual, or more proper. With some clients she will find herself being more verbal. With others, she will talk less. Her rhythm of speech will change. With some teams she will find herself wanting to talk more to one person. In others, she will talk to all team members. She should observe the changes in herself as responses to the team's implicit transactional patterns and should use these external signals as another level of information about the team.

Confirmation

In Nathaniel Branden's brilliant book, "The Six Pillars of Self-Esteem," he states the following:

> "To trust one's mind and to know that one is worthy of happiness is the essence of self-esteem. The power of this conviction about oneself lies in the fact that it is more than a judgment or a feeling. It is a motivator. It inspires behavior. In turn, it is directly affected by how we act. Causation flows in both directions. There is a continuous feedback loop between our actions in the world and our self-esteem. The level of our self-esteem influences how we act, and how we act influences the level of our self-esteem."

> "If I trust my mind and judgment, I am more likely to operate as a thinking being. Exercising my ability to think, bringing appropriate awareness to my activities, my life works better. This reinforces trust in my mind. If I distrust my mind, I am more likely to be mentally passive, to bring less awareness than I need to my activities, and less persistence in the face of difficulties. When my actions lead to disappointing or painful results, I feel justified in distrusting my mind." (p. 4-5, 1994).

A powerful strategy for counteracting the self-defeating feedback loop between self-esteem and actions back to self-esteem is confirmation. Some coaches use confirmation more than others, largely based upon their personality. Very much akin to the concept of self-fulfilling prophecy, or The Pygmalion Effect, confirmation can be either positive or negative and can be delivered in both subtle as well as obvious ways. How subtle is a subjective thing. We are all familiar with our parent who said, "Whatever you want, dear", but with a raised eyebrow that really meant, "Your choice is wrong. You are making a mistake." While it is true that the raised eyebrow may be subtle, the interpretation of the eyebrow is not. The result was that we trusted ourselves less.

In the same way, coaches confirm either the negative or the positive qualities of their clients. And while none of us can take complete responsibility for how clients will interpret our actions, we can gain more awareness of the impact of our verbal and nonverbal behavior.

Entering into a coaching or mentoring relationship with another person means that the coach takes some responsibility for the client's performance improvement and wellbeing. Under such a circumstance, a rather interesting dynamic ensues that involves apprehension. For example, we are all familiar with the parent who is horror stricken upon seeing their toddler waddling toward the street and oncoming traffic. She dashes toward the child, grabs it by the arm and gives him/her a sharp swat on the backside along with an old fashioned scolding. The child cries and if aged one to two, has little understanding of what just happened. The issue is that the parent was scared beyond belief. All sorts of physiological things occurred in a split second. Although our reaction is most heightened when it is our own child who is headed toward danger, we have similar reactions upon seeing any child in the same predicament. The point is that when we take responsibility for another person, apprehension sometimes clouds our objectivity. Under the influence of apprehension and responsibility, we are hypersensitive to those behaviors, attitudes, and feelings that run counter to our personal map of success.

Those coaches who consistently confirm negative qualities are in need of their own coaching. Much like Freudian analysts who must undergo their own analysis, coaches can gain from feedback regarding their skill in confirming a client's positive qualities. Effective coaches search out positives and make a point of recognizing and rewarding them. They also identify areas of pain, difficulty, or stress and acknowledge them and respond to them with sensitivity.

Coaches may even confirm clients they dislike, and, in fact, being aware of these feelings can be a very powerful way to use oneself as a tool in the coaching relationship. Think about the people you currently like and ask how you have programmed yourself to attend to the facets of those people that confirm your view. In other words, how do you ignore the qualities of your friends that are less attractive? When we like someone, we attend to qualities that confirm our viewpoint. We've all seen news reports of interviews with the friends of murder suspects. We've seen these people come to the defense of the accused and we've all had the same reaction, "How can they possibly defend this person? He/she is obviously guilty!" Later, we find out that the accused was found guilty and we cannot imagine how their supporters could be so naïve. But we all experience this to a greater or lesser degree. The same process happens when we dislike people. We scan for negatives while ignoring positives. Even when this person does something nice or altruistic, we assume ulterior motives. We shield ourselves from uncertainty by focusing on those facets of a person or group that confirm them in their position. When a coach recognizes that she is experiencing dislike, she should carefully use herself as an assessment instrument and ask the following questions:

- If I were not aware of my reactions, how would I likely treat or respond to this person?

- What am I really irritated with, frustrated by, or afraid of?

- What does this person trigger for me?

- What does my reaction to this person say about me?

- What kind of non-verbal feedback does this client likely get from other people?

- Does this non-verbal feedback differ depending upon their status (employee or supervisor)?

- What ego defense does this person use to deal with these reactions?

- What is the purpose of the client's behavior? How can negative, self defeating behavior be reframed and viewed in a positive manner?

Coaches who can simultaneously be aware of their personal feelings, yet remain objective and confirm the client's positive qualities can help the client understand how their actions impact those people in their immediate sphere of influence, which creates a feedback loop that in turn affects their self esteem. The first example illustrates a coach who confirms negative qualities.

Jim Snow was an extroverted fire officer of the public education section of a large fire department. The coach reported that Jim was one of the most personable people he had ever met and that upon experiencing Jim's charisma, he became fascinated with how things went awry as reported by the referring fire chief. Jim demonstrated all of the admired qualities, good looks, confidence, eye contact, and a pleasant smile. He was both solicitous of other people's thoughts and interested in hearing about their life experiences. People were drawn to him.

Over time, however, news out of Jim's section was that when he was not in the spotlight, his employees found him to be withdrawn, sullen, and possessing low energy. The coach decided that the best way to observe Jim was through shadow coaching. Several shadow sessions revealed that approximately one-half of Jim's group avoided him outright and went about business in an unfocused manner. Another portion of his group openly defied him whenever he made suggestions, and a smaller portion of people formed an alliance with him and babied him whenever he was upset or sullen.

> *"I would like to share my observations with you," the coach said.*
>
> *"All right, go ahead," Jim replied.*
>
> *"Are you aware of your voice, posture, and facial expressions?"*
>
> *"What about them?"*
>
> *"You seem down, sometimes even angry."*
>
> *"Well, that's probably because I am down and angry," Jim said.*
>
> *"I don't think your ideas are bad, Jim," the coach said, "but I think your demeanor puts people off."*
>
> *"Oh great!" Jim laughed "My worse fear is realized. I'm letting people down."*
>
> *"Jim, you just need to be yourself."*

In this example, the coach unknowingly becomes a part of the negative feedback loop that already affects Jim. Negative reactions from others diminish Jim's self esteem and thus, diminish effective behavior. His trust in himself was so diminished that "being himself" was merely confusing. Jim, like others with diminished self-esteem, don't really know what being one's self is.

In the next example, the coach realizes that because performance is affected by a negative feedback loop, chooses to confirm Jim's positive qualities.

> *"Before sharing my observations," the coach said, "I would like to hear what you are aware of during your meetings."*
>
> *Jim said, "Some people seem uninvolved, others seem downright nasty. Why? What does it mean?"*
>
> *"Let's go there together. Tell me Jim, what were you aware of about yourself?"*

> "I was tired, downright exhausted," Jim said. "Sometimes I feel like the entire universe rests on my back."
>
> "That can be a tremendous burden. What do you think about your staff's ability to succeed without you?"
>
> "No way! They couldn't make their objectives."
>
> "So, could you be taking on the burden for everyone in order to ensure success?" the coach asked.
>
> "Yes, could be."
>
> "I trust that your back is strong. Doing for other people too much can become habitual. How are you teaching people to treat you?"
>
> "I'm probably teaching them that they don't have to be too responsible. I'll handle the work for them," Jim said.
>
> The coach asked, "Would you like to have a choice as to whether you do this?"
>
> "Of course."
>
> "It may be helpful to understand what triggers you to do this. Would you characterize yourself as tending toward pleasing?"
>
> "Absolutely," Jim responded.
>
> "You are a caring person. Do you dislike saying 'no' to people?" the coach asked.
>
> "It's the hardest damned thing for me to do."
>
> "How does your group keep you feeling overwhelmed?"
>
> "They either ignore me or defy me," Jim said. "They're out of control."

In this example, the client's feelings were recognized in an area of difficulty without being criticized or made guilty about it, and he may respond to the coach as if personally confirmed.

Confirmation goes on throughout coaching. The coach continually scans for and emphasizes positive ways of looking at the client's functioning while pursuing the goals of change. It is the one place where the client is allowed to step back and look at contributors to performance, not simply results, results, results, under any and all circumstances. The coach is always a source of support and nurturance as well as the leader and director of the coaching relationship.

"Storying," Not Story

Not long ago, a client called me about twenty-four hours after our meeting sounding perplexed. He could be described as an anxious, impatient, hard driving sort. "It's not working," he said.

"What do you mean?" I replied.

"The coaching. It's not working. Whenever we address an issue and I feel settled, another one pops up."

Frankly, I was a bit relieved. He was evolving and didn't know it. I merely had to reframe that what was happening was to be expected. He, like most of us, wanted a fix all solution for all of our problems until the end of time. I thought about my preschooler who comes to us with a problem and a story about how he was wronged. He wants to feel better as quickly as possible. As such, a story tells us who said or did what, when, where, and in what manner. As in a movie, there is an ending, it is complete. Case closed. Frankly, stories are not very helpful beyond enough details to get a picture of what happened. Furthermore, in adult life and in coaching, no story is ever complete or totally understood.

What is relevant to the coaching meeting is what happens between the coach and client. What becomes most important is change, not as an end in itself, but evolving change to meet ever changing circumstances and challenges. If there is an end, it is that the goal of coaching is to develop confidence in the face of life's challenges -- self-efficacy. According to Branden (1994), "Self-efficacy means confidence in the functioning of my mind, in my ability to think, understand, learn, choose, and make decisions. Confidence in my ability to understand the facts of reality that fall within the sphere of my interests and needs, self-trust, self-reliance (p. 26).

An example is a female firefighter who said that she was not given the same respect as the men. During the meeting with her, I was less focused on whether she was relating an accurate perception of the events and more on the meaning she attributed to the events as she told them. I asked her the following questions to facilitate the meaning of the story she told, her reactions that were ultimately not to her satisfaction, and goal setting:

- Are you a participant in the event that you are going to tell me?

- And what are two words you would use to describe you in the story you are going to tell me?

- Who else is in the story?

- And what are two words you would use to describe him/her in the story you are going to tell me?

- As if extracting only the most important scene, tell me what happened.

- How do you want to be?

- What do you want to happen from coaching?

- How will this (what she wants) make a difference?

- How will you know the problem is solved?

- How are you experiencing some of what you want now?

Arguably the most confirming method to have emerged in recent years and one designed specifically for "storying" is Playback Theater—the improvisational reenactment of personal story—developed by Jonathan Fox. According to Jo Salas, one of Playback Theater's original troupe members, and author of *Improvising Real Life* (1993),

> "The idea of Playback Theatre is very simple. And yet its implications are complex and profound. When people are…invited to tell personal stories to be acted out, there are a number of messages and values that are communicated, many of which are radically at odds with the prevailing messages of our culture. One is the idea that you, your personal experience, is worthy of this kind of attention. We are saying that your life is a fit subject for art, that others may find your story interesting, may learn from it, be moved by it. We are also saying that…story itself is of the profoundest importance, that we need stories to construct meaning in our lives, and that our lives themselves are full of stories, if we can learn to discern them.
>
> People who for some reason cannot tell their story are at a terrible disadvantage. We need to be heard, to be affirmed and welcomed as one who shares the human condition." (pp. 7-19)

Playback Theatre is most effective in team coaching and will be discussed later in this book. But the premise of validating story certainly applies to the individual coaching arena as well. And the job of the coach is more than simply sitting back and listening to someone drone on about details.

In addition to the affirmation that is offered through telling one's story, the "storying" process must offer more. While, the immediate focus is the content of the story, who said or did what, when, where, and how, any experienced coach recognizes that the real work of coaching happens between the lines of content in the realm known as <u>process</u>.

Who, what, when, where, and how is merely that part of a story that is consciously available. The more important aspect of a story, that which is both part and parcel of why we do what we do, and that which is less available to our conscious mind is the meaning that we create as we formulate and tell the story. The language used to tell the story is more than representational of experience. It is itself creational. According to Walter and Peller, in Miller et al (1996),

> "In everyday conversation, most people think of words as representing objects apart from themselves. They think of words as symbols that represent as close as possible an observable world. They assume that everybody who uses the word 'tree' means the same thing

because there is an object out there that the word refers to. When language is thought of as creational, however, the implication is that the word "tree" draws forth the experience of tree. The word "tree" does not take on meaning until it is used. This means that people make meaning of their lives through language...Language does represent experience-it is inseparable from it." (pp12-13)

Therefore, because the client creates her own meaning through language and story and behaves as though her meaning is reality, not just her personal interpretation of reality, the coach cannot dictate meaning without the risk of "mugging" the meeting. The generic purpose of coaching on the way to performance improvement is to help the client evolve from blame and externalization as the explanation of the problem, to a more conscious understanding and personal responsibility. We want the client to live a more conscious life and in doing so, to take responsibility for her actions.

In the example that follows, note how the coach moves the level of transaction from content to interpersonal process, keeping the focus on the same issue. Here the coach is leading the client toward a performance enhancing exploration by helping him gain greater awareness of what he may be doing that gets him the responses he does not want. The client, Fire Marshal Jarrell, is the manager of a new stock brokerage division. It is five minutes into the meeting.

"I'm interested in what you want from coaching," the coach said.

"The higher ups have only one thing in mind," Jarell said, "to get the plans reviewed faster. They set our goal at turning plans around in a week this year. As fast as the city is growing, that's going to be tough. Frankly, I wish plan review was all I had to worry about. I'm managing a bunch of competitive people who will jump ship when they sense that it is sinking. They want to be promoted, not stuck in fire inspections."

"If a miracle happened tonight while you were sleeping and you woke up tomorrow and these problems were solved, how would you know the problems were solved or that your life was going more the way you want?"

"I would be confident," the fire marshal said.

"What problems would this solve?"

"I would quit worrying about how I look to everyone."

"You worry about how you look?" the coach asked.

"Down deep, I think I doubt my ability to pull this off. I mean a one week turnaround on plans, more commercial fire inspections, and it's just a start. The city manager is on our backs."

continued

> *"It sounds like the issue before us is confidence. Would you agree?" the coach asked.*
>
> *"I never tried to put it in that light. But it's something I can control," the fire marshal replied.*
>
> *"Keeping this issue of confidence in mind, do you know what you are doing that contributes to results that you do not want?"*
>
> *"I waver," he said. "I get anxious about the dozens of things I have to attend to and I give in to my veteran inspectors. Don't get me wrong, they're experienced. But their ways are a bit outmoded. I need to trust that my youth and training might serve me well now."*
>
> *The coach asked, "What do you want to do differently and what do you guess could happen?"*
>
> *"I want to listen and then stand firm."*
>
> *"How will you know it's working?" the coach asked.*
>
> *"Two things," the fire marshal replied. "When I am doing things differently and when my inspectors are focused and more productive."*

In this case, the coach gently focuses the responsibility for action on Fire Marshal Jarrell. He knew that, as a general rule, people respond in habitual ways, particularly in the midst of anxiety. As such, Fire Marshal Jarrell has "blind spots" regarding the way he responds. Even in the face of failure, most of us use the same solutions and therefore get the same result. Even in the face of contrary evidence, we follow the script all the way to the bitter end.

In this case, as in many in coaching, the coach had no expertise in the brokerage business. This is not paramount. The coach's job is to take what the client says at face value and to allow the client an opportunity to be a partner in the change process. Initially, it is vital that the coach not impose meaning upon the client's story.

In addition to supporting a client or team, connecting may include challenging, disputing, pushing, etc. Regardless of the technique, the underlying feature of connecting is the conveyance of the possibility of change.

Since the coach's use of self in the change process is the most powerful tool in the process of changing the client or team, coaches need to be knowledgeable about the range of their connecting repertory. Some people `are comfortable and natural with certain clients and situations over others.

One of the true pioneers in the understanding of human nature was Alfred Adler, an Austrian born psychologist. A contemporary of Sigmund Freud, Adler broke from Freud along several dimensions. Adler theorized that human nature and thus, behavior, could not be explained by psychosexual urges, but rather that human behavior is teleo-analytic, that is, moving toward a self-determined goal. The movement toward this goal within a social context explains why we do what we do. Therefore, it is the social context that fixes the meaning of behavior.

Here's how it works! There are a few things to keep in mind:

1. People come to fire service with established, albeit unconscious goals and a set of needs that can only be met in concert with other people.

2. We all need to belong, to be a part of the brotherhood.

3. We also need to express ourselves, to be unique.

4. There must be meaning or purpose in our lives to maintain motivation.

Because the social context is the way in which humans get their needs met, unspoken and unconscious rules are established. Systems are self-correcting. The feedback loop is the way a system gets information necessary to self-correct.

These are not the kinds of things we are conscious of unless we are reading self-help books, attending personal growth seminars, or in counseling, but are nevertheless, powerful contributors to what we do and how we do it. By the same token, goals, which vary somewhat from one person to another, may be thought of as guiding fictions, privately held beliefs that guide our behavior in a forward fashion toward some satisfactory end. Four rather easily recognizable goals include:

1. Power

2. Influence

3. Security

4. Perfection

People in systems tend to respond to these goals in a consistent manner. People who strive for power are usually task oriented, impatient, demanding, commanding, and impulsive. Others respond to them with dependency and avoidance. In turn, the power oriented person views them as weak which means that he/she must become more demanding.

People who seek influence are usually relationship oriented, desire variety and change, avoid rules and restrictions, are trusting, charismatic, less detail oriented, and visionary. Others view them as scattered and irresponsible, and therefore pick up after them. This allows the influential person to avoid responsibility and continue unfettered.

People who seek security are often unassertive, sensitive to the emotional atmosphere, patient, good listeners, fear rejection, and desire familiarity in tasks and environment. Others view them as emotionally weak and unassertive and respond in a dictatorial fashion. The security minded person responds by depending upon others for guidance.

People who seek perfection are often uncomfortable with change, detail oriented, emotionally isolated, rely upon rules and regulations, are observers of the environment, lack spontaneity, and have a harder time seeing the big picture. Others view them as rigid and slow to make decisions. In turn, this person views others as frivolous, pushy and responds by tightening the controls.

The family of origin is the training ground for meeting these needs and establishes specific expectations regarding future success in need satisfaction. Therefore, behavioral, cognitive, emotional, and spiritual patterns are created that are then carried into the workplace and replayed over and over again. The way someone responds to criticism, the manner in which someone leads others, the method by which a person operates within a team, and the degree to which someone is an effective follower is largely determined by goal striving and expectations of need satisfaction.

Chapter 9

The Skills
of Encouragement

The Skills of Encouragement

Introduction

I recently ran into a former colleague of mine from my days as a university teacher. I was curious about how things in the department were going, so I asked him about the new chairperson.

> *"He's a great leader," my friend said.*
>
> *"Excellent." I said. "How so?"*
>
> *"Oh…well, he knows how to motivate everyone."*
>
> *"How so?" I pressed on.*
>
> *"Well…you know…it's one of those things you can't really put a finger on but you know it when it's there."*

Do most of us really know what leadership is? Or what motivation is all about? What is the difference between being a "Leader" and being a "Boss"? Just what are the differences? How does a "Leader" lead? And how does a "Boss" boss? And more importantly, how does this affect the motivation and stress levels of those who are led or bossed. I believe that the major differences that separate the "Leader" from the "Boss" are quite clearly defined as shown below. You are a "Leader" if you:

- Can get and hold the confidence of the people who you have authority over.

- Are able to show them how to do the job in the right way.

- Can instruct them in such a manner that they will want to do the job in the right way.

- Have the necessary people skills to handle those around you in such a way that they will always be "for" you at all times.

- Have the ability to put people at ease.

- Are able to discipline someone in a way that does not cause enmity.

- Can put someone forward for promotion, even if you do not personally like them.

"Leaders" have confidence and trust in their people. They believe in them, and importantly, they let their people know that they believe in them. "Leaders" give credit where credit is due. They do not seek all the credit themselves. "Leaders" do not hand out praise unless it is deserved, but when it is, it is sincerely and appreciatively given. A "Leader" requests and explains. He sells the objective and the organization.

So, how does a "Boss" differ from a "Leader"? A "Boss" uses implied threats. If it is necessary for some to leave the organization, they have to go. But never threaten without reason or intent if you are not prepared to follow through. If you are intending to become a "Leader" instead of a "Boss," you may find it difficult initially. The transition from one to the other is not achieved easily, but if you are prepared to work towards becoming a "Leader" you will find that there will be a substantial improvement in the effectiveness and morale of your people and yourself. To summarize, a "Boss":

- Drives people. Instills fear and uncertainty.

- Says, "Go and do it."

- Makes work a grind and wears people down.

- Relies on the authority of their position i.e. "I am the "Boss," you do what I tell you."

- Constantly says - "I", "I", "I."

Whereas a "Leader":

- Guides people.

- Inspires enthusiasm.

- Says, "Let's go."

- Makes work interesting.

- Says, "We" instead of "You."

True leadership relies on cooperation and feedback. To be a "Leader" you must cultivate the foundations of cooperation that includes understanding, courage, friendliness, confidence, competence, appreciation, and goodwill. These are vitally important to any officer. There are at least ten factors that will help you achieve cooperation:

1. Understanding the source of each person's motivation and why they do what they do

2. The ability to make other people feel important

3. The ability to be tactful and courteous

4. Self-confidence

5. A positive viewpoint

6. The ability to develop people

7. Giving heart-felt praise

8. Being open minded

9. Having genuine enthusiasm

10. Possessing good listening skills

I quote John Fitzgerald Kennedy, "The desire to be important is the strongest urge in human nature." That is why this ability is at the very top of this list. True leadership must be for the benefit of the followers, not for the enrichment of the leaders.

Motivation

Just what is meant by motivation? Most of us assume that pay is the primary motivator. While it is true that paying someone six figures a year goes a long way toward meeting their needs, I believe that motivation is what sparks fire service personnel to want to do something.

At a recent IAFC seminar, one participant said that a member of his command staff was taking extended time off because his Doctor had signed him out due to stress. The participant's response was "How can he be stressed, when he received a significant pay raise last month?"

Pay certainly enables us to buy food, shelter, and our "toys" and, to some extent, it satisfies some social and psychological needs. But we as coaches and leaders are on shaky ground if we believe that money is the sole motivator for the right type of behavior needed for any given position. Money is exciting, but not a motivator to do a job better or the right way. Neither does money help us slog through the tough departmental challenges that require leadership acumen. Money instills neither skills nor desire, at least not for very long.

Everyone knows that we get paid to work. We also know that in order to get people to go to work, we must pay them, although if you ask people what they are paying for, they will invariably give you two groups of answers: "A fair day's pay for a fair day's work" or "We pay for performance."

It is certainly far more complex than either of the above answers. If we pay for a five-day week, we are paying for time, 40 or more hours per week. This means that we might have employees who start at eight, finish at five, and don't do a lot in between (presenteeism).

If we pay for performance, we need to decide what our measures are. Performance standards in many organizations measure anything but performance. Accurate performance assessment is difficult, which is why many people find it easiest to pay for time. What could we pay for? *Time, Productivity, or Customer Service.* We can group the above under one heading: *Performance.* If we are not clear about what it is that we are paying for, we can inadvertently give the wrong signals to people and find that we are paying for something that we do not want.

Is Pay Reward?

Admittedly, many of you will have little to do with pay. Nevertheless, it is important to understand the role that money plays in the total reward strategy. A reward strategy is about developing and integrating a whole range of management tactics to ensure that people deliver. These can include performance appraisals, benchmarking for job fit, and less formal methods like encouragement.

1. Ensure that the organization can recruit the quantity and quality of staff it needs to meet its performance targets.

2. Develop the "fit" between organization and people (integrating interests and aptitudes).

3. Provide rewards for good performance and incentives for further performance improvements.

4. Make sure that similar jobs are paid similar rates (this is a legal requirement).

5. Make sure that the different character of different jobs is recognized.

6. Create flexibility to ensure that the system can accommodate particular needs (for instance, if a company needs an "expert" who will be paid more than the Head of Department).

7. Be robust. This is simple to explain, operate and control.

8. Be cost effective.

The essential elements of effective pay systems are the *balance* and *linkage*. *Balance* means that the pay system should never be allowed to get out of control. Pay should reflect the levels of performance that the individual worker produces. *Linkage* means that there should be a clear and recognizable link between pay and performance. Because of the way in which people are paid, i.e. into bank accounts, people can sometimes lose sight of the links between pay and performance. Numbers appear in their bank or building society account at the end of the month, with no apparent connection to performance at work. Accountabilities are a central feature in maintaining this linkage.

Motivating Through Work Design

Apart from paying people to do the job, what else can an organization do to motivate it's people? First, we can consider the work of Herzburg and his theory on "job enrichment." If jobs are narrow, fragmented and restrictive, it is possible to redesign work to make them more interesting. Herzberg argued for what he referred to as "vertical job loading," in which the employee is given increased authority and challenge within the job, together with more feedback. Hackman (J.R. Hackman & G.R. Oldham, *Work Design*, 1980) took Herzburg's theories further and argued that it was necessary for three more components to be added to ensure that job redesign experiments were successful.

1. People need to see that their work is meaningful and worthwhile e.g. if John is putting box after box on a conveyer belt, he needs to know why he is doing it and how his task fits into the overall functions of the organization.

2. People need to feel personally accountable for the work that they do. Working in organizations can often contribute to a loss of identity.

3. Neither of the above factors can exist without the third, effective feedback, being in place. Without knowledge of progress, it is difficult to feel motivated about work.

Motivating Through Targets—The Perception Of Need

It is generally accepted that people's needs fall into two groups, *Expectancy theories* and *Gestalt theories*. *Expectancy theory* focuses on the connections between goal or objective achievement and performance. In other words, if you supply people with the necessary means to meet their needs, they are likely to behave in a way which will encourage them to continue this behavior, i.e., constantly fulfilling their needs. However, it isn't that simple at all. We all know that different things appeal to different people, i.e., a prestigious car might motivate the super salesman, but it may be a turnoff for the average good performer who would be more switched on by an extra week's holiday for his efforts. A factor that is largely ignored when the annual targets are set is that *people only achieve goals if they consider the goals realistic*. People act as judges in determining whether or not there is a reasonable and realistic probability of them succeeding or failing in the achievement of the task, i.e., the target. Usually, if they consider that it is pointless to attempt to achieve the targets they become apathetic and withdrawn. They become de-motivated.

In the *Gestalt theory*, the belief is that people want to achieve things, i.e., to create stability, simplicity and order in their environment. How often have we heard ourselves and others say "lets keep it simple" meaning this or that is too complicated to achieve easily. Put simply, the Gestalt theory is all about *'closure'* or *completion*. Most of us have a basic need to want to finish things. If we are unable to tie up the loose ends of a problem or situation, we generally feel frustrated and look to other ways of completing the job in hand. But, as most of us are aware, life is full of incomplete situations at work and at home. The Gestalt school views much of our behavior as our attempts to achieve closure or completion in our lives in different ways. It may very well be, that the Gestalt Theory is the reason for Volvo's successful production methods. By having one group of people involved in the completion of most or a major part of the vehicle, instead of having the whole process in separate production facilities that left their employees unable to have the opportunity to complete the task. So, what initially appears to be a simple, i.e. motivational, theory being about managing people's behavior to meet their needs, is far more complex than most of us thought from the start.

Job Characteristics That Contribute to Motivation

- *Variety*—In the job, in the tools used, the place where the job is carried out and the people whom the employee meets.

- *Autonomy*—In the way the task is carried out.

- *Responsibility*—Jobs are often designed to operate within authority structures and this can lead to a reduction in the employee's sense of responsibility for the task. Managers can become swamped with enquiries about "how to do" the task. Unfortunately this is a variant of Parkinson's Law at work, "The availability of a factor will ensure its use."

- *Challenge*—The degree to which a job presents an opportunity for growth and development is a major factor, which contributes greatly to the meaning of the job.

- *Interaction*—This is the way in which people holding a job meet and respond to other people.

- *Task significance*—This again gives meaning to a job. For example the technician who works on the Space Shuttle's life support system is more likely to produce a high quality performance than someone whose job function is to empty the trash. The Space Shuttle technician sees the task as significant.

- *Goals and Feedback*—Without clear accepted goals or objectives, nothing is very likely to succeed. People need to know how they are doing on the job.

Participation and Motivation

William White in his book *Money and Motivation* quotes a classic example of the effects of Participation upon Motivation:

> "A group of staff-all women-were responsible for painting dolls in a toy factory. The women worked a new system whereby each woman took a toy from a tray, painted it, and then put it on a hook passing by on a belt. They received an hourly rate, group bonus and a learning bonus. Production declined dramatically. Staff morale was very low. They complained about the heat and the speed of the belt. Reluctantly, the supervisor met the staff and an agreement was ultimately reached to put fans into the workshop (although the engineer was sure that they would make no difference to the temperature.) The installation of the fans led to a significant increase in morale and further talks led to the women making a radical suggestion - that they be allowed to control the speed of the belt - this was reluctantly agreed to. The staff worked out a complicated schedule in which the belt was fast at some times and slow at other times. Morale shot up and the women were earning more than many "senior" staff members. As a result, the experiment was discontinued. Production dropped, morale plummeted and most of the women left."

The idea of "quality circles" is based upon the above experiment. Groups are encouraged to participate in the planning and implementation of their work; they are not paid for their contribution, although it is often acknowledged in other ways such as in the company magazine, at the annual conference or sweatshirts and T- shirts.

Participation may, however, sometimes bring its own set of problems if it is not put into practice with complete honesty. Most managers generally pay " lipservice" to the concept of participation, i.e., it is fine for them but not for the staff. This is because most managers are reluctant to "trust" and are of two minds about their own attitude towards power and control.

How Do Leadership and Motivation Affect Stress Levels?

Most of the people that I have coached over the years who suffered with work-related stress, have been victims of poor management practices. They have been bossed, not led. They had little or no control over how they did their job. They had rarely been told how their contribution fitted in with the department's/organization's objectives. A major similarity was that most of them felt that they received little or no recognition for their efforts and there was a distinct lack of feedback from their manager. Most felt that they had no opportunity to grow within the organization nor had the chance to develop as individuals. Some felt that their superior officer/boss had placed obstacles in their way. Quite a number of people felt that the management represented a straight-jacket of authority, i.e., everything was decided at the top, without any participation or consultation whatsoever.

For 'Bosses' who want to become 'Leaders' I summarize the essential qualities necessary for the transition. The four most important characteristics of leadership are (ref. James Kouzes and Barry Posner):

- *Honesty-* Leaders are expected to behave in a truthful, ethical and principled way. They must show consistency between word and deed.

- *Competence-* In order to be persuaded to follow a person we must believe that that person is capable of doing what they are responsible for doing.

- *Forward Looking-* We expect our leaders to have a concern for the future and to communicate a clear sense of direction.

- *Inspiration-* We follow people who are enthusiastic, energetic and positive and who inspire confidence and excitement.

Encouragement

Encouragement is such a vital skill and one that is so misunderstood that we decided to insert it as an entire chapter. It is the most vital leadership skill in fire service today and one that coaches must develop. Encouragement is more than just a pat on the back.

The next time you are with a group of people, look for the encourager. He or she is the one whose presence and behavior mobilizes the resources of each person, and who conveys that energy giving optimism that raises performance. The encouraging person is buoyed up by the advantage of being positive, of being certain that life is worth living, that people would rather hope than despair, that fear is the only enemy, and that self-loathing is the true source of relationship problems.

The antidote to fear and self-loathing is courage. Courage is produced by encouragement and is the desire to try and fail and try again. Courage is the knowledge that we are imperfect but that we each have strengths and gifts that lead to success. Courage is synonymous with action and personal accountability. The antithesis of courage is not fear, but rather procrastination, indecision, and negligence. The encouraging leader and coach's gift is a positive attitude coupled with the skills to inspire others to believe in themselves. Actually, this entire book is about how to become an encourager to both yourself and to others. Perhaps there is no other leadership or coaching skill that is more important.

Think about a time when, as a young child, you worked hard to achieve a certain goal. Do you remember the feeling of satisfaction when you finally reached your goal? Who was the first person you wanted to tell about your success?

Now think about a time when you had a problem and needed to talk to someone. Who was the person you usually sought out to discuss your feelings with? Why did you choose that person? What did he or she do to help you? When we are down in the dumps, some people always seem to have the talent to help us re-energize and move on to face our stresses, pressures, and the demands of life.

We call those positive people to whom we are attracted and with whom we share our interests, encouragers. What makes encouragers so appealing to us? Are there common patterns that exist in most encouragers? To discover whether there are patterns in these effective people, we talked to many fire service personnel, perhaps like you, to talking about the encouraging people in their lives. Interestingly, we found that encouragers exist in most all departments. Some people chose parents, friends, teachers, supervisors, fire officers, and fire chiefs, as being the most encouraging to them. To better understand the specific skills of the encourager, we asked people to jot down the ingredients of their relationship with the influencing other person. We asked them to write down what was special about this relationship.

We have listed some of what we feel are representative of the most frequently listed answers to this question. Do any of these observations match your responses?

"This person listened and didn't immediately tell me I was wrong."

"This person understood how I felt."

"In this relationship, I felt like a winner. I think this person felt that I was talented or special somehow."

"I could be honest with this person and wouldn't have to be phony and didn't fear the results. I was even willing to be responsible for what I did if it were wrong."

"I could disagree with this person and wasn't afraid of making him or her angry."

"This person always had time for me."

"This person had a good sense of humor."

"This person was enthusiastic about my experience."

Here are some of the comments people made concerning the characteristics of the most discouraging people in their lives.

"This person never listened to me when I talked and was always too busy."

"This person always expected perfection from me."

"This person only noticed my bad points."

"I was always scared around this person. This person was unpredictable."

By doing this exercise with fire service personnel, it became clear to us that there were characteristics encouragers had that discouragers clearly lacked. An example is listening. Encouragers were described as people who listened without judging or condemning. Discouragers, on the other hand, were described as people who were not effective listeners. From our information, we can list the characteristics of both discouragers as well as encouragers.

<u>Discouragers</u>	<u>Encouragers</u>
Are ineffective listeners	Are effective listeners
Focus on negatives	Focus on positives
Compete and compare	Cooperate
Threaten and manipulate	Accept
Use sarcasm and embarrassment	Use humor and hope
Humiliate	Stimulate
Recognize only well-done tasks	Recognize and reward effort
Are disinterested in feelings	Are interested in feelings
Base worth on performance	Base worth on just being

Encouragement is the key ingredient underlying all positive personal and professional relationships. Did you ever have a doctor who was quite knowledgeable about medicine but had a poor, impersonal bedside manner? This doctor may have been insensitive to your needs and may have created undue anxiety on your part. All the knowledge or leadership skills in the world are ineffective in the hands of an insensitive person who lacks understanding of people.

Change and Encouragement

Organizations spend millions each year in an effort to discover ways of improving our skills in motivating people to a fuller development of talents and resources. And while we assert that while people do not change that much, we also assert that people do not need to change much in order to exhibit outstanding performance. It is job fit that determines, to a great extent, how someone will perform on the job. Thus, it is pessimistic to assume that people who are not right for their job are not right for any position in the organization. The realistic and more optimistic view is that while heredity and environment determine, to a large extent, one's personality, we also possess free will and can adjust accordingly given the proper job fit with our behaviors and aptitudes.

The famous psychologist, Alfred Adler, stated that people do have the capacity for constructive change in their lives and that this change is more likely to occur in a relationship with a person who is encouraging.

This interest in helping people grow and reach a fuller development of their resources is the purpose of this book and of coaching. The world is looking for positive people who bring out the best in others, people who are encouraging.

People who are unhappy and unproductive are not disturbed, rather, they are discouraged. They lack faith in their ability to grow and take risks in more self-fulfilling directions. This immobilization, fear of failure, or negative goal seeking, is reflected in a lifestyle overwhelmed with a theme of "I can't change."

Encouragement is the process of facilitating the development of a person's inner resources and courage toward positive movement. The encouraging person helps the discouraged person remove some of the self imposed attitudinal roadblocks. The goal of encouragement then is to aid the individual to move from a philosophy of "I can't" to the more productive "I will" in order to help people find their own "personal power." With increasing courage, the individual starts to move from irresponsible to responsible; helpless to capable and powerful; self-destructive to helpful to others.

The Psychology of Encouragement

Why do people do the things they do? A firefighter is disciplined for repeated critical incident mistakes yet continues to make the same mistakes.

A chief receives the 360 degree feedback that his leadership is harsh and discouraging, yet he continues to behave in an arrogant and critical manner.

Why they do what they do is difficult to understand. It makes no sense to us as observers. The reason behavior doesn't make sense is because we tend to limit our understanding of human behavior. Most of us don't have an effective theory that enables us to understand as well as predict why people do what they do.

To be an encouraging person, it is essential to have meaningful and effective beliefs about human behavior. Without basic beliefs, we tend to react to behavior instead of respond. We experience behavior that we don't understand, get frustrated, and react, usually with an equal and opposite reaction. Reacting is automatic, with no flexibility. There is no decision or choice.

To be an encouraging person requires understanding the reason for the behavior. We can only become more encouraging as we learn to understand why people behave the way they do. Encouragement then becomes a method for motivating people.

Motivation, from our point of view, means understanding the reason for the behavior. Behavior makes sense to the person behaving. We need to understand the behavior from that person's perception or point of view.

When behavior is understood in terms of cause, the concern is with what caused a particular action instead of the purpose of the action. All behavior has a purpose. It is self-determined and chosen instead of just influenced by some event beyond our control. We choose to decide and move in the direction of our purposes and goals.

Goals give direction and become the basis for final explanation of behavior. What people seek or attempt to achieve explains why they behave in a way that may not make sense to anyone but them. While each of us may not always be aware of our goals, they are created, chosen, or decided upon by us, and they give direction to all of our relationships. You'll recall from the Extended DISC® that each of the four major Personalities (described in detail in Chapter 4) have specific attitudes and behaviors, goals and motives, needs and wants.

It is the fulfillment of needs and wants that makes us feel a sense of belonging, the most basic of goals for every person. All of our psychological movement is pulled by a specific purpose or goal. This is contrary to the belief that behavior is taught. Human behavior is far more than the result of a cause. We choose, decide, and then move in the direction of our goals. Goals are the final cause or explanation of behavior. The goal in itself tells us the why or the reason for the behavior. Understanding goal striving is the underpinning for encouragement.

To Encourage a Person
Optimism

Optimism is a sign of power and potential. To be effective, coaches should focus on the strengths of people within their assessed personality style. All leaders and coaches at one time become over concerned with what doesn't work, or the down side. Fears and limitations become all encompassing.

Martin Seligman, in his book *Learned Optimism* (1991), has developed the scientific basis for optimism. People can either be pessimistic, discouraged and helpless, or optimistic, positive, courageous, and seek solutions.

As Seligman indicates, there are three crucial dimensions to explanatory style: permanence, pervasiveness, and personalization. These become beliefs that direct behavior.

Permanence

Permanence is the belief that things that cause negative or bad events in life are permanent. "There's nothing I can do. I am helpless." Events are seen in terms of always and never, permanent, and pessimistic. The optimistic, courageous person has a certainty that no problem is permanent and things will change. "I can find a way through this." Optimists see the good events in their lives as related to their positive traits and abilities and not to their moods or feelings.

Pervasiveness

This is a tendency to catastrophize. If one thing isn't working, other things aren't working. Soon the negativism has spread like the plague.

Positive people make specific explanations and don't generalize the bad to everything in their lives. Negative beliefs are challenged. They do not see themselves as the problem but believe they are responsible for changing the situation.

Personalization

When bad things happen, you blame yourself. Externalizing is blaming other people and circumstances. Internalizing is self-blame and results in reduced self-esteem. People who blame external events tend to lie to themselves more than those who blame themselves.

As coaches, you have a choice about what you believe and can develop positive expectations. To help you find solutions and options when there are challenges, check whether you are personalizing, believing they are permanent or pervasive. Challenge these beliefs and identify the perceptual alternative—the positive potential in what appears to be negative.

To put these ideas into action, do the following:

- Make a list of your beliefs that help make things work for you.

- Build on your Extended DISC® strengths.

- List those things you tend to avoid and your limiting beliefs and keep those in a place where you can remind yourself to be aware of them.

- Identify the fallacies and mistakes in these beliefs.

Inventory Strengths

Taking inventory means slightly different things depending upon the industry. Often, however, it involves a careful audit of all the things owned by the business or the person. When we move, we give an inventory of what we own to the movers. When sending important documents, we take careful inventory of what is being sent. When we take these inventories, we are making sure to take account of everything we have.

In coaching, it is important to have clients take a self-inventory. This inventory helps clients identify strengths, resources, and potential. It gives clients a good analysis of their strengths.

Some people are more skilled at identifying limitations, liabilities, and deficits. In fact, when asked to identify strengths or limitations, most people are quicker to identify how they are not as attractive as others, not as strong, not as skilled, not as witty, not as outgoing, etc. You may notice that when you ask your clients to inventory the positive things, they are modest in sharing their strengths.

Battalion Chief John Green was let go by a large department as part of a cost reduction move. At first, he was shocked, discouraged, and disappointed. Who would have ever guessed that a fire department would lay people off? Besides, his plans were to finish his work career with the same department. Now he is "on the street" looking for a new position. Will he arm himself with a new appraisal of himself or will he skulk off into a corner and waste time licking his wounds?

Obviously, he is in a better position on the job market or to become an entrepreneur if he can accurately assess his strengths and talents. Doing this goes a long way toward building self-esteem (feeling one's worth and value).

One of the ways to both access and build self-esteem is to take an inventory of strengths, assets, resources, and potential. The assessment discussed earlier in this book is extremely helpful as are the following questions that will help clients begin their self-inventory.

1. What is it they do well? Help clients identify and recognize their "claim to fame". Comparison is with themselves and not with other people. Have your clients identify their traits. One of the things that often limits the ability to function is our tendency to compare ourselves with others. Your clients may think that if they aren't first or best, then they are worst or inadequate.

2. What is it they like about themselves? Have your clients list three to five things. They may find it easier to list a number of things they don't like, but encourage them to ignore that temptation.

3. What is new and good in their lives? Fire service personnel may sometimes think this exercise is silly at first, but we have found that they appreciate it and see the value of it in a very short time. If, on the other hand, they cannot identify anything, what would be new and good in their lives if they had a more positive outlook?

4. What are three to five things they regularly do that they enjoy? This may help clients become more aware of why their lives are more or less enjoyable. Dr. John Gray wrote a book called *Getting What You Want and Wanting What You Have*. He writes that we have ten "tanks" or need areas that we must pay attention to on a regular basis in order to feel fully alive, happy, and satisfied. Much like tending a garden by watering and weeding, we too must pay attention to our

personal, intellectual, social, and spiritual garden in order to remain healthy and happy. Many people load up in one area and neglect other important areas. For example, romantic love is sometimes given enormous time and attention to the detriment of other needs that include friendship, career, intellectual stimulation, spiritual growth, and financial gain. A common stumbling block to success in any endeavor is the tendency to limit oneself to fulfilling only a small number of needs.

Self-esteem is all a product of what people think about themselves. What are some ways your clients can begin to affirm themselves? Discouragement can be a major block in affirming and getting high on themselves. Discouragement is a result of high standards that contribute to the feeling that they are not quite enough. Examples:

- Overambitious—Always wanting to be a little more.

- Pessimism—Feeling it is not going to work anyhow.

- Comparisons—Comparing oneself with those who are better than them.

Discouragers are critical, fault finding, pessimistic people who regularly supply others with put downs and negative comments. The put downs are designed to make the discourager feel better by making others feel less. Discouragers can be likened to vultures that attempt to take the vitality and energy from one's life. One of the essential factors in building self-esteem is to think clearly about the put downs by others. But another, equally important self-esteem builder involves the development of courage.

Courage includes an active, social interest. It is based upon a recognition that others are at least as important as your client and that one of their goals in life is to be actively involved in assisting others. Many fire service personnel may scoff at this suggestion. After all, helping others is what their jobs are all about. But we suggest that helping others extends to both paid as well as voluntary efforts and includes not only a heart felt desire for the well being of others, but the kind of behavioral practice or avocation that demonstrates this desire.

Social interest is the capacity to give and take. Courage helps energize and strengthen one's route to acquiring optimism. Courage also involves practicing new responses. Clients know their typical response to a request at work when asked to do something. If your client's response is negative or based in pessimism, help him to try doing exactly the opposite and take a step toward optimism. Help clients recognize their pattern of thinking and analyze not only what they think but how they think. Are their thoughts positive or negative, optimistic or pessimistic? Help them recognize what happens following pessimistic thinking. And help them in recognizing that negative, pessimistic thinking falls into the following four general categories:

1. To be always right

2. To be always appreciated

3. To be always approved of by others

4. To be always in control of oneself

These four stumbling blocks may be keeping your clients from moving forward. For example, it would be nice to be approved of, but it is neither essential nor required. No one ever achieves complete control. No one is ever completely appreciated by everyone. No one is always right.

Coaches can encourage clients by helping them get in touch with all of their strengths and resources. Encouraging clients to stop comparing and competing with others frees them from self-restrictions. Clients' beliefs and attitudes keep them from functioning more effectively. They create a competitive power seeking world that makes demands on them. As clients move the constrictions of "shoulds," "self-judgments," and blame, they are free to become more of a friend to themselves. Clients who have the courage to be imperfect, who have a concern for others, aren't on a self-escalator that attempts to take them above others, work on an equal plane with others, are less focused on striving for perfection, are focused on being useful rather than on being more than others, and who see mistakes as only a way toward growth, are people who are optimistic and possess a great deal of courage.

The skills and process of encouraging and supporting clients

Discouragement and resultant under performance are, in part, the result of having a constricted perspective on life. Coaches who are optimistic and encouraging work to expand the narrow vision of the client in order to develop a greater range and variety of responses to the challenges of fire service as well as living. The Extended DISC® is one excellent tool for quickly identifying a person's assets. When an individual is not functioning up to par, most often we tend to be focused on identifying weaknesses, limitation, and what's wrong. The mistaken assumption is that we help people by pointing out their weaknesses.

Most of your clients will have been in a relationship that focused on pointing out their weaknesses and mistakes. These relationships become competitive and painful. The major purpose for this book is to overcome the prevalence of the command and control style that tends to focus more on fault finding and criticism. While the intention is to improve the other person, the end result is that the other person becomes resistant, discouraged, and uncooperative.

Effective coaches help clients to be in control of their self-esteem by focusing on the resources of others and helping to build their self-confidence and self-worth.

An essential encouragement skill is being able to spotlight and magnify an individual's strengths, assets, and resources. We all know people who are "nit-pickers" or "fault-finders." They can always spot a mistake, a weakness, or something which isn't as it should be. Optimistic coaches should do the opposite and become individuals who are fine tuned to hearing and seeing resources. Coaches, who train themselves to see the inherent potential and good in a person, are stimulating the ability to encourage. Optimistic coaches may choose to view stubbornness as persistence, talkativeness as informative and friendly, bossy as taking charge, nosy as inquisitive and concerned, socially aggressive as fun to be with.

What we are suggesting is that coaches train themselves to become talent scouts. As talent scouts, coaches must be able to envision the potential of a person with additional training and maturity. The talent scout searches for talent in the raw or diamonds in the rough. This is not to suggest that coaches should be naïve, but too often coaches and leaders overlook the importance of support and encouragement.

The following skills are useful in encouraging and supporting clients:

1. Listen and attend to others. When in contact with people, coaches should stop any preoccupation with what they are doing. Coaches should listen and be in a position to hear the whole message.

2. Before talking with others, clarify the message. For example, "I hear what you are saying, feeling, etc."

3. Use put-ups instead of put-downs. Think about some things that can be said to help build the other person's self-esteem. Think about what can be said that is positive.

4. Respond reflectively, while continuing to stay with the other person's feelings.

5. Look for similarities and places where you can universalize with the client. What are some areas of commonality?

6. Give people honest feedback about how they are coming across to you. Feedback is particularly effective if the client trusts you.

7. Encourage clients for their strengths, not their perfections.

8. Help clients to see perceptual alternatives or more positive, effective ways they can look at the world.

Questions for encouragement

The following are questions for encouragement to stimulate strength and self-knowledge:

- What are your greatest strengths?

- What strengths have others noticed in you?

- What do you deeply enjoy doing?

- What qualities of character do you most admire in others?

- Who is the one person that has made the greatest positive impact on your life? Why?

- What have been the happiest moments of your life? Why?

- If you had unlimited time and resources, what would you choose to do?

- When you daydream, what do you see yourself doing?

- What are the three or four most important things to you?

- When you look at your work life, what activities do you consider of greatest worth?

- When you look at your personal life, what activities do you consider of greatest worth?

- What can you do best that would be of worth to others?

- What talents do you have that no one else really knows about?

- Are there things you feel you really should do? What are they?

- What are your physical needs and capacities? How satisfied are you with your current level of fulfillment in the physical area?

- What quality of life results do you desire that are different from what you now have in this area?

- What principles will create those results?

- What are your social needs and capacities? How satisfied are you with your current level of fulfillment in the social area?

- What are your needs for learning and growing? How satisfied are you with your current level of fulfillment in the learning/growing area?

- What are your spiritual needs and capacities? How satisfied are you with your current level of fulfillment in the spiritual area?

- What are the important lifetime goals you want to fulfill in each role?

- What results are you currently getting in your life that you like? What are you doing to get this?

- What results are you currently getting in your life that you don't like? What are you doing to get this?

- What would you really like to be and do in your life?

- What are the important principles upon which your being and doing are based?

Agreement Skills Create a Bond

Effective coaches and leaders have the skills to quickly connect with clients and subordinates in a way that communicates *we are alike*. By the end of a party, the optimistic person has circulated throughout the room, met everyone and has everyone feeling that they have know this person for years. We call these skills of connecting with others, *agreement skills*.

Agreement skills can be demonstrated in a variety of ways. In this section, we will discuss the type of agreement skills: (1) listening for similarities between you and the other person; (2) finding areas of agreement, even in disagreements; (3) getting people into a "yes" mood; (4) making "we" references; (5) starting with "and" instead of "but" when responsible with a difference of opinion; and (6) employing similar body language, facial gestures, and pace of speech.

Listening For Similarities

Upon meeting someone, the optimistic coach and leader is scanning for ways to connect by finding similarities. Two sources of similarities include common struggles and common interests. The following interaction illustrates common struggles.

> *"I'm frustrated"* Lt. Brown said. *"I would like to be a stronger leader, but these guys won't see me that way. They still think of me as one of them; someone who hangs out on their days off and drinks beer with them."*
>
> *"You wish the shift could see you differently now that you are an officer?"* the Chief asked.
>
> *"That's right. I'm not like them, at least my role is not similar, not the same. But it is difficult to make the turn toward leadership without losing their respect."*
>
> *"Tell me, Lieutenant, have you ever worked for an officer whom you admired who was once your peer?"*   continued

> *"Yeah, I did in fact."*
>
> *"Me too. The thing I liked best about my superior officer was that he was both one of us and, at the same time, separate from us. He sat us all down and told us of his concerns and explained to us what his role was going to be. He asked us to help him be successful."*
>
> *"That's how I feel too, Chief," the lieutenant said. "I want these guys to understand that I care for all of them and would take nothing for the memories I have, but my role is different and I need their help."*
>
> *"And that's exactly how I felt too when I became an officer. In fact, every time I've been promoted, I've had to overcome discomfort and incorporate my new role."*

In this example, the coaching chief did not give direct advice or attempt to solve the problem immediately. Rather, the lieutenant is facilitated to explore his own process toward a solution. This is very important! This new officer is struggling, not for an immediate answer, but for a pathway to leadership maturity. Such a struggle is not solved by a few sentences of advice, but rather through a trustworthy mentor who shares common struggles.

Common Interests

These can include almost anything, including sports related commonalities, similar musical interests, geographical commonalities, or mutual friends. What the commonality is is perhaps less important than the fact that the commonality bonds the two people with regard to shared history or perception. There is an automatic bonding that tends to speed up the process of relationship development and trust.

Finding Areas of Agreement, Even in Disagreement

The coach/client relationship will not always be characterized by peace and tranquility. Sometimes, in the course of daily service operations, coaches must deal with a client who disagrees or who is angry. Thus, in addition to listening for similarities or commonalities with the client, another agreement skill is to find areas of agreement even when disagreeing about an issue.

The idea that opposites attract, while possibly true in the physical sciences, is quite false in the science of human relations. While long lasting relationships have some differences on the surface ("He's outgoing, I'm quiet"), at a deeper level they are quite similar ("We both believe in God." "We both want acceptance." "We both desire the best for our families and our country.") The optimistic person is constantly listening with an ear toward finding areas in which all sides agree. This is especially helpful during strong disagreements.

Agreement skills can also be used in a rather curious and creative way when dealing with a hostile person's direct attack. Watch how the coach takes some of the steam out of the angry client.

> *"The bottom line is that I think you are a micromanaging, controlling person,"* the fire marshal said.
>
> *"I agree,"* the fire chief coach replied.
>
> *"And I think you like being that way. It's a way to wield power."*
>
> *"You're right,"* the chief said. *"I can see how you view me that way."*
>
> *"Okay, then the question is how am I supposed to work with you and stay motivated?"*

An optimistic person can comfortably agree with a person who disagrees with him or her. We call this "flowing with the *resistance*." Disagreeing and trying to force someone to see things your way only results in further frustration and anger. Flowing with the other person's *resistance* helps them to be receptive to working out a solution.

Getting People Into a *Yes* Mood

Good leaders get people to do what they may not want to do under normal circumstances. How do they do it? They do it by getting people to say *yes* and to want to follow the leader's vision. An optimistic person orchestrates an upbeat rhythm in all relationships, skillfully avoiding conversation that is discouraging. The skillful and optimistic leader is always aware of clients' personality style and therefore what they need and want. Skillful coaches then use this knowledge to talk about the other person's interests and by asking questions in such away that they are likely to elicit yes answers.

"No" is a negative. Throughout our life, we use the word "no" to get out of something that is uncomfortable to us. And when we say "no" we tend to stick with it even in the face of changing evidence. We become like a stone fence, standing firm regardless of the changing climate, all because changing to "yes" is giving in, a form of losing face. Optimistic leaders avoid the "no" set and aim for a "yes" set instead. In the following example, the coach is negative.

> *"You don't want those guys to get the best of you do you?"* the negative fire chief said.
>
> *"No,"* said the lieutenant.
>
> *"And you don't want to create conflict with the other shift, do you?"*
>
> *"No."*
>
> *"Then what do you suggest should be done about it?"* the negative fire chief coach asked.
>
> *"Uh, hell if I know."*

In this example, the fire chief coach takes an optimistic tone.

> *"You want to figure out a way to get the shift to perform better?"*
>
> *"Absolutely,"* the lieutenant replied.
>
> *"You've dealt with difficult personnel matters before and come out on top, Lieutenant,"* the optimistic coach said.
>
> *"Yes."*
>
> *"Would you like to look at some ways of handling this situation now?"*
>
> *"Absolutely!"*
>
> *"Then tell me,"* the fire chief said, *"what reaction does their behavior trigger in you?"*

It is important to practice questions that generate "yes" responses. It is also important for the coach to exhibit an optimistic and energetic demeanor.

Making "We" References

To reinforce similarity and agreement, the optimistic coach invites the client under his or her umbrella by using "we," "our," and "us" statements.

> *"Frankly,"* the lieutenant said, *"I'm struggling in this new role. I can't seem to separate my personal feelings in my dealings with some of the firefighters. I'm not quite sure how to deal with them during conflict."*
>
> The coaching fire chief replied, *"We've all had that experience before. I sure have. The thing we all need when taking over leadership positions is support from other leaders to embrace your role, to do some of the things that are difficult."*

Starting With "And" Instead of "But"

When one person makes a point and the other person responds with "but…", the first person tends to tighten, clench fists, back up, get defensive, and prepare for his or own rebuttal. The optimistic coach knows that even when in disagreement, it is more effective to start with the word "and" instead. "And" keeps both parties in an agreement mood, and thus the other person will tend to listen rather than judge.

Using "and" when in disagreement takes much practice but offers rich rewards. Practice by really listening to yourself say the word 'but' and rephrasing it with a big smile on your face, your head nodding in agreement, and starting your response with an "and."

Communicate Respect in Order to Build Confidence

Perhaps you've known someone who believed in you, even more than you believed in yourself at the time. This person communicated to you that you were the right kind of person who "could do it". He/she encouraged you to set high standards, achieve big goals, take risks, and go after your dream. This person saw something unique and special in you. When you were with this person, you were more creative and more certain of yourself. Perhaps this person was equally as interested in you proving it to yourself. Although probably not formally labeled as a "coach," this person made a great coach, leader, or teacher. This person saw past some of your faults and looked deeper into your heart and saw who you really were.

An optimistic coach and leader knows that a prerequisite for being able to genuinely encourage others is confidence and respect. Your confidence is a product of having self-esteem or a sense of personal effectiveness, a belief that you are a capable person who is able to function and meet life's challenges. In certain ways, we live in a confusing culture that conveys the message that if you think less of yourself, feel inadequate, and are overly humble, you are alright. However, if you have self-esteem, self-respect, and self-confidence, you are suspected of having something wrong with you, being less than humble, or perhaps even self-centered.

The optimistic person feels good about himself or herself and is able to assess personal assets, strengths, and resources instead of only limitations. Furthermore, he or she owns, recognizes, and values those assets.

Confidence is built as an individual is encouraged to be more independent and responsible. Insofar as an individual is kept dependent upon others, he or she feels inept and discouraged, with reduced self-esteem. When we encourage independence, we convey "you can do it". Responsibility is freely given instead of earned.

How might you communicate respect and confidence in the following situations?

1. A new young leader has the tendency to give up quickly. He has difficulty separating himself from his charges. He presents this as a leadership difficulty. *What do you say? What do you do?*

2. A firefighter with apparatus maintenance is discouraged. He is expected to do more with less and feels like he gets the blame whenever something breaks down. *What do you say? What do you do?*

These are typical situations that test your desire to encourage. When we see people who are dejected, they are living in the prison of hopelessness and the sentence appears to be for life. Self-confidence comes from the personal reservoir of past successes in mental, physical, occupational, social, emotional, or other areas. Something we are capable of doing may provide us with the necessary self-confidence. As we behave effectively (for example, solving a problem, performing a physical skill, or in relations with others), we increase our self-confidence.

Self-confidence also emerges from our ability to identify and enumerate our resources. As we become sensitive to our vast potential to behave in ways that result in confidence, we will be impressed with the power within our grasp.

A key coaching strategy is to get clients to stop for a moment and think about some of their personality strengths. For example, sensitivity, understanding, and courage can all be personality strengths. In the same way, being a good listener or a caring and concerned person are strengths. Have your client complete the following strength acknowledgment exercise. Have the client list six strengths; these are the resources he or she has that stimulate self-confidence.

Remember, your client is more prepared to list weaknesses, or liabilities, than strengths. Perhaps he or she is unable to develop an adequate list of resources or strengths. If you know your client fully, help by offering some observations of his/her strengths.

You communicate confidence to another person by showing your belief in that person, which stimulates his or her confidence. Communicating this belief involves being perceptive and sincere. Confidence is not communicated by false bravado. Try to communicate confidence in the following scenarios previously presented.

1. A new young leader has the tendency to give up quickly. He has difficulty separating himself from his charges. He presents this as a leadership difficulty. *What do you say? What do you do?*

    Coach: "Your greatest strength is that people like you; they want to be around you. You are inspiring and you appear to like this role. This is not something to get rid of, rather it is important to find a way to utilize this ability to gain the kind of respect you want."

2. A firefighter with apparatus maintenance is discouraged. He is expected to do more with less and feels like he gets the blame whenever something breaks down. *What do you say? What do you do?*

Coach: "It is discouraging to get blamed even when you do your best. I recognize your effort even if circumstances won't permit the result to be as you would like."

Respect comes from believing that all people are equal as human beings and have the right to be treated equally. When you have respect, you show faith in another's worth and potential. Optimistic coaches value and are committed to the client's growth. Since more self-respect is often a reflection of the support and sense of value we get from others, this respect increases the individual's self-respect and self-confidence.

Respect and confidence are essential for communicating encouragement. However, because of self-interest and competitiveness, coaches and leaders often neglect their importance. They are attitudinal outgrowths of what we believe about ourselves and people in general.

Changing Perception

Encouragement doesn't just come from another person's ability to support. It also comes from within and the person's ability to view alternatives. Discouraged people are those who possess a limited view of their alternatives.

Example

John performs poorly in his assessments for promotion. As a result, he is not promoted.

Discouraging perceptual alternative:

"Those tests revealed my true capabilities. I'll never get promoted."

Encouraging perceptual alternative:

"The tests reveal nothing about me. Rather, I must prepare more thoroughly for the next assessment center."

Example

Charlie, a chief, received a community feedback survey about the fire department that was anything but positive.

Discouraging perceptual alternative:

"What do they know? They don't know what we do around here."

Encouraging perceptual alternative:

"We have to learn from this feedback. We can use this feedback to get better. After all, we are here to serve the public and their perception matters."

In general, a situation does not directly cause a feeling. How we interpret the meaning of a situation influences the development of a feeling.

The encouraging person has the ability to view the same situation in several ways. The more ways of viewing the world your clients possess, the greater their capacity for adjusting to life and the ups and downs of fire service. As a coach, your ability to help them develop perceptual alternatives is one of the most important skills for gaining long-term performance and harmony around the department. Your own ability to develop perceptual alternatives is closely linked to your willingness to take risks and grow.

It is important to deal with life's challenges as if there is a solution. Once you are solution-oriented you (as person and coach) are in a position to see a variety of possibilities. However, if you are only problem focused, you may remain forever discouraged.

Consider the following questions:

- Do you usually look for and identify the positive or negative aspects of a situation?

- Are you more aware of the positive or negative traits in a person?

- What habits prevent your ability to encourage?

- Do you tend to think bad events are awful, unchangeable, and broad ranging?

Recognize Discouraging Beliefs

When clients are discouraged, it is not completely because of the way things are; it is because of the way they are looking at things. When we change our beliefs about a situation, we change our discouragement into either acceptance or courage.

The encouraged person looks at failure as a learning experience, a fender bender as an inconvenience, and budget cuts as a way to focus on what is absolutely essential.

One officer, Duke, is frustrated and bitter about the "raw deal' that he believes he is receiving from the chief. He feels that another officer is much more popular than he and that the chief favors the other officer. He constantly complains about all the unfair things that have happened to him. He believes that life in the fire service is unfair.

Chet believes that the worst thing that could happen to him would be to make a mistake. He needs to be perfect in everything. If he does make an error, he relives the mistake over and over again. His work life has become a safe routine, and he never takes any chances. Chet feels that in this way, he need not fear failing. If he does not try, he cannot fail. He believes mistakes are dangerous.

Duke and Chet are just two examples of how negative beliefs can discourage people from living and working fully. They each may live out their days with a handicap, the belief that the world must be fair or that things must be perfect, or that they are no good and worthless, or people should this and ought to do that.

Much discouragement is the result of two basic mistaken beliefs about self, others, and life. The first error is in the failure of people to face and accept reality as it is. The second major mistake is in the failure of people to realize all of the possible alternatives still available to them once they face and accept that reality.

Discouragement occurs when fire service personnel fail to overcome one or both of these errors. The unwillingness of clients to accept reality as it is results from a superiority complex. They place themselves out of perspective in the universe, believing that the world has focused in on them personally. This, of course, is naïve and self defeating and results in the feelings of grandiosity and persecution as is often seen in the paranoid person.

The second mistake that hinders human happiness is the unwillingness of people to realize all of the possible alternatives still available to them once they face and accept that reality. When people make this mistake, they become overwhelmed by the universal reality, giving it too much credit and blame. These people are unaware of their life possibilities and feel hopeless and helpless. They are passive victims to what they see as the powerful forces of life and other people.

Making either mistake, underplaying or overplaying the importance of reality, results in discouragement. The process of overcoming both of these discouraging beliefs is perhaps the most important road to the courageous life. Yet, it is perhaps the most complicated task of life because many of us continue to go on making error #1, disrespecting reality, or error #2, disrespecting ourselves.

Skills in Identifying Some Discouraging Beliefs

As a positive coach, become aware of the following and other faulty beliefs and learn to associate them with certain emotional complaints.

Need for Approval

- Doing or saying something that you believe someone else wants

- Avoiding speaking out for fear of reprisal

- Believing personal opinions are not worthwhile

- Idolizing someone else

Need for Perfection

- Immobilization or inaction

- Ego-involvement as opposed to task-involvement
- Constant planning rather than doing
- Blaming others, the world, or circumstances for errors
- Never relaxed, always on guard
- Highly critical of other's mistakes
- Stereotyped behavior, routinized
- Traumatic behavior change
- Panicking when things and people do not fit into place
- Seeing the world and people in clear cut, black and white ways
- Blaming

Focusing on Effort

Fire service is no different than any other business in that results and the bottom line are what it's all about. After all, lives and property are at stake. We live in a culture that expects us to do our very best. As the old saying goes, anything worth doing is worth doing well.

Consider the crowds at soccer games for a moment. When do they cheer? When a goal is scored, you say. Not completely! It is not unusual for soccer fans to sit through a string of 1-0 games. If they only cheered during goals, they would have little to cheer about. Thus, soccer fans have to focus on not just the end results but the process of good play, of effort. Soccer fans cheer movement down the field, not just the goals.

This is not to suggest that fire service lower its standards and accept less than the best results, but the encouraging coach finds a way to recognize something of value even when others have given up. Movement is the essence of success. It indicates that you are headed toward a goal, and any movement toward a goal is progress. It is essential to recognize that any simple steps in the right direction merit recognition. If a young child who was just beginning to walk, struggled to stand up, took one step, and fell down, you certainly wouldn't say, "Don't try that again until you can do it right and take ten steps at once." Instead, you observe any effort, movement, or progress.

The person who makes an initial effort needs to be encouraged, because encouragement supplies the support to sustain the effort that has begun but may be faltering. Sometimes, a few simple words that recognize the effort being made are all that is needed to sustain the effort.

Encouraging, optimistic coaches tend to see strengths in fire personnel. They tend to frame negative traits into positive intentions. They are focused on highlighting assets, strengths, and effort. Optimistic coaches see how they can improve performance by focusing on strengths and efforts and ignoring what is bad, as long as it doesn't affect the safety of others.

An encourager focuses on:

1. Attempts

2. Tries

3. Any movement

4. Beginnings

5. Observing struggles and supporting the person who moves toward progress

6. Recognizing intentions

Goal Commitment Skills

One of the most important skills that coaches both possess and impart is the ability to get fire service clients to set goals and reach them. Clients who achieve their dreams and goals are those who have them. That's because, without a destination we play no role in our destiny. Our lives are either up to us or up to luck or chance. Positive people know where they are going. They have a goal and they are committed to reaching it. Think of those goals once thought to be unreachable. Climbing Mount Everest, setting foot on the Moon, digging the Panama Canal, and the advent of the personal computer were all goals that generated creativity and enthusiasm. Like an arrow, creativity and drive need a target, without which, all effort is wandering and wasted. Help clients to lock their goals firmly in mind and go for them. Then help them experience the enormous lifting power of their goals, because once goals are established firmly in mind, they lift us by finding the ways and means to achieve them.

Think about the following everyday examples of how the power of goal setting works:

- A fire chief wants to overcome negative press about the department and establishes the goal of better emergency response and customer service.

- The command staff is concerned about the morale of the department and sets the goal of team building and more responsive leadership.

- A lieutenant is frustrated over the amount of complaining and irresponsibility on the part of his shift and establishes shift goal setting as the primary goal in an effort to gain greater esteem through goal accomplishment.

Each of these fire personnel used the same process of goal achievement that the mountain climbers employed to reach the top of Everest. In each case, success began as a firm goal. Imagine what would have happened if these people had not taken a few moments to set goals. What if the command staff had not taken some time to lock the goal of creating better morale firmly in mind? Most likely, they would have never reached better morale! No goal-no lifting power. Without a goal locked firmly in mind, no success is possible.

Your fire personnel's goal locked firmly in their minds makes the difference. Help clients feed off the powerful lift that goal setting can give them. Remember the lift you received from your own goal setting. Sir Edmund Hillary and his Sherpa, Tenzing Norgay, had a goal that gave them extra help. Their goal, like a magnet, attracted all of their actions.

How Goals Make the Difference

Consciously establishing your goals gives you at least three advantages over a person who wanders aimlessly. First, a goal subconsciously lifts you by forcing you, even in your sleep, to find ways to achieve it.

I became conscious of the power of goals while I was in graduate school. One of my closest friends was a "trust fund baby" from the east coast. Tollie, as we called him, was from old Connecticut money. His father's, father's, father were wine merchants and importers and the elder had run one of the most successful and classy Speak Easies during Prohibition, supposedly serving some of New York and Washington D.C.'s wealthiest and most influential politicians.

Tollie reflected his upbringing in almost everything he did. From his thin, French cigarettes to his bottled water that was air expressed directly from the Basque region of Spain, Tollie was a walking cliché of a rich guy who could have anything he wanted. I, on the other hand, was living month to month on a small scholarship that covered books, tuition, and the rent on a three bedroom apartment. I had enough left over for peanut butter and hot dogs.

I was the first person in my family to go to college much less graduate school and I was both proud of this accomplishment and scared to death that I would not make it. And, although I entered my professional program with no career goal in mind, I quickly found my passion was teaching at the university level. I remember the moment it struck me. I was watching my major professor (in my opinion, one of the world's great mentors) teach a class. Suddenly, I could see the big picture; how I could influence people, how I could feel fulfilled, how I could simultaneously work and serve. From then on, the work that had, to that point, been difficult and laborious, became easy and effortless. In hindsight, it wasn't that the work was easier, rather, it just seemed easier because I had a very specific goal that provided me with excitement about meeting and overcoming my academic challenges.

Tollie, on the other hand, spent most of his time sighing, procrastinating, and attempting to personally collect every scotch distilled in the universe. He really didn't drink the stuff that much but he thought it would be cool to have every possible sample. When he decided he wasn't going to finish his dissertation, he had some 350 bottles of the whiskey. He paid me two hundred dollars to make sure the collection was properly packed and shipped to Connecticut while he went to the Festa de Iemanja in Rio de Janiero, essentially a drunken party on New Year's Eve. While Tollie enjoys the *good life*, he jokes to this very day that, "If it weren't for that trust fund, I might have some incentive."

Tollie had no goals and thus, no creativity or motivation. He allowed his money to diminish his goals when, in fact, it could have given him a world of service oriented options for helping the less fortunate, building hospitals, or establishing schools.

Firmly locked in goals give people a lift in another way. It provides additional enthusiasm. Enthusiasm is the power and the energy to ignite fire client's ideas into potential action. The 1980 Olympic Hockey team defeated a bigger, stronger, more skilled opponent because their goal of victory was more firmly locked in. When their goal was lifting them, they had more energy to make it happen. They all played way beyond their usual capabilities. They were more alert, more hyper-vigilant, more focused.

A third way that a firmly locked-in goal lifts your clients is by giving them direction when they are confused or lost. Many people find that their religion does this for them. Goals show us where we are in relation to our destination.

Four Ways to Help Fire Clients Be Goal-Oriented

1. Assess what they do when they run into problems, then help them act, not catastrophize. Life rewards action. While writing this book, I ran into several people who told me they too had book projects in mind. One project in particular sounded very interesting and would contribute nicely to the whole topic of leadership in fire service. When I asked this individual what he had done to make movement toward finishing the book, he indicated that he thought about it occasionally, but that work, kids, etc., usually got in the way. When I asked him what he did on his days off and the kids were in school, his face turned red. Instead of having a real goal and plan for writing his book, he is essentially saying that he would like to have written-past action. This is magical thinking. When your clients run into problems do they blame and procrastinate or do they find ways to tackle the problem? Are their daily activities aimed at meeting the ultimate goal? People who find ways to solve problems are practicing a success-oriented style.

2. Help clients look at what they do, how they think, and how they feel. Our experience is that most fire clients are not aware of *how* they are going about their daily business. They are unconscious of their habitual negative thoughts that results in procrastination and finally, anxiety and depression that creates a vicious cycle that leads to failure and back to negative thoughts.

3. Help your fire client get on course. Life does not allow for straight-line endeavors. There are setbacks along the way and adjustments have to be made. Negative thinking can crop up like a recurring virus.

4. Help them to understand that, no matter the circumstances, we create our own experience. Ask them the following questions:

   a. What is the life or job circumstance that you do not like?

   b. What can you do, think, feel, or perceive differently that will improve the circumstance?

   c. What might you have done to arrange the situation so that it happened in the way that it happened?

   d. What were some warning signs that you ignored?

   e. How might you have failed to be clear about what you wanted?

   f. Did you con yourself because you wanted it to be true?

   g. What choices did you make that directly led to the result you did not want?

   h. Did you choose the wrong person or the wrong place?

   i. Did you choose what you chose for the wrong reasons?

   j. What did you fail to do that directly created the result you did not want?

   k. Did you fail to take the needed action? If so, what was it?

   l. Did you fail to stand up for yourself and claim your rights?

   m. Did you fail to ask for what you wanted?

   n. Did you fail to require enough of yourself?

   o. Are old habits preventing you from experiencing success?

Chapter 10

Positive Leadership Skills and Coaching:
The Core of Leadership

Positive Leadership Skills and Coaching

The Core of Leadership

The purpose of coaching is to help people get better at something. In many cases, coaching helps leaders be better leaders. So what are some commonly targeted leadership goals for fire service leaders? Let's look at the core of leadership.

Leadership is the art of engaging the hearts and minds of ordinary people to achieve extraordinary results. For this book, I've been interviewing gifted leaders from a wide range of industries, including fire. Each has his or her unique organizational responsibilities to carry out. Each has to deal with widely different competitive pressures, customer demands, marketing strategies, service expectations, and workforce requirements. Each represents an organization that is affected in specific ways by the new global economy, the "IT" revolution, the disappearance of stable currency values worldwide, and the collapse of the old industrial business paradigm as an organizing model for their companies.

However, all of the leaders that I have interviewed share one thing in common, an apparently innate set of emotional and intellectual qualities that make up what I call "The Core of Leadership." The components of this core are:

1. Vision

2. Integrity

3. Trust

4. Values

5. Vulnerability

6. Motivation

Together these components produce what we all instantly recognize as leadership.

How leaders exemplify these qualities is easier to note in practice than it is to define in principle. Because we aren't just talking about special skills or strategies that these people exercise, we're talking about individual character. Like the force of gravity or the lump of uranium in a nuclear generator, the leadership core works invisibly. And like any living system, it sometimes works intuitively and mysteriously. But its positive effects upon others can be readily observed, and those observations, in turn, can be put to immediate use by anyone leading fellow employees at any level of an organization.

Leadership as Vision

In contrast to the control-minded authority of the past, today's leaders must exercise power through a shared purpose and vision. An organizational vision is not the same as long range or even strategic planning. Planning is a linear process, a progression toward a goal. Vision is more holistic, a sense of direction that combines a good business strategy with a comprehensive organizational purpose that declares its own importance. A vision describes a fire department as it *could* become over the long term and outlines a feasible way of achieving this goal. To transform a department, leaders must adopt and communicate a vision of the future that impels people beyond the boundaries and limits of the past.

Leaders who articulate such visions aren't mystics, but broad-based thinkers who are willing to take risks. Visionary leaders don't have to be brilliant, highly innovative, or incredibly charismatic. But they do have to be intently focused on what it is they are trying to achieve. Fred Smith, founder and Chief Executive Officer of Federal Express, put it in these very practical terms, "If there is any indication that the leader is not totally committed to achieving the vision, then all the sweet talk in the world will not get people to support it."

Leadership as Integrity

According to the executives that I interviewed, a leader must be seen to stand for something, must act from deep seated principles, and must rely on strong personal beliefs. Leading with integrity implies a willingness to embody the attitudes and behaviors you want to see in employees. The following is an excellent example of leadership integrity in action, described to me by the Training Chief of a large metropolitan Fire Department.

"In our department we try to create relationships that allows us to 'call' one another on behavior that doesn't represent our values. A recent example occurred during the development of our latest strategic plan. Every year we get the top chiefs together once a week, for six to eight weeks. At the end of each of the weekly sessions, we have 'homework' assignments to prepare for the next meeting. At the beginning of one session, a participant told us that at the last meeting he had offered to send us information that we had agreed to review and return with our comments. He went on to say that of the twelve messages he sent out, only three responses had been received. He then asked all of us what we were going to do about this issue of 'irresponsibility.' The meeting stopped and we discussed how to better honor our commitments. Right at the top of the department's leadership, we are aware of the need to mirror whatever behavior we expect to receive in kind."

Leadership as Trust

Until recently, an officer's primary function has been supervision, telling employees what to do and measuring how well they did it. But the new breed of knowledgeable workers increasingly doesn't want or need to be micro-managed. They need to be set free in the sphere of their own authority. They need to be trusted.

Trust is an attitude of confidence in another person, a positive set of expectations about that person's competencies and character. The powerful influence of one person's expectation on another's behavior is known as the "Pygmalion Effect." Eliza Doolittle explains it in George Bernard Shaw's play Pygmalion; "You see, really and truly, apart from the things anyone can pick up, the difference between a lady and a flower girl is not how she behaves but how she's treated. I shall always be a flower girl to Professor Higgins because he always treats me as a flower girl and always will; but I know I can be a lady to you because you always treat me as a lady and always will." The difference between leaders who complain about the lack of responsibility in today's employees and those who speak with pride of the creative contribution and dedication of their staff may lie in the realm of management's expectation.

Leadership as Vulnerability

Recognition of the potential of the workforce for contributing solutions to departmental problems has increased while the infallibility of leaders and the certainty of management tasks have declined. The unquestioned authority of leaders in the department of the past has been replaced by the need to acknowledge the expertise of those below, and to enlist employees as true partners. Moving from a model in which leadership made all the decisions and knew all the answers to a departmental environment of openness, candor, and empowerment takes a willingness by leaders to become and remain highly vulnerable.

There has never been a time in which our departments have experienced more uncertainty and chaos. The fire service leader who can say to his or her employees, "I'm unsure too," will have done more for departmental morale with that single admission than a dozen phony pep talks ever could. Why? Because, as Sue Swenson, President of Leap Wireless, observes, "When leaders are perceived as human and vulnerable, employees identify with those attributes and begin to see the potential for success and leadership in themselves."

Leadership as Values

Webster defines value as "A principle, standard or quality considered inherently worthwhile or desirable." The root is the Latin valor, which means strength. Values are a source of strength for an enterprise or an individual. As leadership strategy moves from coercion to cooperation, the key to bonding people to the goals of the organization automatically becomes the intangibles relationships, commitments and shared values. Values are the heart and soul of an organization. It is not enough for people just to fill functions. They have to know what we are all about.

Leaders must stay focused on values and keep them energized, which is the hardest part. For that, you need to find processes that renew and revitalize values. One process that some of our client departments use is called the "Line Up." Fifteen minutes before a shift begins every day, the supervisor of the line up goes through the basics of that day. Fire service personnel are reminded of the same "value of the day," as prepared by the command staff. Added to that is a "teaching", an issue brought to our awareness, based on customer service input, and then some comments about the daily value that are customized to the individual station.

Leadership as Motivation

The secret to being a great motivator is realizing that motivation isn't something that can be forced or ordered. Motivation is an intrinsic capacity of human beings that can be tapped, nurtured, and developed, but never coerced. In essence, all motivation is *self-motivation*. It manifests when leaders hold a compelling vision of the future, have a strong personal desire to realize the vision, and possess the ability to engage people's individual motivation in the common cause of that vision so that a true interconnection emerges.

Motivational leaders inspire exceptional levels of commitment and performance. Although great motivators probably have answers all the time, they often spend hours talking with personnel, involving them and making them feel as if they are an integral part of a huge change -- as if they are making history. And they get so much out of everyone. For this kind of leader, personnel work 'round the clock. It's exciting, exhausting, incredibly intense, and absolutely thrilling!

As coaches, what is it that we are trying to help fire personnel do and what should we help them try to become? Last year, I heard my daughter's cross-country coach say something I shall never forget. The team had just come in second place to a rival school and the girls were visibly discouraged about their showing. Some cried, others went silent, and still others put on their headphones and sat isolated on top of their gear bags. I observed the coach as he observed the girls. When the bus pulled up the girls shuffled listlessly toward the return bus to make the trip back home. The pall was palpable. After all the girls had boarded, the coach too boarded and ordered all of the girls off the bus. When they had all exited and gathered about, the coach said, "You can get anything you want in life if you simply help everyone else to get what they want. I want to demonstrate what this means in this team before you get back on the bus." Then he strode away.

As one might imagine, the girls appeared somewhat befuddled at first, milling around not knowing what to say or do. But after what seemed like a long time, the team captains began milling about the maudlin group and offering verbal encouragement. Shortly, a chain of events began to occur. Two girls began to cry over their performances while others moved in to listen to them. Thereafter, girls began hugging. Before entering the bus, the captains quieted the group and suggested that they start running like a team instead of a group of separate individuals. The goal and resultant mood was vastly different and the team went on to win the state championship even though not a single individual girl placed in the top ten. The girls had learned to run as a tightly packed team.

Observe groups of people. Find the leaders. They are often the ones who get things done. Leaders not only achieve their own goals but, even more importantly, know how to help other people achieve their goals. Leaders are those rare people who walk, talk, feel, think, and act with positive purpose. Being a leader is not a talent, as some suggest. It is not something that a person is born with. Rather, it is the consistent practice of the skills discussed in this chapter. These are the skills that coaches strive to help their fire clients display.

Your client's leadership skills can be employed in every social setting. Watch how leaders act wherever they go. As you watch the department leaders, you've no doubt recognized that the true leaders are not necessarily the ones who talk the most; they are the ones who keep the group on course and keep everyone energized. You can observe leadership in operation every time two or more people get together to tackle a task.

A department sends the off-duty lieutenants to a wilderness obstacle course training seminar for team building. The group approaches a river with a high volume of water with no readily available means of getting across. One of the emerging leaders says, "The way I figure it, we have about a ten minute lead on everyone else. We're going to lose that lead unless we brainstorm a way across this thing. What would be the best way to do this?"

This key question encourages the group to brainstorm about each member's talents. One person is good at tying rope. Another person is a powerful swimmer. Still another is fast and sure-footed over rocky terrain. Progress occurred because the leader asked the right questions to make things happen. Each member had a purpose, a goal, a direction, rather than wandering aimlessly on the riverbank. The leader makes the difference by taking things off dead center.

Observe leaders in every social situation. They help create solutions rather than dictate them. Leaders create a successful atmosphere by raising key questions, encouraging people to recognize the talents and resources among the group members, and motivating the group to stay on course to achieve their goals. Watch leaders. You will find that true leaders who last as leaders use the powerful approach of encouragement.

Help Them to Think Like a Leader

Accountability is one of today's most popular business buzzwords. Yet in my work as a management consultant, I am frequently struck by how quickly people at all levels abdicate responsibility and blame others for their problems. Self-responsibility is crucial for success in fire service... as well as every other area of life. The meaning of self-responsibility can be summed up in the statement "I am the cause of the effects I desire."

In practice, this means that instead of waiting for someone else to solve a problem, you must ask yourself, "What needs to be done to get the results I want?" and then do it yourself. To become more self-responsible at work:

Assess your current attitudes and beliefs about self-responsibility

This is often difficult to do directly. We tend to avoid facing the areas in which we shirk responsibility. An excellent way to approach this challenge is by using a technique I call "sentence completion." In both clinical and business settings, I've seen this deceptively simple exercise lead to dramatic breakthroughs.

How to do it: Every day for a week, open a notebook and write six to 10 endings to the following incomplete sentence:

If I operated 5% more self-responsibly at work...

Write without stopping to think. Don't worry about whether your endings are accurate, important or reasonable. The idea is to turn off the little voice inside of you that censors your thoughts.

Here are some of the most common endings to these sentences that showed up when I gave this exercise to one group of executives:

... I would look for ways to do more than I was asked to do.

... I would stay focused on the most important issues.

... I would learn more about what is going on around me.

... I would not allow myself to become isolated from my colleagues.

... I would be more honest and upfront with my boss.

... I would get more accomplished.

Another good setup sentence to use for this exercise is...

If I took 5% more responsibility for how I invested my time...

At the end of the week, review and reflect on the endings you have written and any new behaviors they suggest. The discipline of this simple process is often enough to bring about insight and behavior change in a short time.

Banish from your vocabulary the expression "It's not my job"

If somebody who works for or with you makes a mistake or neglects to complete an assignment, self-responsibility dictates that it is up to you to help fix the situation whether or not it's part of your job description.

When someone else's actions or oversights affect us negatively, it's only human to blame that person for letting us down. Blame may indeed be justified but it's rarely productive.

The self-responsible alternative is to ask yourself, "What can I do to correct the situation?" Then ask yourself, "What else can I do?" For example, the department needs parts delivered by Thursday morning in order to repair a truck for the following day's fire training exercises. The parts don't arrive as scheduled. You could complain about the inefficiency of the purchasing department, which will erode interdepartmental relationships, hurt your credibility with the customer and not get the parts there any quicker. Or you could get on the phone with the supplier, track down the wayward delivery and figure out what else you could do to make sure your truck gets out on time.

Refuse to indulge in confusion

Everybody gets confused sometimes, but staying confused is just another way of avoiding responsibility. A self-responsible person takes steps to get unconfused. This might include getting additional facts, comparing notes with others familiar with the situation and confronting, instead of ignoring, the data that challenge our assumptions. Whenever you feel confused, ask yourself, "What am I pretending not to know?"

Be committed to continuous learning

It's always been important to stay abreast of developments in your industry, but in today's rapidly changing environment, this requirement is more urgent than ever before.

Part of self-responsibility is recognizing that you are the author of your career. Identify and address your weaknesses, develop your strengths and be alert for opportunities to make a contribution. Then, communicate those strengths and contributions. Don't wait for your boss, industry headhunters, or anyone else, to recognize your accomplishments. Take it upon yourself to make sure others are aware of your worth.

Offer value in exchange for cooperation

Be a trader, not a parasite. When your goals require other people's involvement, you'll get more enthusiastic participation if you recognize that nobody exists just to serve you. The best way to motivate others is to offer them reasons that are in line with their values.

Give the employees whom you supervise the resources to be self-responsible

Establish clear performance standards for your subordinates. Then, once you've let your team know what needs to be done, allow them to do it.

Micromanaging kills initiative. Your subordinates should always feel free to ask for your help when they need it, but it is just as important for you to encourage them to do their own problem solving.

Communicate clearly

Be consistent about giving corrective feedback. Always do so in a constructive, non-blaming way. In addition, invite feedback from employees on your own performance as a manager; from your subordinates as well as from your boss. Their input can be invaluable and enable you to analyze and improve your effectiveness.

Skill: Listen With Full Attention

Leaders are effective listeners. They give full attention to the speaker's concerns, feelings, and theme. How refreshing it is to be with someone who really listens to you and gives you the ultimate human gifts of time and attention. The listener not only gains respect and popularity in your eyes but learns more as well. No wonder listeners become sought after leaders.

Listening requires a few simple, but important skills:

- Show The Speaker That You Are Fully Attentive. Like a finely coordinated dance with the speaker's words, smile with the humorous words, have heightened energies with the enthusiastic words, show concern with the troublesome words, and display an openness for controversial words.

- Make Eye Contact. A helpful way of showing you are presenting a relationship is through your eyes. Effective listeners have the ability to use an ideal amount of eye contact-not too many breaks and not too much staring.

- Show Presence Through Body Language. Body posture and non-verbal clues say much more about our true intentions than do our words. Thus, if our body posture communicates absence in a relationship, communication will likely be disrupted. Think of pet annoyances (habits or mannerisms) people use that have stopped your train of thought. Was the listener yawning, tapping a pencil, or looking away? Practice avoiding these distancing gestures and learn to demonstrate a relaxed, non-threatening posture.

Skill: Empathizing With People

Most people, fire officers included, are eager to tell us what we should have done. But how many are willing to listen to us with understanding? Not too many. That's why true fire service leaders have the skill of empathic listening and responding. What does empathic responding involve?

First, empathic responding is listening without judging or evaluating the speaker's words. Every time you judge ("You're wrong." "What the hell did you do that for?"), you stop the message and create barriers that keep the speaker's full meaning from being communicated. This only frustrates the speaker. Every day remind yourself to listen and not to immediately judge the words and ideas of others. The most challenging times for you to be nonjudgmental are when you have strong emotions or strong opinions about what the speaker is saying.

This is not a plea from a bleeding heart liberal. You gain an unequaled and powerful ability to lead and motivate the minute that you force yourself to hear, feel, and sense the speaker's words from his or her perspective. When listening, keep the following points in mind:

- Stay on the client's topic.

- Give the client your attention and time.

- Don't be frightened by silences.

- Employ the word "you" or, even better, use the person's name occasionally.

- Keep thinking, "What does what this person is saying mean to him or her?" Instead of "How does this affect me?"

- Don't react out of your own needs.

- Avoid interruptions.

- When listening, don't conclude where people are going before they get there.

Ask yourself the following additional questions about what you say:

1. How does what I said fit in with what the client said?

2. How does it relate to the client's world?

3. Does it have any interest to the client?

4. How did what I said contribute to continuing rather then ending the conversation?

5. In what possible ways might what I said be interpreted?

6. Did I encourage the client by what I said?

7. How did I demonstrate that I listened to the client?

8. How did I sound? Was I enthusiastic?

Skill: Focus on Assets

In addition to listening with full attention and empathizing with people, another essential skill in leadership is being able to spotlight and magnify an individual's strengths, assets, and resources. We all know people who are nit-pickers, and flaw finders, who focus on spotting a mistake, a weakness, or something which isn't as it "should" be. They are quick to offer criticism. Be an individual who is finely tuned to hearing and seeing assets. This is excellent modeling for your clients.

To develop skills in asset focusing, condition your clients to zero in on the assets in people. Think of the most encouraging, asset focusing people you ever met and emulate them. What is their secret? They look past faults and focus on strengths. My own best coaches and mentors have all had this ability. Each one was able to look past my own weaknesses and faults and outright ignore them. The result was both encouraging and empowering for me. Instead of criticism and fault finding, my mentors focused instead on getting me to try again, sometimes even using humor to rib me about my "screw-ups."

Whenever we are called in to coach fire officers and chiefs, we invariably have them take a personality profile of the type discussed earlier in this book. Invariably, these profiles reveal behavioral characteristics that stick out like sore thumbs. It would be easier to simply terminate these people, rehire or promote someone to take their place, and then hope for the best. But this is usually not the best approach. Instead, our experience suggests that in a fair number of situations, the best approach is to look past the faults and look for personality assets and then try to find the best job fit.

Skill: Develop Your Client's Alternative Perceptions

One of the most important leadership skills to develop in your clients is the practice of seeing perceptual alternatives. Help clients to look at people and issues that they face in many new ways. Think of the last time you had a disagreement with someone. Stop for a minute and try to get into the other person's shoes and convincingly present his or her position. If you can, you have taken a giant step toward developing your understanding and coaching style and, most importantly, your client's leadership style.

I recently coached one of the most brilliant chief's I have ever met. Commanding a battalion in a large suburban department, aptitude testing revealed that the chief scored a 9 in mental acuity. This means that the chief is a very fast thinker with a high degree of critical thinking ability. He has excellent problem solving capabilities and can reason through and make good decisions based on knowledge, intuition and reasoning skills. He not only enjoys, but requires, mentally challenging work for job satisfaction. Despite his apparent high IQ and rapid thinking ability, the Chief had a difficult time maintaining the respect of peers, the department officer, or his subordinates. By the time I saw him, he was quite discouraged and felt like a miserable failure.

360 degree feedback results revealed that the Chief was arrogant and cold. Interestingly, when presented with this information, he launched into a tirade about the philosophy of Socrates, in particular, his contribution to the scientific method. With all of his intelligence and learning, he could not see how his professorial demeanor made him appear to be critical and unfeeling. Furthermore, the Chief could not understand that his staff did not possess the same personality style and thus, the same motives or outlook as did he. All of his intelligence, his impressive background, and his knowledge actually worked against him because he didn't use them by starting off in his staff's world.

Our goal was to help the Chief develop the talent of perceptual alternatives. To achieve this end, we catered to his intellectualizing style by showing him some personality style reports and then engaging in the Socratic method of questions and answers. We showed him the benefits of understanding style differences and the fact that different styles both value and are motivated differently. We showed him how people perform better whenever their needs are met and when both work and work relationships meet their motivational needs. We then "shadow coached" with the Chief by following him around over a two day period and giving him immediate feedback whenever he interacted with others in a too cold and intellectualizing manner. The Chief got the message. While he will never be perfect, he reports that he reminds himself each morning to make it a point to perceive the world from his staff's perspective.

Skill: Encouraging Team Spirit

Help clients to build team spirit by emphasizing cooperation as opposed to competition. Observe a shift or battalion with flaring spirit and strong morale, and you will find a talented leader in the picture. No doubt one talent the leader possesses is the ability to de-emphasize competition among teammates and put the accent on cooperation.

Build team power by giving group credit and encouraging each member to do the same. The United States ranks foremost among nations in valuing individual achievement and accomplishment (Hofstede). But team spirit is eroded whenever individuals attempt to take credit for the success of the group. This is not to say that individual achievement should not be recognized, but team power is often greater than the sum of the parts. Help clients think in terms of "we" not "me" or "I".

Skill: Recognize the Power of Conveying Confidence in People

Harness the power of self-fulfilling prophecies. A self-fulfilling prophecy causes people to perform according to expectations. As a leader, your confidence or lack of confidence in people actually is one of the most important factors in terms of how they will perform.

This phenomenon has been observed in numerous instances. Bosses, mentors, supervisors, and leaders have taken others who are considered incorrigible and turned them into productive people. Teachers have taken pupils labeled as "un-teachable" and helped them progress. How? By conveying their belief in the individual by communicating, "I know you can do it!"

Remember your own experience to see how this confidence works. Did you ever have a teacher or a supervisor who didn't have confidence in you? Everything you did was put down. The harder you tried, the more this person focused on what went wrong. Eventually your performance level dropped and you became discouraged.

On the other hand, did you ever have a teacher, supervisor, or leader who truly believed in your abilities, who thought you were special, and conveyed this belief to you? What happened? In this situation, you were probably more creative, less anxious, and actually more productive.

Bibliography and Recommended Readings

Shaw, George Bernard. Pygmalion. Mineola, NY: Dover Thrift, 1938.

Chapter 11

Generational Differences: Can the Mix Really Work?

Generational Differences Can The Mix Really Work?

[Reprinted By Permission of Texas Fire Chief]

Introduction

We included this chapter for one very simple reason: the fire service is screaming for help to solve generationally based conflicts and misunderstandings. We could have included a chapter on racial and ethnic differences, but these issues are either covered in other fine books or simply are not receiving as much attention as is generational differences.

We've become known as leading experts on young fire service personnel — first Generation X and now Generation Y. Today's young firefighters and officers have no baggage from the workplace of the past and seem more comfortable in the new high-tech, high-speed, super-fluid, fiercely competitive service business world. Why? They've never known it any other way.

But what about the Baby Boomers and those of the Silent (Veterans) Generation, who still account for more than half of the workforce? Those with more age and experience are decades into their careers and they are well aware of the profound changes transforming the working world. Some are happy to change along with the real new economy, while others are digging in their heels and pining for the old rules of business (dues paying, seniority, and job security).

The generational clash playing out in the workplace today is not merely a matter of young versus old. This clash pits the old-fashioned expectations, values and practices of stability against the new reality of constant change and the consequent need for agility. In this economic downturn, some observers expected that the upstart free agent movement would be stopped dead in its tracks and we would all go back to the paternalistic, "business as usual," employer-employee relationship. But look what's happened instead. Employers in every industry have demonstrated their new organizational agility by downsizing and restructuring on a dime to adapt to changing market conditions.

How are employees reacting? Those who were already thinking like free agents are saying, "I told you so. I must fend for myself aggressively because there is no such thing as job security anymore." Those still digging in their heels are more terrified than ever.

What's the punch line? In the real new economy, every worker of every age must become more self-sufficient, flexible, entrepreneurial, and techno-savvy to remain viable. That's not a generational preference. That's just the order of the day. The new generation gap at work is a mirror of the various individual responses to this order and a reflection of the fundamental tension between the need for stability and the need for agility.

If you are experiencing a clash between the young and not so young in your organization, don't treat it as just another diversity issue. Use it. We recommend the following action plan:

1. Clear the air. Hold a team meeting and ask individuals to focus on two key questions: What do you feel you have to offer that will be of particular value to those of other generations? How can YOU benefit from the differences of other generations?

2. Get everybody focused on the shared mission. What is the organization's mission? What is the team's mission? What is your individual role?

3. Make sure everybody understands that the arbiter of all differences hereafter will be the work itself. What decision helps us get more work done better and faster?

Today's fire service is unique and singular. Never before has there been a workplace and workforce so diverse in so many ways. The mix of races, genders, ethnicities, and generations in today's fire service is stunning. The latter, generational diversity, and the tension, challenge, opportunity, and promise it presents are the focus of this article.

Like a two by four between the eyes, there is the realization that the gulf of misunderstanding and resentment between older, not so old, and younger employees in the workplace is growing and problematic. It is a rift that will not heal itself or just go away, as so many departments fervently hope. It is a problem based in economics, demographics, and world-views that must be confronted to be solved.

The problem among older and younger personnel is a problem of differences in values, ambitions, views, and mind-sets stemming directly from generational personality differences. Generational personality! Yes, there is such a thing, and right now all these generations are vying for position in a workplace of shrinking upward opportunity. Previously, things like the "old guard", military hierarchy, and shorter life spans kept a given generational cohort isolated from others. These factors no longer exist, or they exist in a much less rigid, more permeable manner. Merit is creeping in as a variable in advancement decisions. The negative outcomes are obvious. Intergenerational conflict, differences in values and views, and ways of working, talking, and thinking sets fire personnel in opposition to one another and challenges the department's best interests.

On the positive side however, one outcome of this largely accidental generational blending is creativity, or at least it can be. People of different perspectives have the potential to bring different thoughts and ideas to problem solving and future opportunity. Studies reveal that heterogeneity holds more promise for creativity than does homogeneity.

The four generations and their birth dates include: Veterans (1922-1943), Boomers (1943-1960), Xers (1960-1980), and Nexters (1980-2000). Each has a unique work ethic, a different perspective on work, a distinct and preferred way of managing and being managed, an idiosyncratic style, and a unique way of viewing such "work-world" issues as quality, service, and, well just showing up for work.

What generations are represented in your department? It should come as no surprise that the majority is probably Boomers, particularly when considering that they make up the largest percentage of the population according to US Census statistics. And when we talk about your organization's mature workers we can't forget the Boomers' parents who are still hard at work throughout many organizations. With a trend towards later retirements, the Veterans generation still serves a vital role in the workforce.

How about the younger generations? According to a recent Washington Post article, some organizations are soon to experience an enormous retirement rate. This means that succession planning must be a primary consideration. For some organizations this is foreign territory because they have never developed a coaching or mentoring culture for bringing people up within the organization to teach them to become leaders.

The Generation Xers must be ready to step up to the leadership challenge. Xers represent roughly 20% of the working population, yet, in a short time, they will make up the bulk of our workforce.

Generation Y, the youngest workers, will have to develop even more quickly than the Generation X predecessors to help fill the leadership positions because there are far fewer Generation Xers than Baby Boomers in our society. These are the people that are coming out of colleges and training academies as we speak. Some refer to this generation as the super Xers. These are the cyber kids who grew up with the Internet and speed and access to information is something that they are accustomed to.

What Do the Members of Each Generation Value?

Fundamental value differences exist between those of different generations. Driven by our value system and our value programming, these values differences may help us understand conflicts and misunderstanding that arise in the workplace.

If we examine the value system shared by generational groups then we can better understand the diverse beliefs and behaviors. We don't have to agree with the values of different generations but we can strive to understand the mind-sets of different generations and how each group sees the world based on their experiences. While it's important to recognize that many dimensions of diversity from race, sex, sexual orientation, geographic location, etc., shape who we are and how we behave, we can generalize values based on generations as well. Let's take a look at some of the espoused values or beliefs held by each of the generations so that you will be better able to appreciate the challenge that we face as an organization trying to create an inclusive environment. Please note that these are generalizations and may not apply to all employees of a particular generation.

Veterans

Veterans' values are influenced by the experiences of their parents whose values go back to the 1800s. This generation experienced the Great Depression and World War II, both of which shape how they view the world.

Veterans value...

- Privacy: Veterans are the private, silent generation. Don't expect members of this generation to share their inner thoughts.

- Hard Work: They believe in paying their dues and become irritated when they perceive others are wasting their time. Members of this generation often feel that their career identifies who they are.

- Trust: A leader's word is his/her bond.

- Formality: Whether written or in oral communication, a formal communication style is preferred. This generation values formal dress and organizational structures.

- Authority and institutional leadership: Veterans have a great deal of respect for authority.

- Social Order: Other generations may view this desire for social order and placement as bias, prejudice or even racism or sexism.

- Things: This group loves their stuff and they won't get rid of it. Some may call them pack rats but others would argue that they remember the depression days and going without. You never know when you might need it.

Supportive behaviors & tips for communicating with veterans...

By nature Veterans are private, the "silent generation". Don't expect members of this generation to share their thoughts immediately.

- For the Veterans, a leader's word is his/her bond, so it's important to focus on words rather than body language or inferences.

- Face to face or written communication is preferred.

- Don't waste their time, or let them feel as though their time is being wasted.

Baby Boomers

Some call this group the Nu-agers. This generation represents the children of our World War II veterans. They did not go through economically hard times as their parents did, they had the good life. The Veterans wanted them to have the best and as a result the "Me" decade arrived.

Baby boomers value...

- Competition: Boomers value peer competition and can be seen by others as being egocentric.

- Change: Boomers thrive for possibilities and constant change.

- Hard Work: Boomers started the "workaholic" trend. The difference between Veterans and Boomers is that Boomers value the hard work because they view it as necessary for moving to the next level of success while Veterans work hard because they feel that it is the right thing to do.

- Success: This generation is committed to climbing the ladder of success.

- Body Language: Boomers are the show me generation and body language is important.

- Teamwork: This group embraces a team-based approach to business. They are eager to get rid of the command and control style of their Veterans predecessors.

- Anti Rules & Regulations: They don't appreciate rules for the sake of having rules and they will challenge the system.

- Inclusion: This generation will accept people on an equal basis as long as they can perform to their standards.

- Will Fight For A Cause: While they don't like problems, if you give them a cause they will fight for it.

Supportive behaviors & tips for communicating with baby boomers...

- Boomers are the "show me" generation, so your body language is important when communicating.

- Speak in an open, direct style but avoid controlling language.

- Answer questions thoroughly and expect to be pressed for the details.

- Present options to demonstrate flexibility in your thinking.

Generation Xers

This group is sometimes called the Syn-Tech generation. They tend to be economically conservative, remembering double-digit inflation and the stress that their parents faced during times of on and off unemployment. Unlike their predecessors, they will not rely on institutions for their long-term security. This makes them appear disloyal.

Generation Xers value...

- Entrepreneurial Spirit: Xers believe in investing in their own development rather than in their organization's. While others may see them as disloyal they are cautious about investing in relationships with employers because experience has shown that these relationships are not reliable.

- Independence and Creativity: Xers have clear goals and prefer managing their own time and solving their own problems rather than having them managed by a supervisor.

- Information: They value access to information and love plenty of it.

- Feedback: This group needs continuous feedback and they use the feedback to adapt to new situations. This generation is flexible.

- Quality of Work life: This generation works hard but they would rather find quicker more efficient ways of working so that they have time for fun. While Boomers are working hard to move up the ladder, Xers are working hard so that they can have more time to balance work and life responsibilities.

Supportive behaviors & tips for communicating with Generation X...

- Use email as a primary communication tool.

- Talk in short sound bites to keep their attention.

- Ask them for their feedback and provide them with regular feedback.

- Share information with them on a regular basis and strive to keep them in the loop.

- Use an informal communication style.

Generation Y (Also Called Nexters)

If you think that Generation Xers were challenging for Boomers to manage just wait until Generation Y moves into the workplace. Generation Y represents people who have grown up during the high tech revolution. They have never known a world without high-speed video games, speed dial and ATMs. The secret to motivating this group is to provide systematic and frequent feedback, as it happens.

Generation Y values...

- Positive Reinforcement: Members of this cyber generation value positive reinforcement at accelerated rates compared to older generations.

- Autonomy: This group wants more input into how they do their job and the independence to do it.

- Positive Attitudes: This group grew up during tranquil times and, as a result, has a very optimistic outlook on life in general.

- Diversity: This group grew up with more diversity than their predecessors and if not exposed to it in their community, then they were introduced to diverse people and cultures through the media.

- Money: This group is used to making and spending money.

- Technology: Technology is valued and is used as a tool for multi-tasking.

Supportive behaviors & tips for communicating with Generation Y...

- Use action words and challenge them at every opportunity.

- They will resent it if you talk down to them.

- They prefer email communication.

- Seek their feedback constantly and provide them with regular feedback.

- Use humor and create a fun work environment. Don't take yourself too seriously.

- Encourage them to take risks and break the rules so that they can explore new ways of doing things.

Managing the Generational Mix

How do we keep a generationally diverse group of employees motivated and productive in today's environment? The first step to making the generational diversity work is to understand what motivates members of different generations and to institute practices that are flexible enough to meet their needs. Gone are the days when the Veterans are in charge and everyone who is not a Boomer reports to a Boomer. In today's complex mix of generations, Veterans also report to Boomers and Boomers report to Generation Xers. Trends toward later retirements mean that Veterans are still happy working and Generation Xers are quickly moving into positions of power and influence where they are supervising members of older generations.

Departments are beginning to recognize that the changing demographics of the workplace can affect morale and productivity. The HarBeck Company has incorporated an intergenerational component to leadership training for many of the fire service clients. Officers experience how different generations react and interact with each other. Some officers focus on opening the channels of communication by encouraging employees of all levels to forward e-mail questions and comments. Departments have also focused on creating a more fun working environment to address the needs of incoming generations. For example, some departments strive to match people with their jobs and to ensure that they are continuously challenged. This is vital for techno-literate employees who are perhaps more easily bored.

Other departments understand that it is important to focus not only on what needs to get done, but also on accommodating the work styles of various generations. This is not to suggest that employees should not be held accountable for those processes that are non-negotiable, but many departments are beginning to revisit what those non-negotiable processes really are. And some processes that were considered non-negotiable in the past are now given more flexibility.

Chapter 12

Performance Evaluations

Performance Evaluations

Let's understand one thing from the start—performance evaluations don't work. That's right! They don't work. Although everyone uses them and countless hours are spent on them, they are woefully inadequate for anything other than using numbers to justify whether or not to give a raise. They have little to do with performance improvement and even less to do with motivation.

Giving and receiving feedback has long been considered an essential skill for leaders. As they strive to achieve the goals of the organization, employees need to know how they are doing. They need to know if their performance is what their leaders expect from them and, if not, they need suggestions on how to improve it. Traditionally, this information has been communicated in the form of feedback from leaders to their employees. And leaders, themselves, need feedback from their employees, in the form of suggestions on how to improve procedures and processes, innovative ideas for new products and services, and input on their own leadership styles. This has become increasingly common with the advent of 360 degree feedback.

But there is a fundamental problem with feedback. Feedback focuses on the *past*, on what has already occurred, not on the infinite variety of things that can be, in the future. As such, feedback can be limited and static, as opposed to expansive and dynamic.

Over the past several years, I have observed more than five thousand leaders participate in a fascinating experiential exercise. In the exercise, each participant is asked to play two roles. In one role, they are asked to provide *feed forward*, that is, to give someone else suggestions for the future and *help as much as they can*. In the second role, they are asked to accept feed forward, that is, to listen to the suggestions for the future and learn as much as they can. The exercise typically lasts 10-15 minutes, and the average participant has 6-7 dialogue sessions. In the exercise, participants are asked to:

- Pick one behavior that you would like to change. *Change in this behavior should make a significant, positive difference in their life.*

- Describe this behavior to randomly selected fellow participants. *This is done in one on one dialogues and may be done simply (e.g. "I want to be a better listener").*

- Ask for feed forward by requesting two suggestions for the future that might help you achieve a positive change in your selected behavior. *If participants have worked together in the past, they are not allowed to give ANY feedback about the past. They are only allowed to give ideas for the future.*

- Listen attentively to the suggestions and take notes. *Participants are not allowed to comment on the suggestions in any way. They are not allowed to critique the suggestions or even to make positive judgmental statements, such as, "That's a good idea."*

- Thank the other participants for their suggestions.

- Ask the other persons what they would like to change.

- Provide feed forward by making two suggestions aimed at helping them change.

- Say, "You are welcome" when thanked for the suggestions. *The entire process of both giving and receiving feed forward usually takes about two minutes.*

- Find another participant and keep repeating the process until the exercise is stopped.

When the exercise is finished, I ask participants to provide one word that best describes their reaction to this experience. I ask them to complete the sentence, "This exercise was …". The words provided are almost always extremely positive, such as "great," "energizing," "useful," or "helpful." The most common word mentioned is "fun!" What is the last word that most of us think about when we receive coaching and developmental ideas? Fun!

Ten Reasons to Try to Feed Forward

Participants are then asked why this exercise is seen as fun and helpful as opposed to painful, embarrassing or uncomfortable. Their answers provide a great explanation of why feed forward can often be more useful than feedback.

1. ***We can change the future.*** *We can't change the past.* Feed forward helps people envision and focus on a positive future,

not a failed past. Athletes are often trained using feed forward. Racecar drivers are taught to "look at the road, not the wall." Basketball players are taught to envision the ball going in the hoop and to imagine the perfect shot. By giving people ideas on how they can be even more successful, we can increase their chances of achieving this success in the future.

2. ***It can be more productive to help people be "right," than prove they were "wrong."*** Negative feedback often becomes an exercise in "let me prove you were wrong." This tends to produce defensiveness on the part of the receiver and discomfort on the part of the sender. Even constructively delivered feedback is often seen as negative as it necessarily involves a discussion of mistakes, shortfalls, and problems. Feed forward, on the other hand, is almost always seen positively because it focuses on solutions.

3. ***Feed forward is especially suited to successful people.*** Successful people like getting ideas that are aimed at helping them achieve their goals. They tend to resist negative judgment. We all tend to accept feedback that is consistent with the way we see ourselves. We also tend to reject or deny feedback that is inconsistent with the way we see ourselves. Successful people tend to have a very positive self-image. I have observed many successful executives respond to (and even enjoy) feed forward. I am not sure that these same people would have had such a positive reaction to feedback.

4. ***Feed forward can come from anyone who knows about the task.*** It does not require personal experience with the individual. One very common positive reaction to the previously described exercise is that participants are amazed by how much they can learn from people that they don't even know! For example, if you want to be a better listener, almost any fellow leader can give you ideas on how you can improve. They don't have to know you. Feedback requires knowing about the person. Feed forward just requires having good ideas for achieving the task.

5. ***People do not take feed forward as personally as feedback.*** In theory, constructive feedback is supposed to "focus on the performance, not the person." In practice, almost all feedback is taken personally (no matter how it is delivered). Successful people's sense of identity is highly connected with their work. The more successful people are, the more this tends to be true. It is hard to give a dedicated professional feedback that is not taken personally. Feed forward cannot involve a

personal critique, since it is discussing something that has not yet happened!

6. ***Feedback can reinforce personal stereotyping and negative self-fulfilling prophecies.*** Feed forward can reinforce the possibility of change. Feedback can reinforce the feeling of failure. How many of us have been "helped" by a spouse, significant other, or friend, who seems to have a near photographic memory of our previous "sins" that they share with us in order to point out the history of our shortcomings. Negative feedback can be used to reinforce the message, "this is just the way you are." Feed forward is based on the assumption that people can make positive changes in the future.

7. ***Face it! Most of us hate getting negative feedback, and we don't like to give it.*** I have reviewed summary 360 degree feedback reports for over 50 companies. The items, "provides developmental feedback in a timely manner" and "encourages and accepts constructive criticism" almost always score near the bottom on co-worker satisfaction with leaders. Traditional training does not seem to make a great deal of difference. If leaders got better at providing feedback every time the performance appraisal forms were "improved," most should be perfect by now! Leaders are not very good at giving or receiving negative feedback. It is unlikely that this will change in the near future.

8. ***Feed forward can cover almost all of the same "material" as feedback.*** Imagine that you have just made a terrible presentation in front of the executive committee. Your manager is in the room. Rather than make you "relive" this humiliating experience, your manager might help you prepare for future presentations by giving you suggestions for the future. These suggestions can be very specific and still delivered in a positive way. In this way your manager can "cover the same points" without feeling as embarrassed and without making you feel even more humiliated.

9. ***Feed forward tends to be much faster and more efficient than feedback.*** An excellent technique for giving ideas to successful people is to say, "Here are four ideas for the future. Please accept these in the positive spirit that they are given. If you can only use two of the ideas, you are still two ahead. Just ignore what doesn't make sense for you." With this approach, almost no time gets wasted on judging the quality of the ideas or "proving that the ideas are wrong." This "debate" time is usually negative, it can take up a lot of time, and it is often

not very productive. By eliminating judgment of the ideas, the process becomes much more positive for the sender as well as the receiver. Successful people tend to have a high need for self-determination and will tend to accept ideas that they "buy" while rejecting ideas that feel "forced" upon them.

10. ***Feed forward can be a useful tool to apply with managers, peers, and team members.*** Rightly or wrongly, feedback is associated with judgment. This can lead to very negative, unintended consequences when applied to managers or peers. Feed forward does not imply superiority of judgment. It is more focused on being a helpful "fellow traveler" than an "expert." As such it can be easier to hear from a person who is not in a position of power or authority. An excellent team building exercise is to have each team member ask, "How can I better help our team in the future?" and listen to feed forward from fellow team members (in one on one dialogues.)

In summary, the intent of this article is not to imply that leaders should never give feedback or that performance appraisals should be abandoned. The intent is to show how feed forward can often be preferable to feedback in day-to-day interactions. Aside from its effectiveness and efficiency, feed forward can make life a lot more enjoyable. When managers are asked, "How did you feel the last time you received feedback?," their most common responses are very negative. When managers are asked how they felt after receiving feed forward, they reply that feed forward was not only useful, it was also fun!

Quality communication between and among people at all levels and every department and division is the glue that holds organizations together. By using feed forward, and by encouraging others to use it, leaders can dramatically improve the quality of communication in their organizations, ensuring that the right message is conveyed, and that those who receive it are receptive to its content. The result is a much more dynamic, much more open organization, one whose employees focus on the promise of the future rather than the mistakes of the past.

Chapter 13

Putting Some
Skills Together

Putting Some Skills Together

Chapter 13

Introduction

It's time to show you what these skills look like in operation. Over the next few pages, we are going to step inside an initial coaching meeting and illustrate the following twelve coaching skills:

1. Questioning

2. Contracting the work

3. Joining

4. Getting familiar with the client's challenges

5. Concreteness

6. Empathy

7. Confrontation

8. Respect

9. Testing the client's ability to own their part of the issue or objective

10. Encouraging clients to set measurable goals

11. Clarifying the purpose of coaching and/or of coaching meetings

12. Verbalizing expectations

Application

Twenty years ago, George Bailey became the chief of a little country town some twenty-five miles from the inner city. Within the city, he was heralded as the guardian of the city's traditions. Keeping things the same was valued and George was just the man to do so. He had leisurely lunches every day with a member of the city council, the city manager, or one of the community's prominent business people.

The discussion of fire department or city business made up only a small portion of the lunch hour. Golf handicaps and pro football lines were more the interest of discussion. Everything was fine and would have remained so except that the little town's growth skyrocketed and it received state and national recognition as the fastest growing community in the U.S. based on per capita percentage growth. What the little community had to offer looked attractive to residents desiring bigger houses for less money, and for businesses looking to build bigger headquarters for less money and a greater tax break than could be had from the big city. Naturally, local politics reared its ugly head as older, long-time residents wanted certain protections for their beloved small town environment. When George took the job, change had only begun to knock on the doors of the resident's psyche. Their reaction was one of stubborn resolve.

These Eastern European descendents wanted no part of globalization and cared not about the situation in the Middle East except for the gasoline price fluctuations at the local pumps. The town's most long settled families had inhabited the black farmland for six generations and their plan was to continue to do so for at least six more. Sons of long established farmers and merchants married the daughters of long-established farmers and merchants, went to work, and had babies that were named James IV or Margaret Elizabeth, and time went on. New model tractors and the seasons were the only changes either welcomed or tolerated. The most popular burger in town was named after a notorious bootlegger of the 1920's whose descendents still ran the local hole in the wall joint, and whose grandson (of the same name) was none other than the fire chief.

Until recently, the biggest controversy to sweep the city was whether to change the name of the high school mascot from Redskins to Native-Americans or simply to go with the less offensive lions or tigers. A brawl ensued over the issue at the school board. As one of the most vociferous board members was led away by his brother-in-law, the Assistant Chief of Police, he shouted, "Pride, greed, and lust are deadly sins! Things should remain as they are." He was released from jail within twenty minutes on his own recognizance. Charges were never brought against him and he is a city councilman at the time of this writing.

New residents wanted things to move a little faster. Unlike the long term residents, they wanted all of the amenities of the big city, even though they had rushed to flee that very environment. And, as is the way of city politics, money has a way of influencing decisions.

The fire department expanded at a rapid pace in keeping with the growth of the city and was not subject to civil service guidelines on hiring and promotion. New, young firefighters were hired at an incredible pace and then promoted within an unheard of time span. One such new hire was the son of a city councilman, also a relative newcomer to the community. By all accounts, this young firefighter was irresponsible, reprehensible, unlikable, and a goof-off. Firefighters who would have been subordinate to him had he been promoted, gave a sigh of relief when he was not. Prior to the next city council meeting, the father of the young firefighter spread the news that he was going to lop off the head of the fire chief. Of course he didn't admit that his was a vendetta against the chief for failing to promote his son. Instead, he claimed to report the complaints of a majority of firefighters about the morale of the department and the demeanor of the chief.

The news of the councilman's intentions spread throughout the community and citizens started arriving ninety minutes prior to the scheduled start. Like the guests of the bride and groom, supporters of the chief sat on the left while supporters of the councilman sat on the right. It didn't take long for all hell to break loose and the police had to clear the room of citizens while a closed-door session ensued.

The mayor listened to the complaints of the city councilman and then asked the chief to speak on his own behalf. Then Chief Bailey rose from his seat near the back of the chamber, shifted the dip of Skoal that he had planted, prior to the meeting, from his left cheek to the right. He then strode past the microphone that he was supposed to use when addressing the council and stopped directly in front of his adversary. Eyeing the notes the councilman had brought to make his case, the chief leaned over the desk and sent a stream of solid dark brown spit across the neat stack of pages. He then turned and left. The left side of the room erupted in cheers and the next day, the chief was referred for coaching.

> *"I bet you've heard why I'm here," Chief Bailey said.*
>
> *"I hear you found an interesting spittoon," the coach said.*
>
> > *(Joining)*
>
> *"He got off easy," the chief said, "In the old days, they would have been cleaning up more than a stack of papers."*
>
> *"Looks to me like you made your point," the coach said.*
>
> > *(Joining)*
>
> *The chief laughed, "I won't ever forget the look on his face."*
>
> *"I can only imagine," the coach replied.*
>
> > *(Empathy)*
>
> *"Like father like son, huh," the chief said. "The little guy went to the big guy instead of coming to me, like a man. He gets daddy to confront the city manager."*   continued

The coach asked, "He should have come to you about his promotion."

(Joining)

"Yes, and even before that, he and the rest of the firefighters should have come to me if they were so dissatisfied."

"You're experiencing betrayal," the coach said.

(Empathy)

Chief Bailey shifted in his chair and cleared his throat. His hands gripped the chair arms tightly making his knuckles pop up and turn porcelain white. Hard, band-like jaw muscles twitched behind skin bronzed from exposure to the sun.

"Damn right I am! I mean, I have my faults, don't get me wrong. I can be hard to deal with, I know that, but I can't respect a weakling. Besides, my faults aren't as big as he makes them out to be. No, he's just mad because he didn't get promoted."

"Just revenge on his part?" the coach asked. "Nothing more?"

(Testing the client's ability to take responsibility)

"I think that's it," the chief said. "Like I say, I have my faults, but, hey we all do, don't we? Anyway, the city manager bends to the whims of the council."

"Nothing fair about this. You would do things the same now that you look back?"

(Testing the client's ability to take responsibility)

George raised his finger and tightened his lips as if to defend himself once again. But hesitating, his finger dropped and his face softened, smoothing over hard jaw muscles.

"No, I wouldn't do things the same way," he said.

"How so?" the coach asked.

(Questioning)

(Concreteness)

"Don't get me wrong. I'm still mad at the kid and his old man."

"I understand," the coach said. "We can come back to that. But I guess I'm interested in your personal assessment of your performance."

(Empathy)

(Testing the client's ability to take responsibility)

"And I hate these damn politics," Chief Bailey said.

continued

"I'll give you that," agreed the coach.

(Empathy)

"I've got to be honest with myself, don't I?"

"Why do you?" the coach asked. *"That's what you have to ask yourself when you're considering change. Why?"*

(Testing the client's ability to take responsibility)

"Look, I don't want to get philosophical about it," the chief said. *"I just need to be honest with myself. I should. Let's just say that the kid is not the only one who is upset. Several firefighters have formally complained to my command staff about me, saying that I'm weak in my leadership and too harsh in my demeanor. And there is a lot of bickering and infighting among the people in the department. The director of human resources is one of my best friends and he called me in the other day and asked me point blank what the hell was going on, that many of my staff were wearing out his carpet with complaints about me and each other."*

"What would you like to get out of this coaching?"

(Contracting)

George stood and walked to the window.

"What I'd like to say is that I want the kid to find another job," the chief said. *"But what I know is that I need to improve on some things."*

"Be more specific if you can," the coach prompted.

(Concreteness)

Chief Bailey said, "I've got to tighten up in some areas, be more organized, oversee things a bit more. On the other hand, and I've had this feedback before, I need to be more encouraging, less critical."

"Okay, Chief, very good. That sounds like a good set of general goals to begin with. Why?"

(Encouraging goal setting)

"Pardon me? What do you mean?"

"Why? Why do you want to do these things?" the coach asked.

(Questioning)

"Well, for a variety of reasons," Chief Bailey said. *"I want to keep my job and I'd prefer to stay out of hot water. But more than anything, I would like to be a different kind of chief; one that my firefighters respect instead of just fear. I want to be the kind of leader who facilitates people to want to do things."*

continued

"Very well, Chief. Given your years of experience in management, I know that you have overcome challenges like this before. What I want you to think about is how?"

(Respect and Questioning)

"Actually I've never had to really. But get one thing straight," the chief said. "I'm no dummy. I realize that my style works in the good-ole boy, small town kind of atmosphere but not so much here. I just forget it sometimes."

"You're telling me that the feedback you've received is not a surprise to you and that you are fully aware that your style is what?" the coach asked "How would you describe it?"

(Familiarizing the coach with the client's challenge)

"Abrasive, I guess you'd say," Chief Bailey said.

"Tell me, Chief, what do you want to change?"

(Contracting and Encouraging goal setting)

"Between you and me," the chief said quietly, "and this is all confidential, right?"

"Yes."

"I want to deal with fear," the chief said.

"Say more," the coach said.

(Concreteness)

"Okay, I have a reputation as a tough person and frankly I like it. It's who I am, and I can't say that one hundred percent of me wants to change, but who I am doesn't work like it used to, at least it appears that way. I don't even know if I'm capable of being the "sensitive" chief that they are asking for."

"You possess specific traits that will help you solve this challenge, Chief," the coach said. "What are they?"

(Respect)

"I know that I'm mule-headed and demanding. Does that count for anything? Besides, I thought you might tell me how to fix me."

"Right now I'm not witnessing mule-headedness, or direction," the coach said. "Rather, I think I'm seeing discouragement or avoidance."

(Confrontation)

"Okay, okay, I'm sorry," the chief said. "Actually I think I bring a lot. That's not to say that there aren't things for me to learn. Clearly there

continued

are. But nobody understands the fire department's role in city government better than I do."

The coach nodded, "Be more specific, Chief."

(Concreteness)

"I mean I can accomplish what I want to when I set my mind to it."

"And how will you know when you'll want to," the coach asked, "because the purpose of coaching is to help you get better at something? But, that something must come from you. Coaching is a collaborative process whereby I facilitate very specific improvements that you target."

(Contracting, Encouraging goal setting, and Clarifying purpose)

"I know what I don't want," Chief Bailey said. "I don't want them to pull a stunt like this any more."

"All right then, here's another question for you to consider," the coach said. "How will you know when things have improved for you?"

(Getting the client to verbalize expectations)

Summary

At this point, no work has been done toward accomplishing a goal. Nevertheless, a lot of work has been done. Coaches must question, contract, join, familiarize themselves with the client's challenge, be concrete, empathic, occasionally confront, communicate respect, test the client to take responsibility, clarify the purpose, and facilitate the client to verbalize expectations before working on goal accomplishment. Moving too quickly to set goals often ends in failure because the foundation of coaching has not been established. In fact, our experience suggests that if the foundation is firmly established, specific goal setting and movement toward those goals is made much easier.

Chapter 14

The Habits of
Successful Coaches

The Habits of Successful Coaches

In coaching it is important to have a reliable and replicable process for improving the client's performance. Toward this end, this chapter presents the habits of highly successful coaches. And perhaps it would be helpful to start by discussing two things: (1) what clients want from coaching, and (2) what highly successful coaches do. In this way, you can emulate a general blueprint for success.

What Fire Service Personnel Want From Coaching

Almost nothing can be gleaned from the coaching literature regarding fire officer perceptions of coaching. Because of this paucity of research, I conducted an opinion survey in order to begin building an understanding of fire service personnel's needs, desires, and requirements in this learning system (coaching relationship). This "research" should in no way be considered the final answer but rather as a mere starting point upon which to build coaching models for success with fire service personnel.

During the summer of 2002, a survey questionnaire was distributed to five hundred fire service personnel who had participated in individual and/or team coaching with me during the previous twelve months. One hundred fifty items pertaining to coaching were presented. The questionnaire simply asked respondents to put a check mark next to those items that they deemed "most important" in a supervisor/coach.

The only restriction was that respondents could only use a maximum of seventy-five checks. This prevented respondents from checking all items as most important and forced them to consider the most important items. Forty-one out of the one-hundred and fifty items were checked by at least 60% of the respondents as important in the coaching process. This percentage was arbitrarily chosen to reveal a majority opinion. The break down of the 500 respondents is listed below.

- 18 departments were included in the survey

- 10 respondents were chiefs

- 10 respondents were assistant chiefs

- 80 respondents were battalion chiefs

- 117 respondents were lieutenants

- 283 respondents were firefighter/EMTs

- Average age of the firefighter/EMTs and Lieutenants was 34.6 years

- Average age of the chiefs was 51.2 years

Table 1 reveals the results of the survey. The items are listed in no particular order although they were grouped according to the coach's function following the completion of the survey. The number of respondents who checked the item and corresponding percentage is listed beside each item. Three general groups were considered in the analysis of results: Overall (all respondents), firefighters/EMTs and Lieutenants, and Command staff personnel that included battalion chiefs, assistant chiefs, and chiefs.

First, let's look at overall responses without further breakdown based on rank. This may further reveal what is perceived as important in coaching by fire service personnel.

Items 1-4 pertaining to basic initiating behavior on the part of the coach were checked by 75% of the respondents.

Items 5-9 pertaining to general, non-specifically focused conversations with subordinates were checked by 83% of the respondents. These items garnered the highest percentage of respondents and indicated that the most important coaching functions include sensitivity to others, giving full attention to the speaker, problem solving rather than blaming, and encouraging mutual communication. It can be safely assumed that checks of these particular items indicate the desire for a pleasant atmosphere with little conflict where they feel valued by their supervisors.

Items 10-16 that pertained to problem-oriented discussions with subordinates or peers were checked by 79% of the respondents. Item #15 (helping people take responsibility for solving their own problems) was checked by 90% of the survey group while 94% checked item 16 (serves as a resource for new ideas). This suggests that these fire service personnel prefer to solve their own problems rather than simply being told what to do and provided with the solutions. The fact that other items were checked frequently, appears to indicate that the respondents prefer to have input into problem solving and that their supervisors serve as resource guides.

Results on items 17-19 indicated that 71.6% of respondents felt that it was important for the coach to initiate conversations about the

Table 1
% importance assigned to items by rank
Only those items chosen by at least 60% of respondents (overall) are listed

	Overall: All fire service personnel	Firefighter/EMT & Lieutenants N=400	Chief Officers i.e, Battalion Chiefs, Assistant Chiefs, & Chiefs N=100
1. Initiates conversations with subordinates or co-workers to help them resolve their concerns.	392 / 78%	352 / 88%	40 / 40%
2. Makes it easy for other to be candid with him or her.	415 / 83%	372 / 93%	43 / 43%
3. Makes it easy for others to acknowledge that they lack knowledge.	385 / 77%	347 / 86%	38 / 38%
4. Makes it easy for others to inform him or her about others.	320 / 64%	259 / 64%	61 / 61%
5. Does not put them down with behaviors like sarcasm or ridicule.	470 / 94%	380 / 95%	90 / 90%
6. Gives full attention to them when they are speaking.	356 / 71%	306 / 76%	50 / 50%
7. Shows appropriate sensitivity to their feelings.	380 / 76%	340 / 85%	40 / 40%
8. Emphasizes solving problems rather than blaming people.	445 / 89%	389 / 97%	56 / 56%
9. Encourages mutual, two-way communication.	425 / 85%	355 / 88%	70 / 70%
10. Develops a full understanding of the problems before helping to solve them.	410 / 82%	376 / 94%	34 / 34%
11. Requests their opinions before expressing his/her own.	305 / 61%	266 / 66%	39 / 39%
12. Helps them find their own solutions to their problems.	375 / 75%	298 / 74%	77 / 77%
13. Helps them gain a deeper understanding of their own feelings about the problems.	350 / 70%	317 / 79%	33 / 33%
14. Helps them explore alternative solutions to the problems.	405 / 81%	350 / 87%	55 / 55%
15. Helps them take responsibility for solving their own problems.	450 / 90%	369 / 92%	81 / 81%

The Habits of Successful Coaches

Table 1
% importance assigned to items by rank
Only those items chosen by at least 60% of respondents (overall) are listed

	Overall: All fire service personnel	Firefighter/EMT & Lieutenants N=400	Chief Officers i.e, Battalion Chiefs, Assistant Chiefs, & Chiefs N=100
16. Serves as a resource for new ideas.	470 / 94%	389 / 97%	81 / 81%
17. Helps them understand the political issues that must be taken into account in making decisions.	405 / 81%	385 / 96%	20 / 20%
18. Helps them understand the departmental history behind issues and problems.	305 / 61%	274 / 68%	31 / 31%
19. Helps them become sensitive to the aspects of the department's culture that affect their success.	365 / 73%	327 / 81%	38 / 38%
20. Helps them develop their own personal networks for accomplishing their jobs.	345 / 69%	328 / 82%	17 / 17%
21. Helps them take personal responsibility in managing their own careers.	330 / 66%	240 / 60%	88 / 88%
22. Helps them gain commitment to the department's goals and values.	395 / 79%	301 / 75%	94 / 94%
23. Makes them aware of the chief's likes and dislikes.	480 / 96%	389 / 97%	91 / 91%
24. Provides them with practical career advice.	344 / 68%	300 / 75%	44 / 44%
25. Encourages them to apply for positions that would enhance their careers, even if such encouragement might mean losing competent subordinates or co-workers.	322 / 64%	256 / 64%	66 / 66%
26. Helps them identify what new knowledge or skill they need to acquire.	440 / 88%	346 / 86%	94 / 94%
27. Serves as a resource to them on technical matters.	345 / 69%	264 / 66%	81 / 81%
28. Serves as a resource to them on administrative matters.	300 / 60%	274 / 68%	26 / 26%
29. Helps them gain expert status in their areas of responsibility.	400 / 80%	362 / 90%	38 / 38%

Table 1
% importance assigned to items by rank
Only those items chosen by at least 60% of respondents (overall) are listed

	Overall: All fire service personnel	Firefighter/EMT & Lieutenants N=400	Chief Officers i.e, Battalion Chiefs, Assistant Chiefs, & Chiefs N=100
30. Encourages them to test new knowledge and skills that they acquire.	300 / 60%	220 / 55%	80 / 80%
31. Encourages them to look for new learning opportunities.	310 / 62%	233 / 58%	77 / 77%
32. Praises them when they have acquired knowledge and skills.	445 / 89%	390 / 97%	55 / 55%
33. Mutually clarifies expectations about performance with them.	370 / 74%	326 / 81%	44 / 44%
34. Promptly identifies performance problems with them as these problems occur.	303 / 60%	213 / 53%	90 / 90%
35. Challenges them to take on more and more difficult tasks.	340 / 68%	249 / 62%	91 / 91%
36. Develops strategies with them to improve their performance.	343 / 68%	287 / 71%	56 / 56%
37. Confronts performance problems in a way that maintains a positive relationship between them and himself/herself.	305 / 61%	228 / 57%	77 / 77%
38. Is concrete and specific in talking about performance problems.	405 / 81%	316 / 79%	89 / 89%
39. Emphasizes improvement in the future rather than failure in the past.	395 / 79%	329 / 82%	66 / 66%
40. Helps them find their own best ways to improve their performance.	405 / 81%	316 / 79%	89 / 89%
41. Develops concrete strategies for solving performance problems.	350 / 70%	265 / 66%	85 / 85%

department's politics, history, and culture. Some of the greatest variance was found between command staff respondents and firefighter/EMTs and lieutenants. It was somewhat surprising that these three items were thought to be of the most important items in the survey until the breakdown of rank is considered. Chiefs, assistant chiefs, battalion chiefs and lieutenants ranked these items most important of all and thus skewed the results higher. Nevertheless, even 51% of firefighter/EMTs indicated that these items were important, perhaps reflecting today's emphasis on political and cultural awareness in the workplace.

Items 20-32 are those that pertain to acquiring and testing new knowledge and skills and 73% of respondents felt that these were of the most important coaching functions. These items pertain mostly to career management and meeting both personal and departmental goals and objectives. The single item checked by more respondents than any other was 23 (makes them aware of the chief's likes and dislikes). When 96% of the respondents indicate that this item is important, it indicates that they view either advancement, job satisfaction, or overall happiness in their career as being closely tied to the chief.

It is unknown, through this research project, whether knowing the chief's likes and dislikes were perceived as his personality, his vision for the department, or both. Nevertheless, it is interesting to note that 82% of the firefighter/EMTs and lieutenants were subject to some sort of civil service regulations pertaining to hiring and advancement. It was my assumption going into the project that when assessment determines advancement, most personnel would give little thought to what the chief wanted. This is apparently not the case. It appears that no matter how people are hired or promoted, the boss's demeanor or vision still matters.

Finally, items 33-41 pertain to helping subordinate fire service personnel identify performance problems and developing concrete strategies for solving them and 71% of respondents overall indicated that these were important coaching functions. These items have to do with specific performance oriented discussions and indicate that personnel desire specific and concrete feedback and helpful suggestions for improving their performance. Item 38 and 40 were checked by 81% of respondents. One gets the sense from seeing how important these three items are to the respondents, that the command staff as well as firefighters/EMTs and Lieutenants desire a collaborative, as opposed to an admonishing. approach to solving performance problems.

This is not a surprising finding. Most of us would probably indicate that we respond better to help and assistance as opposed to reprimands when it comes to "raising our game" or overcoming unsatisfactory performance. But fire service, having historically utilized a command and transactional style of leadership, has not been at the forefront of constructive, collaborative performance improvement.

This initial research suggests that altering supervisory practices toward the constructive coaching approach as outlined in this book might be a helpful move for improving the relationship between supervisor/coach and subordinate. While common sense suggests that improved supervisor/subordinate relationships will result in improved personnel performance, further research is needed to verify this.

Finally, items 1-4 were checked by 71.5% of the respondents. These items reveal that fire service personnel desire informality in their relationships with supervisors. Additional research might be able to tease out generational differences with regard to the importance of informality in supervisor/subordinate relationships. Although not verified, it is generally assumed from the wealth of anecdotal reports, that Generation X (those people born between 1964-1982) prefers informal relationships, few hard and fast rules, and mentoring as the preferred method of supervision. This is in opposition to the Veterans Generation (those people born between 1922-1943) who operated in a more formal style where the chain of command was clearly delineated and adhered to. For this group, conflict was handled more by reprimand than by negotiation, subordinates did not readily state differences of opinion and veterans preferred formality where there was a delineation between work and friendship relationships.

When breaking down responses based upon rank, battalion chiefs, assistant chiefs, and chiefs (command staff) gave much less importance to items 1-4 and 5-9. This is not surprising given that they are on the opposite side of the coaching dyad. But could the differences also be associated with advancing age and generation gaps? Could it be that as one advances in rank, one changes with regard to what is perceived to be important in leadership? Further investigation is required.

But a few assumptions can be considered. For example, the average age of command-staff officers is, of course, older than the average age of lieutenants and firefighter/EMTs. Being on the upper end of the baby boomer generation, these officers may tend to practice the transactional style of leadership that they have advanced through on their way up. This style is most commonly associated with command and control, military organizations. The younger officers and non-supervisory personnel, on the other hand, indicate a strong desire to be heard and for their opinions to count for something.

This may be an outgrowth of a generation raised within a country that diverged from the command and control style toward what might be called a "corporate" style that takes into consideration the information age and tends to reward technical, administrative, and people expertise with a greater degree of empowerment and inclusion in decision making. Thus, the two groups differ greatly not only in their practice, but also their preference of the encouraging and motivating leadership style. The command style motivates through orders and consequences for failing to follow orders. The inclusive style motivates by appealing to personality traits, values differences and job fit. Each having its detractors, the former style is considered harsh and cold whereas the latter style is considered spineless and wishy-washy. A method that combines the strengths of both styles is the aim of this book and the Constructive Coaching approach.

Command staff personnel indicated that the most important coaching items were 21 (helps them gain personal responsibility in managing their own careers, 88%); 22 (helps them gain commitment to the department's goals and values, 94%); 26 (helps them identify what new knowledge or skill they need to acquire, 94%); 30 (encourages them to test new knowledge and skills that they acquire, 80%); 34 (promptly identifies performance problems with them as these problems occur, 90%); 40 (helps them find their own best ways to improve their performance, 89%); and 41 (develops concrete strategies for solving performance problems, 85%).

From these data it appears that command-staff officers place the greatest importance on those coaching functions that directly improve performance whereas non command staff personnel place the greatest importance on relationship elements including listening, attention to their ideas and input, encouragement and praise, and understanding the chief's likes and dislikes.

Summary

From this initial research some tentative assumptions can be made about coaching as a primary leadership method. It is safe to assume that these findings can be translated into coaching behavior with potential for positive performance results in the entire department. Non-supervisory personnel state that listening, sensitivity, mutual problem-solving, encouraging communication, having a resource on whom to depend, and having the ability to understand the likes and dislikes of their chief are the most important coaching functions.

On the other hand, command staff personnel state that the most important coaching functions are those that have a direct and immediate bearing on performance enhancement. One tends to be relationship oriented, while the other is task oriented. It is the premise of this book that the two can be combined to enhance relationships as well as performance.

A second step took a slightly different angle. Clients were asked to then rank order the same items in answer to the following prompt- "Using the following scale, rate each item as it pertains to helping you succeed in your career. 1 = Very important, 2 = Important, 3 = Neutral, 4 = Unimportant, and 5 = Very unimportant."

In answer to what coaching methods are important for your job success, the items fell out as follows:

1. A relationship based on mutual respect

2. A coach who presses them to stretch

3. Someone who serves as a resource in people, administrative, managerial, and technical matters

4. Someone who helps them find their own solutions to problems

5. A coach who develops strategies with them to improve their performance

6. The coach to listen and encourage communication, even if it's bad

7. The coach to assume that they (clients) are competent

8. The coach to embody a servant-leader style

9. A coach who confronts performance problems in a way that maintain a positive relationship between them and himself or herself

10. A coach who develops concrete strategies for solving performance problems

11. Someone who encourages them to test new knowledge and skills that they acquire

12. Someone who emphasizes improvement in the future rather than failure in the past

13. A process that generates specific, measurable goals

14. Encouragement, affirmation, empowerment

15. Encourages them to test new knowledge and skills that they acquire

The difference between the two sets of lists is rather interesting. In answering what they want from coaching, respondents express the desire for relationship-oriented factors including, listening, encouragement, mutual respect, communication, and support. But when answering what will help them be most successful, respondents focus on coaching as a method for increasing skills, strategies and solutions to problems. In the first, the focus is on relationship development while in the second, the focus is on skill development. But certain items that are both desirable as well as necessary appear in both lists. These include, a relationship based on mutual respect, someone who serves as a resource, someone who helps them find solutions to their own problems, a listener and encourager of communication, a servant leader style (as opposed to a controlling, micro-coach), and someone who helps the client set measurable goals.

Appendix I

The Principles of
Diversity Competent Coaches

The Principles
of Diversity
Competent Coaches

Diversity Competent Coaches must learn and practice the following points in regards to race, ethnic and cultural heritage, gender, socioeconomic status (SEC), abilities, religion, and spiritual beliefs.

I. Awareness of Self

    A.   Attitudes And Beliefs

    1.   Demonstrate movement from being unaware to being increasingly aware and sensitive to their selves and others and to valuing and respecting differences.

    2.   Demonstrate increased awareness of how they and others are impacted by their own experiences and histories which in turn influence (coaching) processes and dynamics.

    3.   Recognize the limits of their competencies and expertise with regard to working with (clients) who are different from them.

    4.   Demonstrate comfort, tolerance, and sensitivity with differences that exist between themselves and (clients).

    B.   Knowledge

    1.   Identify specific knowledge about their own race, ethnicity, SES, gender, sexual orientation, abilities, religion, and spirituality, and how they personally and professionally affect their definitions of "normality" and (coaching process).

    2.   Demonstrate knowledge and understanding regarding how oppression in any form - such as racism, classism, discrimination, and stereotyping - affect them personally and professionally.

3. Demonstrate knowledge about their social impact on others. They are knowledgeable about communication style differences, how their style may inhibit or foster the (coaching) process with (clients) who are different from themselves along with the different dimensions of diversity, and how to anticipate the impact they may have on others.

C. Skills

1. Seek out educational, consultative, and training experiences to improve their understanding and effectiveness in working with (clients) who self-identify in regards to race, ethnicity and/or disability. Within this context, (coaches) are able to recognize the limits of their competencies and (a) seek consultation, (b) seek further training or education, (c) refer members to more qualified group workers, or (d) engage in a combination of these.

2. Constantly seeking to understand themselves within their multiple identities (apparent and unapparent differences) and are constantly and actively striving to unlearn the various behaviors and processes they covertly and overtly communicate that perpetuate oppression and particularly racism.

II. Awareness of Client's World View

A. Attitudes and Beliefs

1. Exhibit awareness of any possible negative emotional reactions toward those different to themselves and a willingness to contrast in a nonjudgmental manner their own beliefs and attitudes with all others who are group members.

2. Demonstrate awareness of their stereotypes and preconceived notions that they may hold towards others different from themselves.

B. Knowledge

1. Possess specific knowledge and information about Indigenous Peoples, African-Americans, Asian-Americans, Hispanics, Latinos/Latinas, gender differences, and persons with disabilities with whom they are working and be aware of the life experiences, cultural heritage, and sociopolitical backgrounds. This particular knowledge-based competency is strongly linked to the various racial/minority and sexual identity development models available in the literature.

2. Exhibit an understanding of how race, ethnicity, culture, gender, different abilities, SES, and other immutable personal characteristics may affect personality formation, vocational

choices, and the appropriateness or inappropriateness of the various types of theoretical approaches to (coaching).

3. Demonstrate competency in diversity, understand and have the knowledge about sociopolitical influences that impinge upon the lives of all others. Immigration issues, poverty, racism, oppression, stereotyping, and/or powerlessness adversely impact many individuals and therefore impacts the (coaching) process and dynamics.

C. Skills

1. Diversity-skilled (coaches) familiarize themselves with relevant research and the latest findings regarding mental-health issues of all others and actively seek out educational experiences that foster their knowledge and understanding of skills facilitating groups across differences.

2. Become actively involved with all others outside of their work (coaching) so that their perspective of minorities is more than academic or experience through a third party.

III. Diversity-Appropriate Intervention Strategies

A. Attitudes and Beliefs

1. Respect clients' religious and/or spiritual beliefs and values, because they affect worldview, psychosocial functioning, and expressions of distress.

2. Respect helping practices of various people and identify and utilize community intrinsic help-giving networks.

3. Value bilingualism and sign language and do not view another language as an impediment to (coaching).

B. Knowledge

1. Demonstrate a clear and explicit knowledge and understanding of generic characteristics of (coaching) and how they may clash with the beliefs, values, and traditions of others.

2. Exhibit an awareness of institutional barriers that prevent people from actively participating in or using coaching services.

3. Demonstrate knowledge of the potential bias in assessment instruments and use procedures and interpret findings, or actively participate in various types of evaluations of group outcome or success, keeping in mind the linguistic, cultural, and other self-identified characteristics of the group member.

4. Exhibit knowledge of the family structures, hierarchies, values, and beliefs. Be knowledgeable about the community characteristics and resources as the family.

C. Skills

1. Diversity-competent coaches are able to engage in a variety of verbal and nonverbal coaching functions dependent upon the kind of coaching (individual, pair, team, group, and career), and the multiple, self-identified status of various clients. They are able to demonstrate the ability to send and receive both verbal and nonverbal messages accurately, appropriately, and across/between the differences represented in the group. They are not tied down to one method or approach to coaching and recognize that helping styles and approaches may be culture-bound. When they sense that their coaching style is limited and potentially inappropriate, they can anticipate and ameliorate its negative impact by drawing upon other culturally relevant skill sets.

2. Diversity-competent coaches are trained and have expertise in the use of traditional assessment and testing instruments related to coaching and are aware of the cultural biases/limitations of these tools and processes. This allows them to use the tools for the welfare of diverse clients following culturally appropriate procedures.

3. Attend to, as well as work to eliminate biases, prejudices, oppression, and discriminatory practices. Be cognizant of how sociopolitical contexts may affect evaluation and provision of group work and develop sensitivity to issues of oppression, racism, sexism, heterosexism, classism, and so forth.

Appendix II

Core Competencies
for Fire Officers

Core Competencies
for Fire Officers

Instructions:

Using a scale of 1 to 5, please rate yourself in terms of the degree to which you demonstrate each of the supporting behaviors listed under each of the core competencies we've identified for fire officers. The results are yours, alone, and serve as the basis for your professional development planning activities. You should focus on your role as an officer in your self-evaluation.

1 = Never exhibit the behavior

2 = Seldom exhibit the behavior

3 = Sometimes exhibit the behavior

4 = Often exhibit the behavior

5 = Always exhibit the behavior

COMPETENCY: Organizational Awareness	*"As an officer, I..."*	Self Score
1	Possess a strong understanding of the culture, values, history, and core business of the Organization.	
2	Scan the external environment in order to anticipate opportunities and potential threats to the Organization's core business—regulatory issues, emerging trends, employment laws, etc.	
3	Establish a strong network within the Organization so that I maintain an in-depth knowledge of core strategy, business processes, and ways to influence them on behalf of the company.	

COMPETENCY: Organizational Awareness	"As an officer, I..."	Self Score
4	Build and maintain a network of contacts internally and external communications, and encourage staff to do likewise.	
5	Keep current with company goals, initiatives, internal and external communications, and encourage staff to do likewise.	
6	Actively participate in committees, task forces, project teams, and professional associations.	
7	Contribute to the success of other business lines in the Organization.	
8	Review public policy, case law, periodicals, and professional journals to assess the viewpoints of decision-makers and policy shapers.	

Total in this Section (score should not exceed 40)

COMPETENCY: Team Building	"As an officer, I..."	Self Score
1	Promote teamwork and shared vision by actively supporting and encouraging inter and intra-departmental collaboration.	
2	Demonstrate strong listening skills and welcome ideas other than my own.	
3	Ensure teamwork in meetings by facilitating interaction and collaboration.	
4	Demonstrate strong meeting management skills (develop an agenda, facilitate discussion, address counterproductive behaviors, etc.).	
5	Help team members understand/act on team goals.	
6	Value diversity in teams.	
7	Champion and serve as an advocate for team goals at all levels of the Organization.	
8	Actively work to remove barriers to the team's/department's success.	

Total in this Section (score should not exceed 40)

COMPETENCY: Action and Implementation	"As an officer, I..."	Self Score
1	Align actions with organizational goals and values and provide strategic organizational context for direct reports.	
2	Involve team by discussing goals/strategies.	
3	Clarify objectives and give both positive and corrective feedback to keep activities on track and monitor performance and evaluate results on an ongoing basis.	
4	Outline purpose and objectives when delegating responsibility.	
5	Manage human, financial, information, technology and material resources.	
6	Identify potential barriers that may threaten the success of a plan.	
7	Set priorities while considering the implications of specific courses of action on the larger system.	
8	Evaluate courses of action within the context of organizational strategy, vision, and values.	

Total in this Section (score should not exceed 40)

COMPETENCY: Communication Skills	"As an officer, I..."	Self Score
1	Adhere to principles of good communication (use simple, clear language and listening skills to convey openness, honesty, and sensitivity to other points of view.	
2	Communicate often with staff; adhere to a regular schedule for staff meetings, e-mail communications, and one-on-one or small group interactions.	
3	Organize thoughts before speaking in a way that the listener can understand.	
4	Demonstrate genuine concern for other people's ideas by asking questions, encouraging feedback, and outwardly promoting other people's opinions.	
5	When necessary, I ask a trusted colleague to review my written and/or verbal communication in advance to evaluate effectiveness, appropriateness, and clarity.	
6	Am able to "think on my feet" when confronted with challenging situations, tough questions, and/or ambiguous issues.	
7	Promote ideas effectively by considering the audience, structuring thoughts in advance, and considering other people's perspectives.	
8	Communicate effectively with all levels in the Organization.	

Total in this Section (score should not exceed 40)

COMPETENCY: Creativity and Problem-Solving   *"As an officer, I...*   Self Score

1	Am able to apply the most useful parts of yesterday's solutions to today's problems.	
2	Remain open-minded about ideas that may challenge the status quo.	
3	Encourage self and others to view challenges from a variety of perspectives and take a disciplined approach to addressing and solving problems — challenge first impressions and avoid jumping to conclusions.	
4	Foster creativity in self and others by creating a work environment that encourages it.	
5	Consider pre-existing solutions to current challenges, regardless of the problems they were originally designed to address.	
6	Recognize and build on what has worked well in the past, but not to the exclusion of new ideas.	
7	Demonstrate support for an environment that reinforces "out-of-the-box" thinking.	
8	Create an environment where continuous learning is an expectation.	

Total in this Section (score should not exceed 40)

COMPETENCY: Ethics and Values   *"As an officer, I...*   Self Score

1	Follow through on commitments to others and to the Organization (e.g., complete performance reviews on time, address performance problems swiftly, etc.)	
2	Set an example for others by never asking them to do something I would not do in their position.	
3	Possess a strong working knowledge of the Department's Compliance program and the "Code of Conduct."	
4	Maintain confidentiality of information regarding direct reports and other employees and do not discuss confidential issues except with Human Resources or my own command staff when necessary.	
5	Consider the ethics of my management decisions at all times.	
6	Treat others fairly and expect them to do the same.	
7	Hold myself and others accountable to the highest ethical standards and "call the behavior" when I see someone acting unethically or in a way that is inconsistent with our Corporate values.	
8	"Walk the talk" by doing what I say I will do and operating in the best interests of the Organization, my staff, and our shareholders at all times.	

Total in this Section (score should not exceed 40)

COMPETENCY: Managing Change	"As an officer, I...	Self Score
1	Adapt well to change by acknowledging and working with ambiguity.	
2	Constantly gauge my own and others' reactions to change, especially when I may not embrace the change or feel threatened by it.	
3	Maintain an open mind by considering other points of view and multiple solutions.	
4	Balance the need to help staff through change initiatives with achieving organizational goals within necessary timeframes.	
5	Communicate with staff regularly about organizational change initiatives to support early adoption of the change.	
6	Create an environment where employees feel free to ask questions, voice concerns, share reactions about change initiatives, etc.	
7	Ensure that strategies, processes, structure, people, culture, and reward systems are aligned to support the desired change.	
8	Openly express support for change and maintain a positive attitude regardless of my personal opinions.	

Total in this Section (score should not exceed 40)

COMPETENCY: Interpersonal Skills	"As an officer, I...	Self Score
1	Demonstrate sensitivity, respect, and candor when dealing with others.	
2	Build cross-company relationships informally and formally and encourage interaction with others.	
3	Continuously look for ways to improve working relationships, especially with individuals with whom I currently have a poor working relationship.	
4	Am able to adapt my behavior and communication style to the style needs of those with whom I interact.	
5	Acknowledge other points of view and encourage dialogue rather than merely advancing my agenda.	
6	Give/receive feedback and encourage an open and respectful exchange of ideas and opinions.	
7	Challenge and coach staff in a non-confrontational manner when they show an intolerance for other's embrace diversity in the workplace.	
8	Spend time preparing for negotiations in advance.	

Total in this Section (score should not exceed 40)

Transfer the score for each competency area in the corresponding space (as shown below).

EXAMPLE:

COMPETENCY:	5 10 15 20 25 30 35 40
Organizational Awareness	-------------------|
Team Building	---------------------------|
Action & Implementation	---------|
Communicaton Skills	---------------------------------------|
Creativity/Problem Solving	-------------------|
Ethics & Values	---|
Managing Change	---------------------------|
Interpersonal Skills	---------------------------------------|

YOUR SCORES:

COMPETENCY:	5 10 15 20 25 30 35 40
Organizational Awareness	
Team Building	
Action & Implementation	
Communicaton Skills	
Creativity/Problem Solving	
Ethics & Values	
Managing Change	
Interpersonal Skills	

Bibliography and Recommended Readings

Adler, A. Understanding Human Nature. Hazelden Information Education; Reprint edition, 1998.

Buckingham, Marcus and Curt Coffman. First, Break All the Rules. New York: Simon & Schuster, 1999.

Index

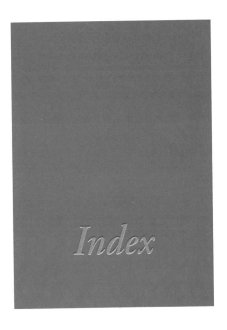

Index

A

accountability, 254
action planning, 124–125
Adler, Alfred, 29, 210–211, 224
age. See ageism; generational differences
ageism, 54–55, 263–270
agreement skills
    assessing client personality style, 235–236
    finding common interests, 234
    and hostility, 234–235
    listening for similarities, 233–234
    "we" references, 236
alternative perceptions, encouraging clients', 258–259
altruism, 15
American Counseling Association, 29
American Society for Training and Development (ASTD), 29
anger management, 150
Apple Computers, 25
apprehension (during coaching process), 169–170, 177–178
assessments
    behavioral, 77–80
    benefits of, 78
    as part of coaching process, 124
    personality, 77–80, 165
asset focusing, 258
Association for Specialists in Group Work, 29

B

Baby Boomers, 265, 267-268
balance (of pay system), 218
Beck, Aaron, 29
behavior patterns
    conventionals, 81, 86–88
    drivers, 80, 81–83
    influencers, 80, 83–84

    and personality, 116
    steadfasts, 80, 84–86
beliefs, faulty, xi–xii
belonging, as goal, xi
Blanchard, Ken, 154
bottom line goals, 141–142
Branden, Nathaniel, 202, 207
brotherhood of the fire service, 47
Buckingham, Marcus, x, xiii

C

Campanella, Roy, 6
challenges faced by coaches, 31–32
change
    coach's theory of, 30
    and encouragement, 224–225
    first order, xiii–xiv
    resistance to, 153–154
city planning, 51
clarification, 183–184
classism, 56–57
client
    comfort level of, 169–170, 177–178
    developing alternative perceptions, 258-259
    expectations of, 168-169
    See also contracting
closure (Gestalt theory), 219–220
coach
    acceptance of, 197–198
    attractiveness of, 169
    basic skills of, 177–193
    defined, 20
    personal feelings of, 204–205
    preconceptions of, 57
    qualifications for, 20
    selection of, 38–39
    style of, 30, 117–119

on conflict, 67-68
for encouragement, 232-233
importance of, 128–129

R

racism, 56
reflection, 179–181
relationship combinations, 89–115
    conventional-conventional, 110–111
    conventional-influencer, 111–114
    driver-conventional, 97–100
    driver-driver, 90–93
    driver-influencer, 100–102
    driver-steadfast, 93–97
    influencer-influencer, 114–115
    steadfast-conventional, 103–107
    steadfast-influencer, 107–110
    steadfast-steadfast, 102–103
relationships, triangle, 61–62, 63
respect, 134
responding, by coach, 13–15
responsibility, ability to take, 134–136, 254
retention of firefighters, xx, 79, 151
retreating, by coach, 139
review, importance of, 125–126
Robinson, Jackie, 5–6, 18
role models, 5–6, 45
role-play, 163

S

Salas, Jo, 208
self-analysis, 79
self-confidence, 238, 260
self-disclosure (by coach), 187–188
self-efficacy, 207
self-esteem, 228, 229
self-fulfilling prophecy, 203, 260
self-motivation, 252
self-sacrifice, 47
Seligman, Martin, 226
September 11, 45, 46
service goals, 140–141
sexism, 55–56
sexual harassment, 51, 55–56
shadowing, 5, 124, 205
signature presence (of coach), 30
silence, coach's use of, 181–183
Six Pillars of Self-Esteem, The (Branden), 202
60 Minutes, 16–17
skills, coaching
    clarifying, 183–184
    delegating, 188–193
    listening, active, 177–179
    mini-lecturing, 185–187
    modeling, 187–188
    reflecting, 179–181

    self-disclosure, 187–188
    silence, 181–183
    summarizing, 184–185
skills practice, 24
Smith, Fred, 250
social interest, 229
Society For Human Resources Management (SHRM), 29
Socrates, 11, 18
Socratic method, 11–12
Stand and Deliver, 14–15
steadfast behavior pattern, 80, 84–86
storying, 197–198, 206–212
strengths, inventorying, 227–230
stress, 48
subordinates, coaching, 139, 169-170
succession planning, 27
Sullivan, Anne, 7–8, 18
summarizing, 184–185
support, departmental, 36–37
Syn-Tech generation, 268–269

T

teaching, as part of coaching, 9–12
    review, importance of, 12
    terms and acronyms, 11
teaching case, xviii
teaching methods, 10
team spirit, 259
technology, 52–53
tests, personality trait, 77–80
    benefits of, 78
traditional coaching, 37
training, compared to coaching, 27–28
transactional command-style, ix
triangulation, 26, 61-62, 63
trust, 251

V

values, 252
vertical job loading, 219
Veterans, 265, 297
vulnerability, 251–252

W

Wazniak, Steven, 25
weight control, 52
Weiner, Norbert, 33
White, William, 221
women in the fire service, 47, 51, 53, 55–56, 207
Work Design (Hackman and Oldham), 219
work process goals, 141–142
workplace, optimum, xiii
World Trade Center attack, 45